Forgotten Friendships

Forgotten Friendships

Yugoslavia and the Anticolonial Francophone World

Alexandra Perišić

Amherst College Press

To my grandparents who fought against fascism
And to my daughter Zaria, so she knows she has a history

The complete manuscript of this work was subjected to a partly closed ("single-anonymous") review process. For more information, visit https://acpress.amherst.edu/peerreview/.

Published in the United States of America by Amherst College Press
Manufactured in the United States of America

Library of Congress Control Number: 2024950672
DOI: https://doi.org/10.3998/mpub.12988661

ISBN 979-8-89506-016-2 (paperback)
ISBN 979-8-89506-017-9 (open access)
ISBN 979-8-89506-018-6 (hardcover)

CONTENTS

FIGURES

ACKNOWLEDGMENTS

I have been incredibly fortunate to be surrounded by friends, colleagues, and interlocutors who have helped shape my ideas and bring this book to life. The idea for this project first emerged while I was an Assistant Professor at the University of Miami and I am grateful to my colleagues and graduate students in the Department of Modern Languages and Literatures for engaging me in thought-provoking discussions over the years.

This journey began with the chapter on René Depestre, which was made possible by his generosity in hosting me in the South of France and sharing his memories of Yugoslavia. My former professors and mentors, Kaiama Glover and Souleymane Bachir Diagne, provided invaluable feedback on various chapters of the book. Chiara Bonfiglioli directed me to the crucial archives, while the staff at the Archives of Yugoslavia, the Museum of African Art, and the Homeland Museum in Petrovac na Mlavi—notably Milica Naumov and Darko Stokić—helped me find precisely what I needed. Lawrence Kiiru and Nika Autor generously shared their documentaries. Special thanks go to Sima Kokotović for inviting me to present part of Chapter Four at the Museum of Yugoslavia in Belgrade and for helping shape the introduction. Olivier Hadouchi's expertise, Kimberly Storr's editing skills, and Paul Stubbs's helpful suggestions have greatly enriched this book. I am also deeply grateful to Nemanja Radonjić for sharing archival documents on Guberina's trip to Senegal, which were damaged in a flood. The many conversations with Bojana Videkanić have been a constant source of inspiration. My wonderful editor, Hannah Brooks-Motl, has been supportive of this project from the beginning, and I am deeply grateful for her effort and invaluable advice. A special thank you also goes to the talented Andrej Dolinka who created the beautiful cover image.

I also extend my gratitude to my colleagues at the Faculty of Media and Communications in Belgrade; due to their exceptional aptitudes, I have had time to write this book. My life partner, Jacques Laroche, has shown me what decolonial friendships look like in everyday life, and I am thankful every day for his presence.

Parts of Chapters One and Five were initially published in *Small Axe* and *Expressions Maghrébines*, while my interview with René Depestre first appeared in *Transitions*. I would like to thank Duke University Press, Indiana University Press, and *Expressions Maghrébines* for allowing me to reproduce this material.

Above all, my deepest gratitude goes to the friends—in thought, struggle, and care—whose political friendships have sustained, challenged, and transformed me over the years.

PREFACE

I never intended to write about Yugoslavia. Until now, it has not been the focus of my research. When I left Yugoslavia for France in 1999, I vowed *not* to focus on it, as the events of the 1990s were emotionally fraught and it seemed impossible that I could ever view the region objectively. So, I studied Francophone literature, which became a home for me in those days. It spoke to me, particularly when it dealt with the challenges of immigration, helping me to understand my own experience as an immigrant in France. Through it, I understood better the ideology of European supremacy and why my French math teacher was flabbergasted that someone from a "backwards, war-torn" country could have received the highest grade on his test. Ultimately, I made a career of it. I wrote my doctoral dissertation and first book on Francophone (and Latin American) literature and taught Francophone literature for years in several universities.

And then, the most unexpected thing happened: Francophone literature brought me back to Yugoslavia. At first, it was Aimé Césaire who, I learned, began writing his *Cahier d'un Retour au Pays Natal* in Dalmatia, of all places. When I was asked to write an introduction to the Serbian translation of Césaire's *Discourse on Colonialism* in 2015, I discovered yet another interesting detail linking Francophone authors to Yugoslavia. In 1947, Haitian writer and intellectual René Depestre had participated in the building of the Šamac-Sarajevo railroad in Bosnia as part of a communist youth brigade. I wrote him a letter, asking about this experience but hardly expecting an answer, and was pleasantly surprised to receive a very enthusiastic response a few months later. Yugoslavia played a tremendous role in his political experience and thinking, he wrote, and it was also there that he had his first love affair with a European woman. References to Yugoslavia by Francophone authors just multiplied from there. Léopold Sédar Senghor was drawn to Yugoslav self-management, for instance; during the Algerian War of Independence, Frantz Fanon had collaborated with Zdravko Pečar, the founder of the Museum of African Art in Belgrade—which holds an incredible and deeply understudied archive of the Algerian revolution. By turning toward the Francophone world, I had not escaped Yugoslavia. In fact, my affinity toward Francophone literatures and cultures wasn't accidental; rather, it belonged to a much larger history of Francophone-Yugoslav connections. These connections emerged from shared experiences, albeit not identical, alongside a united fight against capitalism and colonialism.

The friendships I uncovered resonated with the stories of antifascist struggle, internationalism, and solidarity that I heard from my grandparents during my childhood. These values, which I was raised on, I still uphold, notably in light of the mounting nationalisms and growing right-wing politics in the region and beyond. In 1947, to borrow from Nika Autor's wonderful documentary, "at the dawn of their visions of the future," the youth building the Šamac-Sarajevo railroad "planned for us a future of security, justice and infrastructure."[1] While we are not currently living this future, dismissing their enthusiasm as naive, youthful exuberance would be reductive.

The friendships and societal visions described in this book contained many contradictions. Despite this, there is a lot we can learn from both their successes and their shortcomings. Times have changed, and past models cannot simply be reproduced. Yet, this does not render them worthless, because their belief in the possibility of a world based on interethnic and interracial solidarities, as well as their willingness to fight for it, is something we desperately need today.

Introduction: Revolutionary Friendships

The following photo, of Zdravko Pečar, the Yugoslav journalist and diplomat, was taken near the Tunisian-Algerian border in 1958. During the Algerian War of Independence, Pečar accompanied a battalion of the National Liberation Army (ALN) led by Major Abderrahmane Bensalem, which frequently crossed from Tunisia into Algeria to attack French troops. The photograph is signed by an ALN fighter, who wrote: "To my friend, Mr. Zdravko Pečar, who lived with us in the mountains burned and bloodied by the blood of their Algerian sons fighting for their freedom."[1] He describes Pečar not as an ally or a comrade, but much more intimately, as a friend.

Within its politics of non-alignment, Yugoslavia supported the ALN by sending weapons, providing care for the wounded, and dispatching journalists like Pečar to help counter French propaganda. On the edges of these official arrangements, friendships formed, and as this photo shows, many Algerian fighters saw Pečar as their friend in arms. He and his wife Veda Zagorac were eager to join in the anticolonial struggle; they are but one example of Yugoslavs who developed friendships with their counterparts in the Global South and jointly organized against imperialism and capitalism. The Martinican politician and poet Aimé Césaire had a decades-long friendship with Yugoslav-Croatian linguist Petar Guberina, for example. Poet and longtime president of Senegal Léopold Sédar Senghor was friends for years with the Yugoslav-Macedonian poet Aco Šopov. And Malian midwife and anticolonial activist Aoua Kéita had enduring friendships with both Veda Zagorac and Vida Tomšič. These were personal, but also political friendships, with important local and global ramifications.

Figure 1. Portrait of Zdravko Pečar near the Tunisian-Algerian border, 1958. The Veda and dr Zdravko Pečar Collection, Belgrade Museum of African Art.

Forgotten Friendships explores the significance of Yugoslavia for Césaire's and Senghor's Négritude, Depestre's communism, Kéita's struggle for female emancipation, as well as the Algerian struggle for independence. I argue that these Yugoslav connections allow us to reevaluate Négritude, the Algerian War of Independence, African Socialisms, and Socialist Feminisms as movements and events that extended beyond national, regional, and even diasporic spaces to become globally connected and open to the world in ways that remain understudied. The intellectuals featured in this text each conceptualized, mobilized, and lived friendship as a political category at the center of their postcolonial and socialist "worldmaking."[2]

The friendships described in this book challenged the racial segregation of the world and the binarism perpetuated by colonial ideology, and they complicated the center–periphery divide. The Yugoslavs in these friendships were speaking from Europe, but not from its center, yet they were ambivalent regarding the Global South at large; meaning, they actively supported anticolonial struggles but were unable to free themselves entirely from the influence of European racial ideology. Still, they were willing to work with and learn from their Francophone friends, who were interested in the alternative vision of Europe that stemmed from its periphery.

Most studies dealing with Yugoslav connections to the rest of the Global South focus on its role in the non-aligned movement (NAM).[3] In fact, during the Cold War, Yugoslavia represented a "third space," outside the West–East binary, having co-founded NAM, supported struggles for decolonization, and opened space for interracial solidarities. In *Forgotten Friendships*, I take a wider historical approach as Césaire and Depestre grew interested in Yugoslavia before the advent of NAM. Indeed, Césaire first visited Yugoslavia before World War II, when it was still a kingdom. It was the peripherality of Yugoslavia vis-à-vis Europe that made it such a fruitful detour for Césaire, who discovered internal contradictions of white supremacy as a project, which helped him reimagine a global perspective originating from his native island of Martinique. Later on, it was the Yugoslav turn toward self-management after WWII, and its support for decolonization, that kept Césaire interested in the country throughout his life. Similarly, when Depestre participated in building the Šamac-Sarajevo Railroad in 1947, Yugoslavia had not yet split from the Soviet Union. It was youth involvement in the antifascist struggle and the country's postwar national reconstruction effort that initially attracted him, but like Césaire, Depestre continued to follow from afar as Yugoslavia attempted to build a decentralized form of socialism. Senghor similarly viewed Yugoslav federalism as an important example for Africans. And while Yugoslavia was initially skeptical that his government was too supportive of French neocolonial interests, Senghor received an official invitation to visit the country in 1974. Yugoslav-Algerian and Yugoslav-Malian connections described in this text were the most explicitly linked to the NAM, as both countries represented an important focus of Yugoslav foreign policy in the years after the movement was launched. When dealing with the NAM, I consider Yugoslav involvement in the movement not exclusively through the frame of government policy but through the views and experiences of Yugoslavs engaged in building transnational solidarity; I also approach the movement not solely from the standpoint of Yugoslavia, by asking what Yugoslav non-alignment meant to Francophone writers, thinkers, and political theorists in the African diaspora.

On both sides of these friendships was an awareness that the world's peripheries cannot survive in autarchy. To break oppressive bonds with the center, peripheries needed to create alternative political communities—and they did. The countries of the Global South were not passive recipients of Western politics, but active participants in projects to build political and economic alternatives. They did this by establishing systems, organizations, and networks, and by drawing on personal friendships.

The Global South Before the Global South

The friendships and exchanges analyzed in this book bring into question the East–West axis as the only relevant global demarcation during the Cold War, as well as the notion that all anticolonial and postcolonial discourse was directed at former colonizers. In fact, African and Caribbean intellectuals were thinking well beyond imperial centers and even beyond the African diaspora.

Within Francophone studies, attempts have recently been made to "unhome" the discipline and place it in a comparative context.[4] This book enters into this conversation by showing that Francophone literatures and cultures have always been comparative, and in ways that exceed imperial and postcolonial routes. More specifically, I bring into dialogue two fields that have thus far remained mostly separate: Francophone and Slavic

Studies. Adam Kola has recently noted the relative absence of the so-called Second World from comparative literature studies.[5] And while since then, some groundbreaking works have placed Slavic Studies in a more comparative focus, a lot of work remains to be done.[6] In *Forgotten Friendships,* I hope to bring us one step further in this direction.

In this endeavor to move beyond literary regionalisms and monolingualisms, I build on the methodologies of Global South studies, which gained visibility in the aftermath of the 2008 financial crisis, as well as the anticapitalist protests and racial justice organizing that followed.[7] Similarly to other scholars working within the field, I perform comparative readings "of subaltern subjects not merely relative to a majority culture as in orthodox postcolonial approaches, but occupying their own agentic spaces within it—and more importantly, in relation to *each other.*"[8] The figures analyzed in this book were thinking across peripheries as they formed international friendships, which were "conceived as a space from which to theorize alternative futures."[9] Colonial difference certainly retained an important role as newly decolonized countries strove to move beyond their colonial legacies, yet former colonial powers were no longer the sole audience, and former metropoles were no longer the only model. Francophone intellectuals who engaged in anticolonial struggles joined in global conversations, while at the same time working to adapt what they learned to local circumstances. And one thing was certain: they needed the Third World/Global South to survive as a project, to avoid a geopolitical imbalance of neocolonial power.[10]

While the primary focus of Global South studies has been to provide comparative frameworks for understanding our contemporary era of neoliberal globalization (or global neoliberalization, as I have called it in the past), the connections outlined in this book offer a longer view of the Global South as "a direct response to the category of postcoloniality" which "captures both a political collectivity and ideological formulation that arises from lateral solidarities among the world's multiple Souths."[11] I thus join the ranks of scholars who have outlined a continuity between the Third World and the Global South as projects of peripheral solidarities that circumvented imperial centers (which is why I use the two terms interchangeably).

For instance, Anne Garland Mahler has examined the Tricontinental as an example of the "transnational struggle for racial justice" that took place during the Cold War.[12] Though I focus on a different Cold War network of solidarity, I similarly offer a history of anticolonial and anticapitalist transnational struggle that places the concept of the Global South into an elongated temporal *durée*.[13] In fact, the Tricontinental and the NAM operated simultaneously but at times antagonistically, given that the Cuban and Yugoslav visions of socialism did not always align after the Tito-Stalin split. The coexistence of these movements positions the Global South as "a shifting geography" and moreover as "a polyvalent and even protean term, whose meanings shift across time and context."[14] Here, I also draw on Leo Zeilig's work, which examines Frantz Fanon's efforts to forge a Global South project by building solidarities between Algeria and sub-Saharan Africa.[15]

In other words, Cold War projects aiming to build "a transnational political subjectivity emerging from recognition of analogous circumstances" were multiple; sometimes overlapping and sometimes diverging.[16] My objective here is not to position connections to Yugoslavia as central to the work of Césaire, Senghor, Depestre, or Kéita, and thereby replace the existing theoretical frameworks through which their work has been read, but to highlight how this connection brings new insights into their work by speaking to the multiplicity of their interests and the breadth of their internationalisms.

I further borrow from Boaventura de Sousa Santos, who defines the South as "a metaphor for the human suffering caused by capitalism and colonialism on the global level, as well as for the resistance to overcoming or minimising such suffering." This South is "anti-capitalist, anti-colonialist, anti-patriarchal, and anti-imperialist."[17] De Sousa Santos also introduces the idea of multiple Europes, resulting from internal imperialism on the Continent, by which he positions Southern Europe as part of the Global South. I map out a similar Southern geography that extends into the Global North (and East) by way of Yugoslavia, which mobilized its peripheral position within Europe and its histories of imperial subjugation and antifascist struggle to position itself as an ally of anticolonial actors and newly decolonized nations.

It should be noted that for these Francophone authors, Yugoslavia was not the only Eastern European connection.[18] Aoua Kéita collaborated with Soviet women's organizations.[19] René Depestre spent several years in Czechoslovakia, before leaving with his Jewish partner due to rising antisemitism. Léopold Sédar Senghor maintained a correspondence with the Soviet Africanist Ivan Potekhin and the poet Yevgeny Yevtushenko.[20] However, as we will see in the chapters to follow, these intellectuals frequently turned to Yugoslavia when they became disillusioned with the Soviet Union and its satellite states. Yugoslavia was of particular interest due to its history of imperial dependence, its post-WWII attempt to build a more decentralized form of socialism, and the important role it played in the NAM.

At the Periphery of Europe

Though the Balkans did not experience colonialism in the modern sense, its populations were subjugated over centuries by the Ottoman, Habsburg, and Venetian empires.[21] With this subjugation came varying ideological discourses about the inferiority of the people and cultures of the Balkans. Maria Todorova has reflected on the legacy of this discourse, declaring that "a specter is haunting Western culture—the specter of the Balkans."[22] Arguing that the region cannot be fully understood through the prism of Orientalism, Todorova proposes Balkanism as a discourse and methodology with its own set of characteristics. If the Orient is the Occident's Other, the Balkans are its distorted mirror image. The West and the Orient are "usually presented as incompatible entities, antiworlds, but completed antiworlds," while the Balkans are portrayed as a land of transitions, a space in-between, the link between East and West, Europe and Asia.[23] Thus, "the Balkans are also a bridge between stages of growth, and this invokes labels such as semideveloped, semicolonial, semicivilized, semioriental."[24] The Balkanist discourse embraces this ambiguity and exists outside the domain of dichotomies. It is "[t]his in-betweenness of the Balkans, their transitionary character," as Todorova notes, that "could have made them simply an incomplete other; instead they are constructed not as other but as incomplete self."[25] This leaves the Balkans an almost-Europe, stuck in arrested development.

Since the publication of Todorova's book, various other scholars have contributed to our understanding of Balkanism. Dušan Bjelić contends that Balkanism is comparable to Orientalism in that it is indeed based on a series of binaries (e.g., center/periphery, rational/irrational, civilized/barbaric).[26] K. E. Fleming has characterized the Balkans as an "outsider within" due to the region's simultaneous proximity and distance from Western Europe, noting that this positioning has "both heightened and literalized" the "intimate estrangement" Edward Said used to characterize the West's relationship to the Orient. In the case of the Balkans, Fleming asserts that this intimacy originates from "a perception of similarity, while estrangement stems from the awkwardness and ill ease with which that similarity is greeted."[27] The Balkans are "Europe's resident alien, an internal other that is an affront and challenge by virtue of its claim to be part of the West, as well as by its apparent ability to dramatically affect Western history."[28] Both Fleming and Milica Bakić-Hayden have underscored that the Balkans tend to be associated with violence, which is depicted not only as "a social condition but [as] inherent in the nature of its people."[29] The Balkans are seen through this lens as Western Europe's embarrassing cousin: an unacknowledged and misjudged relative in the East who cannot be disowned if the West seeks to cement its supremacy.

Situated in the Balkans, Yugoslavia was, during its existence, indisputably peripheral and disputably European. Catherine Baker writes, for instance, that:

> Yugoslavia was a European power in a region (the Balkans) perceived in the Western discourses of modernity as European and not-European simultaneously; on territory formerly subject to one empire centred in central Europe and another centred in west Asia; where members of majority ethnonational groups (including their diasporas) were usually racialised as white but whose whiteness had still been conditional or "white, but not quite."[30]

Due to this liminal positioning, Césaire saw certain similarities between Yugoslavia and Martinique, both of which he characterized as "handicapped societies."[31] When he visited Yugoslavia, Senghor similarly drew certain parallels between the Yugoslav history of imperial subjugation and Senegal's colonial past. This doesn't mean the Balkans have historically been immune to racial ideology. Like the rest of the white world, the region has participated in the economy of racial capitalism.[32] Yet, in Yugoslavia, like the rest of Eastern Europe, whiteness "is more conditional and contingent on place, historical context, and specific social relations."[33] Thus, people who have been racialized as "non-white" by the rest of Europe, often identified as white in relation to the rest of the Global South. As a result, complex histories of external domination (fostering solidarities with colonized peoples) collide with enduring internal racisms (such as a long history of discrimination against Albanians and

Romas) in the region.[34] After WWII and particularly in the context of non-alignment, Yugoslavia mobilized this liminality to its advantage, strategically navigating "the shifting boundaries between 'white'/'not-quite,' 'European'/'non-European,' and 'developed'/'underdeveloped worlds'."[35] For the Francophone intellectuals, the position of Yugoslavia highlighted the fact that whiteness is not monolithic, and that Europe is a construction with its own internal contradictions. While some of the collaborations described in this book began prior to WWII, many more developed in the context of Yugoslav participation in NAM, whose brief history I outline in the following section.

Yugoslavia and Non-Alignment

When World War II finally ended in May 1945 and Yugoslavia had been liberated from Nazi occupation by the communist-led Partisan resistance, it was the Communist Party of Yugoslavia that emerged victorious. Socialist Yugoslavia was officially established the following year, with Josip Broz Tito at its head. This victory of the People's Liberation Struggle created a "rupture," as Gal Kirn puts it, that "far overreached the Yugoslav context, contributing significantly to the social revolutions of the working classes and the anti-imperialist struggles of the second half of the twentieth century."[36]

For its first two years, Yugoslavia followed the political and economic path established by the Soviet Union, its main ally. But in 1948, a split between Tito and Stalin led Yugoslavia to turn away from the Eastern Bloc, toward the Third World, and ultimately to adopt non-alignment. The reasons for this split were numerous and included Stalin's refusal to support a plan by Tito for a Socialist Balkan federation comprising Yugoslavia, Albania, Bulgaria, and Greece; Moscow's insistence on preferential trade treaties; and the fact that Stalin and Churchill had divided the Balkans into respective spheres of influence during the Yalta Conference. But more than anything, Tito would not allow Yugoslavia to be a satellite state, and this resulted in Yugoslavia's expulsion from the Cominform, a decision that shocked many observers and resonated across the socialist world.

Internationally isolated, Yugoslavia knew it would not be able to survive on its own as an underdeveloped, newly socialist country, situated (literally) between the two prevailing blocs. It needed to find an alternative political and economic path, and looked to decolonizing territories in Asia and Africa, which were simultaneously seeking ways to preserve local sovereignty and independence in an increasingly polarized context. As Kirn writes, "the Yugoslav leadership found itself in front of an abyss and decided to leap into a void."[37]

Various events set the stage for the full emergence of non-alignment in these years, most notably the 1955 Afro-Asian Bandung Conference,[38] a 1956 meeting between Tito, Nasser, and Nehru on the Adriatic Island of Brijuni (which Vijay Prashad has described as "Third World Yalta"[39]), and the 1960 meeting with Nasser, Nehru, Nkrumah, and Sukarno, which Tito convoked during the fifteenth United Nations General Assembly.[40] Tito had also used his 1954 and 1955 tours of India and Egypt to introduce the notion of an alliance outside the blocs, as Yugoslavia worked to position itself as an ally of the Global South on multiple fronts. For instance, the Yugoslavs sent arms to Burma and to Egypt, and supported Congo and Angola in the UN.[41] Most notably, as we will see in Chapter Four, Yugoslavia offered considerable help to the Algerian National Liberation Front (FLN), ranging from shipments of arms to medical assistance to political recognition.[42]

The NAM was officially launched during the 1961 conference in Belgrade, which was chosen in part because the city's communications infrastructure could meet the event's media requirements.[43] Tito, Nasser, and Nehru welcomed delegates from twenty-two Latin American, Asian, and African countries, including monarchs, "heads of bourgeois nationalist parties, leaders of coups, and representatives of mass nationalist movements."[44] As their political views were not all in harmony, the NAM turned its attention to two specific, interconnected issues on which these delegates could agree: global nuclear disarmament and the democratization of the UN. Non-aligned states would work to end the arms race, insisting on the connection between nuclear disarmament and "the principles of self-determination, non-interference in other states, and, crucially, the freeing of resources spent on armaments for social and economic needs."[45] But as they engaged in most of their advocacy at the UN, the UN would need to be democratized to better serve the interests of the Global South. The NAM thus lobbied to increase the number of non-permanent UN members and the number of Economic and Social Council (ECOSOC) members, and strove to limit the influence of the Security Council, which held veto power.[46]

More broadly, the NAM advocated for the right of all nations to self-determination and promoted economic and political non-interference. Accordingly, it condemned colonialism and warned about the dangers of neocolonial interventions. The NAM also encouraged and facilitated cultural, artistic, and scientific exchanges across the Global South, striving to build "alternative imaginaries" and "to 'provincialize' universal history."[47] Works of art and popular culture were used to "create a unified structure of feeling—a new transnational imagined community that began developing in the mid-1950s."[48] In this sense, the NAM can be thought of as a form of "prior globalization, a globalization otherwise, an alter-globalization before alter-globalization."[49] Meaning, the NAM created South–South dialogues and exchanges that circumvented former imperial centers. In this context, in the 1960s and 1970s, "Belgrade functioned as a transnational space of interaction for highly mobile international revolutionaries."[50]

One of the main proponents and theoreticians of non-alignment was Edvard Kardelj, who served as a key architect of Yugoslavia's foreign policy after the split with Stalin. Kardelj describes the NAM as a product of Cold War politics, but also as the result of a longer struggle of various peoples "to achieve full national liberty and to carve out the right, in such liberty, to develop socially according to their own lights; not to be, or to cease being, an economic and political appendage of the great world powers."[51] Countries that emerged victorious from their anticolonial and antifascist struggles, Kardelj argues, had encountered an existing international order that did not serve their interests. Hence, this order needed to be transformed according to the principle of "peaceful coexistence."

For Kardelj, peaceful coexistence is an active principle, based on the right to economic and political self-determination, and an impossibility within a system in which former colonial powers maintain economic influence over their former colonies.[52] The main objective of the NAM, he explains, is to tackle this uneven global economic development through structural changes to international relations and the global economy. Kardelj thus positions the NAM as a project of worldmaking, with the survival of the Third World conditioned on a reimagining of global power relations. NAM is fighting for a new world order based on "democratic elements," including a less exploitative international division of labor, economic aid for developing countries and stronger cultural ties between countries.[53]

Ultimately, for Kardelj, the NAM "was to serve both as a buffer and as an accelerator. As a 'buffer', the NAM would act against the hegemonic pretentions both of the capitalist and communist camps," and as an "accelerator," it would promote more rapid development in underdeveloped countries.[54] Non-aligned states could not rely on the East or the West for this development, however; their only way out of political and economic dependence was Third World cooperation.

The Yugoslav turn toward non-alignment corresponded to its rejection of Soviet-style centralization, in favor of worker self-management, and it is no accident that Kardelj was among the main proponents of self-management.[55] He viewed it as a means of realizing both the principle of free association as conceptualized by Marx and Engels, and "the withering away of the state" envisioned by Lenin.[56] At the 7th Congress of the League of Communists of Yugoslavia, held in Ljubljana in 1958, self-management was framed as a necessary counter to "bureaucratization" and "centralization." Unlike the centralized Soviet model, Yugoslavia thus promoted a decentralized system where workers had a significant role in managing enterprises through workers' councils, which made decisions on production, distribution, and investment. The objective was to reduce the state's direct control over economic activities by transferring authority to local institutions, including municipalities and regional governments, as well as workplaces.[57] By the late 1950s, self-management expanded from the economy into other spheres, leading to what James Robertson has termed "small socialism" and "a greater appreciation for the local, the peripheral and the minor in Yugoslav culture."[58]

Along with peaceful coexistence and self-management, Kardelj advanced the "many roads to socialism" doctrine—which contends that, as there is neither a single history nor a single model of socialism, socialist systems should be adapted to the historical and social circumstances of each country. This was an attractive idea to newly decolonized states looking to embark on their own socialist paths. Moreover, it positioned Yugoslavia as an ally to African and Asian nations that had embraced the idea that "the principles of Marxism-Leninism could be realized only through concrete experience which reflected the historical uniqueness and complexity of each adherent to socialism."[59] Yugoslav self-management became an example of such a localized socialism.

Like many other Yugoslav officials, Kardelj positioned his country as part of the imperially dominated world. He thus characterizes Yugoslavia as a "semi-colonial" country, due to its history of both Ottoman and Austro-Hungarian rule:

> The break-up of the colonial system in Europe and other continents was paralleled by the collapse – swift in some places, slower in others – of vestiges of semi-colonial relations of economic and political dependence characteristic, for instance, of the pre-war Yugoslavia. In some countries, like China, Yugoslavia, Vietnam and a few others in other parts of the world, genuinely people's and socialist revolutions were the outgrowth of national liberation wars.[60]

While never claiming that Yugoslavia shares the colonial history of other non-aligned states, Kardelj emphasizes that the Yugoslav experience of political and economic dependence makes Yugoslavia an ideal ally.

Kardelj thus makes a connection between antifascist, anticolonial, and socialist revolutions, not equating them entirely but highlighting that they are parallel fights guided by similar principles, as a way of justifying Yugoslavia's presence in the NAM. He writes that the forces of "fascist imperialism" had tried, through World War II, "to impose their political hegemony," but that quite the opposite had occurred, as a series of guerrilla movements fighting both imperialism and colonialism were unleashed across the globe.[61] Certainly, there are many differences between the historical experiences of Yugoslavia and those of former European colonies, but when Kardelj characterizes Yugoslavia as semicolonial, he is not merely alluding to history but is engaging in an interpolative exercise to strengthen Yugoslav identification with the Global South. This comparison was taken up by Senghor, for instance, in one of his diplomatic speeches in Yugoslavia.[62] At the same time, Kardelj frequently adopted a linear, progressive understanding of history and often characterized countries of the Global South as "backwards," pointing to his ambivalent position in relation to European colonial discourse.[63]

Debate has waged regarding the extent to which Yugoslavia's participation in the NAM was motivated by self-interest. Once it had been cut off from Soviet economic aid and expertise, and had refused this aid from the United States, Yugoslavia needed new markets in which to grow its export driven economy. Hence, Yugoslav policies toward African and Asian states have been characterized as "status-seeking solidarity performances" meant to deliver "positive recognition for Tito's regime and its alternative socialist modernity project."[64] While there is no doubt that Yugoslavia saw an opportunity to place its products in emerging markets and thus assure its economic independence from the world's two hegemonic blocks, it did also invest in the public infrastructure of developing countries, made its experts available, and provided loans at very favorable commercial terms that could be repaid through barter or at a much later date.[65] Yugoslavia thus supported its non-aligned allies in very concrete ways. Still, as a white, European country in the NAM, Yugoslavia practiced what Paul Stubbs has called "liminal hegemony," occupying "a space between the Global North and the Global South yet providing leadership of the South – in terms both of Yugoslavia's impact on the Movement and the impact of the Movement on internal developments within Yugoslavia itself."[66]

Yugoslavia's participation in the building of the Third World thus implicated "contradictory points of identification."[67] For example, Yugoslavia offered thousands of scholarships in engineering and medicine to students from other non-aligned countries to contribute to modernizing the Global South, but was unable to free itself entirely from the legacy of several centuries of racial capitalism, so that its official shift toward non-alignment did not eradicate racism within its six republics.[68] At the same time, Nemanja Radonjić has shown that in its fight against racism, Yugoslavia was not passive. Quite the contrary, researchers and policymakers actively discussed the presence of racism in the country and continuously debated the best ways to promote antiracist ideas and actions.[69] Peter Wright has made a similar argument when questioning the scholarly tendency where "a static socialist 'East' is opposed to a dynamic and transnational global order that formed unencumbered by the weight of socialism."[70] By contrast, Wright shows that the 1960s and 1970s were marked by "a dynamic and explicit self-interrogation of Yugoslavs' racial attitudes and identity," prompted notably by the activism of Black African students in Yugoslavia. In other words, it was through dialogues and interactions with people from the Global South that the Yugoslavs began interrogating their own racial identity and prejudices.[71] Thus, we need to understand Yugoslavia's "enrolment in the decolonial struggle as 'a gradual process,'" marked by "shifting understandings over time."[72] This was certainly the case for the Yugoslavs mentioned in this book.

On the Francophone side, the authors discussed in this book were well-aware of the liminality of Yugoslavia and recognized the Eurocentrisms of their Yugoslav friends, and it was precisely this intermediacy that they found intriguing. Senghor frequently reiterated the differences between African and Yugoslav socialism, but this did not prevent him from viewing Yugoslav federalism and socialism as useful examples to Africans. And while Césaire and Depestre both emphasized the specificity of the historical experience and positioning of the African diaspora, the peripheral positioning of their Yugoslav counterparts—and shared values of anticapitalism, antiracism, and anticolonialism—facilitated the development of these friendships.

Why Friends Matter

"For without friends no one would choose to live, though he had all other goods," wrote Aristotle.[73] Yet while there is a growing body of literature on friendships/enmities between states[74] and also a growing body on the ethical stakes of personal friendships,[75] the friend has essentially disappeared from our political vocabulary.[76] Therefore, I was surprised to see the term "friend" used so frequently in the context of Yugoslav–Francophone relations. In fact, in the letters, photographs, and video footage I drew from for this project, Francophone and Yugoslav intellectuals regularly referred to each other as friends. I wondered why they chose this term of engagement (as opposed to comrade, ally, partner, or brother/sister, for example) as well as why we no longer do the same in contemporary political struggle. In *Forgotten Friendships*, I bring to the fore friendships that have been overlooked in Francophone and Slavic studies, in an effort to rethink the "friend" as a political category.

In the binary reality of colonial relations, the colonized and the colonizer sat in opposition, divided, in a Manichean world of uncrossable lines.[77] In such a world, even friendships can disrupt established hierarchies, and the friendships described in this book did just that. They challenged racial divisions, as well as the notion that countries of the Global South could do little more than imitate models produced in the North. These Francophone authors and their Yugoslav counterparts shared "common concerns for building economic sovereignty that kept the Leninist emphasis on national self-determination as a foundation for socialist internationalism; a shared sense of peripherality and backwardness that required a collective endeavor to be overcome."[78]

Forgotten Friendships builds on the work of scholars who have theorized postcolonial and decolonial friendships. For instance, Leela Gandhi has focused on anti-imperial South Asian and European friendships that developed in the late nineteenth and early twentieth centuries to form "dissident cross-cultural collaborations."[79] Gandhi tells the often forgotten history of anti-imperial thought in Europe, particularly the emergence of "utopian-socialist critiques of Empire," and challenges the notion of European ideological uniformity. Many Europeans, especially those already on the margins of society, renounced their colonial privilege to stand in solidarity with the colonized. Gandhi thus conceptualizes friendship "as a countermand against social exclusion,"[80] ultimately proposing that "[a]ffective singularity, anarchist relationality, and other-directedness are...the constitutive elements of the utopic community that we are conjuring under the sign of friendship."[81]

Similarly, though in a somewhat different context, Paula Moya argues that interracial friendships are one way to "engage in a decolonial project with respect to race."[82] She says further that "both the epistemic and emotional dimensions of interracial friendships are central to forging an effective decolonial antiracist project."[83] Astrid Nordin has also written about the need to decolonize friendship, and contends that doing so requires that we challenge three assumptions: "(1) friendship is the less important, residual, and feminised other of enmity; (2) friends need to be significantly similar to the Self; and (3) friends are valuable because they affirm a stable sense of Self."[84] Nordin thus argues that the friend must be accepted in their alterity, while the sense of self can remain fluid.

I expand upon the work of these scholars by examining how the Francophone and Yugoslav intellectuals it features navigated sameness and alterity. Following Gandhi, I further develop the argument that Europe was never politically and ideologically homogeneous. However, unlike the valuable examples Gandhi offers, the perspective of Yugoslavs was not rooted merely in a critique of Empire. Together with their friends in the Global South, Yugoslavs actively participated in anticolonial struggles and in building a more just postcolonial world order. And it was not only individuals on the margins of society who did so; rather, many held official government positions, and even had state resources at their disposal due to Yugoslavia's involvement in the NAM. They distributed these resources to engage in what Gary Wilder has called "concrete utopianism," which "seeks to identify possibilities for alternative arrangements that may already dwell within, or be emerging from, the nonidentical order that actually exists."[85]

The authors featured in this book used the term "friend" to imply the inseparability of the private and the public, the personal and the political, in much the same way feminists deployed the slogan that the "personal is political." In other words, they referred to each other as friends to underline the fact that a common struggle builds strong personal bonds. Friends do not help each other only in private and personal matters, but also in the political arena, and it is in fact through collective struggle and collaboration that one achieves personal transformation. The fight is therefore public and at the same time intimate; collective and at the same time individual. Indeed, to borrow from Am Johal and Matt Hern, friendship simultaneously embodies freedom and constraint, creating spaces for intimacy and distance. Though often lacking a clear purpose, it is always poised for potential mobilization or dissolution, making it inherently political.[86] In this sense, these friends strived to realize Jacques Derrida's "democracy to come."

The same contradiction, argues Derrida, is at the heart of both friendship and democracy, in that they require sameness to survive and alterity to be transformative. While true democracy and true friendships must respect singularity, "there is no democracy without the 'community of friends' (*koina ta philon*), without the calculation of majorities, without identifiable, stabilizable, representable subjects, all equal."[87] Democracy cannot exist without absolute alterity, which must be eliminated in order to create a community of recognizable subjects. Derrida nonetheless believes in the possibility of a "democracy to come," based not on associations of blood, land, and nation, and the figure of the friend plays a significant role in this democracy as indistinguishable from the figure of alterity. To conceive of democracy outside of homogeneity and sameness, friendship must be positioned as an opening toward the future, which cannot be predetermined. Still, in many ways, this democracy exists only in that space between the preservation and elimination of alterity, or perhaps in the tension generated there, and so it remains an "*unfulfillable* promise."[88] For Derrida, this fundamentally different model of friendship remains hypothetical, though, as he cannot find any examples of it.[89] But the problem is not that examples do not exist, it is that he does not step outside the Western canon to discover them, as if friendship were a purely Western concept. I argue that Derrida would have been able to find concrete examples of radical friendship had he looked toward the Global South.[90]

This does not mean that the friendships described in this book were without problems or contradictions, though, and Yugoslavia undoubtedly demonstrated a certain ambivalence regarding both Europe and the Global South. In fact, these friends' historic, geographic and economic situations also differed in many respects. The brutality of European colonialism and the afterlives of slavery were not experienced in the same way by Yugoslavs. And yet, a process of mutual influence, cooperation, and translation occurred, nonetheless. Négritude could simultaneously address the historical specificity of the African diaspora and be in dialogue with multiple peripheries of the world. African socialism could look to Yugoslav federalism as an example, while adapting to local African conditions. The importance of internationalism, of building a network of cooperation across the Global South, reemerges in every chapter of this text. The friend is not merely an extension of the self; yet, friendship is also not love of the absolute stranger. These friendships are about lives intersecting, experiences communicated across difference, and interwoven attempts to envision and realize a more just global order. Within these friendships, difference was not merely tolerated but "seen as a fund of necessary polarities between which...creativity can spark like a dialectic."[91]

The goal of these friends was to initiate a global dialogue and establish ways of learning across the world's peripheries; and so it seems impossible to exclude Martinican thinker and writer Édouard Glissant from this discussion. Glissant writes that "rhizomatic thought is the principle behind... the Poetics of Relation, in which each and every identity is extended through a relationship with the Other."[92] In many ways, these friendships illustrate Glissant's understanding of Relation, where the primary elements do not only create a third element as they enter into a relationship but are furthermore themselves transformed in this process. In fact, through their friendships, the figures in this book were involved in a continuous practice of undoing capitalist and colonial ideology. Hence, returning to Moya's argument, these friendships allow us to "engage in a decolonial project with respect to race," where decoloniality is not an endstage but an ongoing process.

Césaire once said that he and Petar Guberina had led parallel lives. Lives at a distance yet moving in the same direction; aware of the other and adjusting in response; aiming to accomplish the same things in similar but different contexts; and throughout, learning from one another. These friends, like the other authors, intellectuals, and politicians featured in this text, did not reside in the same place, for the most part—one of the conditions for successful friendship set out by Aristotle[93]—but they followed the work of their friends and the destinies of their respective countries, from afar. Even when separated by distance, they engaged in a form of conviviality as described by Paul Gilroy, which "makes a nonsense of closed, fixed, and reified identity and turns attention toward the always unpredictable mechanisms of identification."[94] These were lifelong friendships, not always in the foreground, but continuously in the background, and in some cases reemerging at crucial times.

It was Petar Guberina's presence in 1930s Paris, for instance, that ignited the interest of both Senghor and Césaire in Yugoslavia. Senghor would turn toward Yugoslavia at the very beginning and very end of his political career. Similarly, Yugoslavia played an important early role for Césaire as the genesis of his *Cahier*, then reappeared (if briefly) in his famous letter to Maurice Thorez declaring his resignation from the French Communist Party, and then came to the fore near the end of his life when he participated in a documentary about his decades-long friendship with Guberina. Yugoslavia also played an important role for Depestre at the beginning of his political and literary career, as it was there that he had one of his first experiences of collective political action. Yet, it was only much later that he would write about it, in a collection of short stories he authored in the 1990s. Throughout the 1960s, Aoua Kéita established friendships with members of the Conference for the Social Activity of the Women of Yugoslavia that endured long after she was stripped of her official duties. Finally, Zdravko Pečar, who participated directly in the Algerian War for Independence, continued to write about Algeria long afterward, and Algerian officials continued to call upon him to share his account of the Algerian revolution.

In other words, these friendships spanned decades, and were a source of hope and inspiration drawn upon when needed. Notably, these friendships also challenge the story often told about the relationship of Francophone authors to communism: Césaire was a Marxist until his disappointment with the French Communist Party led to his staunch resignation, marking his break with communism and his realization that a revolution led by the European proletariat would not necessarily solve the problems of colonized people; and Depestre was a devoted communist, until he abandoned politics, disappointed with the direction the Cuban revolution had taken. These narratives are rooted in an identification of communism with Stalinism and dismiss the extent to which these authors developed a nuanced understanding of communism and its various iterations, just as they developed a nuanced understanding of Europe and its internal divisions. They were critical of the Soviet Union, but they viewed its politics as a specific and problematic implementation of communist thought and, throughout their lives, continued to search for alternatives. This is not to say that Yugoslav socialism was the ideal alternative, or without its problems, of course, but simply that the complex and nuanced relationship of Francophone intellectuals like Césaire, Senghor, Depestre and Kéita to communism and socialism is often omitted or overlooked. While they rejected Stalinism and adherence to the Soviet Union, they never rejected socialism entirely, and remained interested and even invested in various possible applications of Marxism.

It should also be noted that the official rhetoric of the Yugoslav government toward newly decolonized countries was one of friendship. Asian and African states were among those deemed "*prijateljske zemlje*" ("friendly countries"), and this guided the diplomatic stance of Yugoslavia. Thus, when Tito undertook a 72-day trip to various African countries in the spring of 1961, to promote the idea of non-alignment in anticipation of the 1961 conference in Belgrade, most of his visits were described in official sources as "visits to friends," and this theme of friendship reverberated across the continent. During his visit to Ethiopia, for instance, Tito declared that the two countries were "linked together by deep friendship based on common aspirations which came to expression more than once in the past, and particularly in the struggle against the forces of aggression on the eve and during World War II."[95] This rhetoric of friendship extended beyond official documents and speeches and even came directly from Yugoslavs themselves. While traveling on his yacht, *Galeb*, Tito received dozens of daily telegrams from across Yugoslavia with messages of friendship directed to Africans. For example, people in the village of Grljan, in eastern Serbia near the border with Bulgaria, wrote that they were deeply upset by the assassination of Congolese Prime Minister Lumumba, and lauded Tito for undertaking this voyage "to once again contribute to the cause of peace and friendship with the peoples of Africa."[96] The Vukovar military post office collective sent a similar message, wishing Tito "a nice, happy and successful trip to the distant but friendly and always close countries of Africa."[97]

I am not suggesting that the friendships explored in this book merely reproduced official government rhetoric. Far from it. But they did develop in specific sociopolitical contexts that allowed for them to materialize, and moved within but also beyond those contexts, continuously envisioning possibilities for the future, yet to be realized.

Transnational Friendships and/as Comparative Methods

Friendship is both the topic and the method of this book. In fact, the way these intellectuals thought and acted across national borders and local differences can serve as a lesson for all of us working in literary studies, across languages and regions. In this regard I build on the work of literary scholar Gayatri Chakravorty Spivak who has argued that Derrida's "teleiopoesis" could function as a model for a renewed comparative literature.[98] Derrida's neologism encompasses three different terms (tele/telos/poiesis), allowing him to merge the objective (telos) with distance (tele). In teleopoiesis, the telos of the imaginative act is always deferred, always at a distance. For Derrida, friendship is linked to teleopoiesis; it can bring about an alternative future, but this outcome remains a *perhaps*, its realization always uncertain. There is no friendship without risk, as the anticipated future may never be realized, and therein lies the political value of friendship, as any predetermined political project is but a "a programme or a causality, a development, a process without an event."[99]

Comparative literature, Spivak argues, should draw from Derrida's discussion of teleopoiesis and friendship, in order to invoke "acts of the imagination that cross time and space with uncertain outcomes."[100] A comparative literature influenced by Derrida's politics of friendship could, thus, offer models of "reconstellating, copying and pasting for editing, teleopoiesis."[101] The intellectuals analyzed in this book did precisely this by showing how global conversations can have local applications. The friendships discussed in this book were a balancing act between similarity and singularity, between global projects and local particularities, as they posed "questions of solidarity and community from the interstitial perspective."[102] Arvind Sharma has introduced the term "reciprocal illumination" to refer to ways in which ideas from one tradition or region can shed light on those from another.[103] My argument is, foremost, that through their friendships, the intellectuals studied in this book engaged in a process of "reciprocal illumination." At the same time, studying these collaborations brings the fields of Francophone and Slavic studies into that same process. In this way, these stories of international friendships also become stories of comparative methods, which allow us to consider the role of comparative literature in "advocating for a depoliticization of a politics of hostility toward a politics of friendship to come."[104] Thus, while I offer a lot of historical information in this book, *Forgotten Friendships* is not a traditional historiography. Rather, it is an interdisciplinary study grounded in the field of comparative literature, which uses close reading as its primary method of analysis.

To tell the story of these friendships, I read across a corpus of literary texts, archival materials, newspaper articles, interviews, and photographs in four languages: French, English, Serbo-Croatian, and Macedonian. Various official government documents—notably those from the Archives of Yugoslavia—are used in combination with secondary sources to establish historical context, as for instance of Yugoslav involvement in the Algerian War of Independence. The book's research also relies heavily on (auto)biographies, interviews, and private correspondence. These friendships were personal and it is in personal accounts and recollections that their intimate aspect is best expressed. Furthermore, this approach, which focuses on specific figures, complements and counterbalances existing narratives of Yugoslavia and the NAM, which focus on government policy.[105]

Many of the personal accounts that follow are of an anecdotal nature. Here, following Jane Gallop, I strive to "think through anecdotes," reading them for the theoretical insights they offer.[106] According to Joel Fineman, the anecdote, defined as "the narration of a singular event," is "the literary form or genre that uniquely refers to the real."[107] The anecdote has literary characteristics yet it also exceeds its literary status, thereby connecting the fictional to the historical. In fact, the anecdote is uniquely connected to history because it "lets history happen by virtue of the way it introduces an opening into the teleological, and therefore timeless, narration of beginning, middle, and end."[108] *Forgotten Friendships* is not a book about anecdotes per se. But it does use personal accounts of Césaire's, Depestre's, Senghor's, and Kéita's visits to Yugoslavia as well as Pečar's time spent in Algeria, to understand what these places and friendships meant to them, personally. Furthermore, I argue, close readings of these documents uncover important theoretical insights on internationalism, solidarity, and friendship, enabling interpretive breakthroughs. Surrounding fictional texts like Césaire's *Cahier* or Depestre's *Eros* with other types of narratives (historical and personal), creates openings that allow for more nuanced and transnational readings of these texts. In fact, from this diverse corpus of texts and images, emerge stories of interconnected lives and intersecting geographies.

Archival, cultural, and documentary texts are thus interwoven in each chapter of this book. In Chapter One, I combine readings of Aimé

Césaire's *Cahier d'un Retour au Pays Natal* with excerpts from *Martinska-Martinique*, a documentary film about the friendship between Césaire and Petar Guberina, made by Zagreb-based Kenyan director Lawrence Kiiru. The focus of Chapter Two is on archival materials documenting the visits of both Prime Minister Mamadou Dia and President Léopold Sédar Senghor of Senegal, to Yugoslavia. Chapter Three alternates between a short story by René Depestre that describes his experience in Yugoslavia and an interview I conducted with him in 2017. In Chapter Four, I bring together Aoua Kéita's autobiography with archival materials documenting her collaboration with the Yugoslav Conference for the Social Activity of Women. Finally, Chapter Five discusses the extensive photographic archive of the Algerian War of Independence found in the Belgrade Museum of African Art.

By combining the literary and archival, my aim is not merely to assess whether literary narratives correspond to their historical circumstances. Rather, reading these literary narratives in conjunction with documentary materials opens an array of new interpretations. The "autobiographical example," as Saidiya Hartman observes, "is not a personal story that folds onto itself; it's not about navel gazing, it's really about trying to look at historical and social process and one's own formation as a window onto social and historical processes, as an example of them."[109] While not all the texts mentioned here are necessarily autobiographical, this superposition of documentary and literary materials gives us new insights into both. Césaire, Depestre, Senghor, Pečar, and Kéita were writing in response to their historical conditions; their literary texts can and should be read in relation to their interviews, recollections, and personal writings. It is in these private exchanges and personal recountings that important theoretical insights frequently appear.

I thus offer close analysis of some archival documents, such as speeches delivered by Senghor during his official visit to Yugoslavia. These belong to the specific genre of diplomatic speeches but could also be read as essays, clarifying Senghor's conceptualization of Négritude, the Civilization of the Universal, and *métissage*, as well as his interest in Yugoslavia. Following Yohann Ripert, I treat these speeches, as well as other archival materials, less as factual documents and more as literary texts that "open a fictional world," searching "for meaning within the rhetorical and ideological framings that the text deploys."[110] The personal and the documentary are thus intertwined throughout this book, and together form an understudied archive of revolutionary friendships. Different forms of friendship are also highlighted, from individual friendships between Césaire, Senghor, Guberina, and Šopov, in the context of both Négritude and the rise of African socialism, to the edges that exist between friendship, love, and camaraderie, as manifest in Depestre's two narratives of his experience in Bosnia (one fictional and one he offered in our interview) and the introduction of a Yugoslav antifascist revolutionary and woman, Kostandinka Crnojević. Female friendships via a network of Malian-Yugoslav connections, centered on Malian anticolonial activist and midwife, Aoua Kéita, are also explored. Finally, the book takes a culturally reversed approach by tracking a network of Yugoslavs who were considered friends of the Algerian revolution. In particular, the photographs found in Pečar's archive position friendship at the center of Algerian revolution.

In Chapter One, Yugoslavia is shown to have represented an important detour for Césaire, who began writing his *Cahier* in Dalmatia, after he discovered Martinska, a local island that reminded him of his native Martinique. Yet, an analysis of this Balkan genesis of *Cahier* is absent from most critical interpretations of the work. In Dalmatia, Césaire viewed Europe from its periphery, and found a different Europe with which he had some things in common. His relationship with Yugoslavia, and with Guberina, allows us to understand better his internationalism, and his attempts to think across the world's peripheries.

Léopold Sédar Senghor's long friendships with Petar Guberina and Macedonian poet Aco Šopov anchor the following chapter. Even before he entered the Senegalese presidency, Senghor's conceptualization of African socialism was deeply influenced by Yugoslav federalism and self-management, and this chapter presents official documents from the visits of Mamadou Dia and Senghor to Yugoslavia. There, Senghor gave a number of speeches on the importance of internationalism, solidarity, and friendship. Yugoslavia played an important role at the beginning of his political career, but also at the end, when Senghor returned to some of his initial postulates about African socialism. His visit to Yugoslavia was facilitated by Šopov, who like Senghor, was both a poet and a politician, and served as the Yugoslav ambassador to Senegal. Their relationship and collaboration shaped both of their careers.

Chapter Three focuses on Haitian poet and intellectual René Depestre, who participated in the 1947 construction of the Šamac-Sarajevo railroad in Bosnia alongside other local and international youth volunteers. This experience of socialist rebuilding after World War II deeply impacted Depestre, who remained attached to Yugoslavia throughout his life. Indeed, his enduring connection to Yugoslavia complicates the story of his supposed break from politics after his departure from Cuba. By combining a close reading of "La jupe," a short story Depestre wrote regarding his experience in Yugoslavia, and an interview I conducted with him in 2017, I question the existing apolitical interpretations of his later stories.

In Chapter Four, female friendships between African and Yugoslav communists come to the fore through a focus on the Malian midwife and anticolonial activist Aoua Kéita and her friendships with Veda Zagorac and Vida Tomšič. After Mali declared independence, Kéita's work became increasingly internationalized, in part through her work as Secretary-General of the Women's Social Commission within the US-RDA.[111] In this context, she worked with many women's organizations, including the Yugoslav Conference for the Social Activity of Women, and official collaborations led to the development of personal friendships in some cases. Kéita's connection with various Yugoslav women contributes to our understanding of transnational feminisms, which think and act across difference without homogenizing women as a category.

Chapter Five shines a light on the role of Zdravko Pečar and Veda Zagorac in the Algerian War of Independence and their efforts to mediatize the accomplishments of the ALN. As journalists and diplomats, they both spent years reporting from Algeria and facilitating the official aid provided by the Yugoslav government to the FLN. Furthermore, Pečar—who wrote a PhD dissertation on the history and revolutionary struggle of Algeria, which was later published as his book *Algeria to Independence*—organized the visit of a Yugoslav Newsreels crew to document the Algerian War. The resulting collection, which I see as an archive of friendship and revolution, counters French propaganda by representing the ALN in a different light and focusing mostly on the bonds and joy of revolution, rather than its bloody consequences.

Together, these five chapters tell the story of internationalisms untold, globalizations otherwise, and revolutionary friendships overlooked. I tell these stories in part to challenge a current of contemporary pessimism on the left that "dismisses solidarity politics and internationalist projects as intrinsically Western, elite, or liberal—as alibis for hierarchy and pathways to imperialism."[112] Gary Wilder has recently criticized this form of pessimism, which relies on "Left culturalism, presentism and realism." As he describes it, Left culturalism relies on "quasi ontological claims about incommensurable lifeworlds and categorical claims about epistemological differences."[113] Any positive assessment of these internationalist projects is characterized as romanticized, naive, and foolish, hindering "our capacity to forge transversal political alignments in the service of other possible worlds."[114]

I share Wilder's view of the perils of this type of pessimism, which "perversely mirrors neoliberalism's end-of-history triumphalism precisely when our times call for new practices of concrete utopianism in the service of new forms of Left internationalism."[115] While we should not romanticize the past or ignore the contradictions of earlier internationalist projects, it is not helpful to assume that any belief in the possibility of solidarity is naive and that any value found in historical examples is uncritical. After all, when we lack examples of history, futures are more difficult to imagine, even though past mistakes must be acknowledged if we are to avoid repeating them. By rejecting the utility of any past examples and "by identifying pessimism with radicalism, political realists seek to disparage utopian imagination as naïve about or complicit with dominant power relations."[116] Studies of solidarity projects and friendships across the Global South are necessary precisely because they challenge culturalism and pessimism. This does not mean these projects are without incongruities, or these friendships without conflict. Yet they can still widen our political horizons, both globally and locally.

This task seems particularly relevant if we are to respond to recent calls to envision a new politics of solidarity across the Global South. For instance, before his passing, Marxist scholar Samir Amin advocated for the creation of a new political organization which would amalgamate progressive and revolutionary movements worldwide and the current iteration of the global capitalist system.[117] Since then, scholars have debated Amin's call for an International Alliance of Workers and Peoples, mostly agreeing on the need to increase cooperation across the Global South, yet diverging on the organizational structure that could support this effort.[118] While friendship alone may not be enough to sustain Amin's Fifth International, I hope that the next five chapters will show the importance of nurturing friendships in the context of Global South solidarity.

CHAPTER ONE

Across Peripheries: Aimé Césaire and the Balkan Genesis of the *Cahier*

Alexandra Perisic: I've always found it very interesting that it was in Dalmatia (i.e., in Croatia) that Césaire started writing *Cahier d'un Retour au Pays Natal* [*Notebook of a Return to the Native Land*].[1] What do you think about this?

René Depestre: I think it's extraordinary! When he opened his window at Guberina's parents' house, Césaire could see out to the ocean, spotting an island in the distance...It's up to you to tell that amazing story. The work is a masterpiece of decolonization, before Senghor and Frantz Fanon even entered the scene. It's the most important book ever written on the phenomenon of colonialism. And it was born in Croatia!

Alexandra Perisic: Do you think there's a historical reason for this connection?

René Depestre: Césaire was deeply attached to his friend Guberina's country. The emotion he felt being there, and the whole Martinique island connection, would have made Aimé Césaire feel an unprecedented degree of nostalgia and rebellion.

This exchange—from an interview I conducted in 2017 with Haitian writer René Depestre (whose own Yugoslav story I tell in Chapter Three)—and his comment that Césaire felt "an unprecedented degree of nostalgia and rebellion" in Yugoslavia, which inspired him to write *Cahier*, guides the analysis in this chapter.[2] The story of *Cahier*'s origins has been recounted in numerous studies of Césaire's work, including in Robin D. G. Kelley's brilliant introduction to *Discourse on Colonialism*.[3] Yet this Yugoslav connection tends to be framed as merely anecdotal, circumstantial, and ultimately irrelevant to the meaning and form of the text in *Cahier*, which was written primarily in Paris.[4]

I have been aware of this story for many years, and for all those years it has intrigued me. Why was it in Yugoslavia, of all places in the world, that Césaire felt inspired to begin *Cahier*? In this chapter, I argue that this was not sheer chance, and that Yugoslavia represented an important detour for Césaire.[5] Césaire's friendship with Petar Guberina and his discovery of Martinska allowed him to see how the particularity of his experience as a member of the African diaspora could serve as a basis for solidarity with other oppressed people. His Martinican-ness, it turned out, was relevant far beyond the island, and in unexpected places like Dalmatia.

Reading Césaire through the lens of this Yugoslav detour adds another layer to existing interpretations of *Cahier*. Notably, it allows us to better understand Césaire's commitment in the poem to a specific kind of universality, one that doesn't negate the particularities of various historical experiences. To borrow from Yohann Ripert, Césaire's connection to Yugoslavia helped him "uncover a nascent image of globality as it is grasped in the (ex-)colonies."[6] And while the accusation of racial essentialism has long followed the founders of the Négritude movement due to Jean Paul Sartre's now famous "Black Orpheus" essay, the Yugoslav connection invites a more layered and nuanced reading of *Cahier*, the unusual origins of which resonate throughout its verses.[7] The poem, and its view from Martinska, invites an archipelagic interpretation, underlining its transnational dimensions. When Césaire found his Martinique in Dalmatia, it struck him that the island followed him everywhere. Though Martinska is actually located on a peninsula, Césaire describes it as a separate island, pointing to the strength of his imagination. This inability to ever really leave Martinique, which reappeared in the most unusual places—such as off the coast of Croatia—inspired Césaire to explore the (im)possibility of "return" and use it to develop a more global understanding of oppression and resistance.

Clearly, Yugoslavia was not Césaire's sole inspiration for *Cahier*, but the Balkans are woven into the background of the poem. This may seem unusual if we consider Négritude to be a movement advocating a return to a mythologized Africa. If, however, we embrace Souleymane Bahir Diagne's conception of Négritude as a "philosophy of becoming," marked both by an acceptance of one's historical positioning as "nègre" and an opening toward the world, the Yugoslav connection begins to make sense.[8] In fact, it is not by accident that Martinique reappeared to Césaire in Yugoslavia. As Anja Jovic Humphrey notes, it was in Dalmatia that Césaire discovered "another face of Europe;"[9] which is not merely to say that he discovered a "good" Europe, as opposed to the "bad" Europe incarnated by France. Rather, he discovered Europe's internal other, a part of Europe that was subjugated both by the East and the West, pointing to the instability of Europe and whiteness as constructs and ideologies.

This was the Europe that was home to Petar Guberina, renowned linguist and among Césaire's closest friends. Césaire admired his work, and not surprisingly so, as Guberina's research had shown that rhythm, intonation, and the body played a crucial role in European linguistics, despite their common association with non-European cultures. Guberina found that these attributes, ostensibly particular to non-European societies and deemed inferior by Europeans to mind and reason, were universally important to our understanding of human languages. His research thus supported Césaire's belief that, only by embracing his own particularity, could he reach what Gary Wilder has called a "concrete universality."[10]

The friendship of Césaire and Guberina is outlined in this chapter. This is followed by a reading of *Cahier*, inflected by its Yugoslav origins. Finally, Guberina's research in linguistics and its relevance for the Négritude movement is discussed.

An Unusual Friendship

Aimé Césaire was born in Basse-Pointe, Martinique, in 1913. His family moved to Fort-de-France when he was still a boy, so that he could attend the Lycée Schoelcher. There in the capital, Césaire encountered the Martinican bourgeoisie, provoking a deep sense of disdain in him: "I started to hate—and I'm not using the word lightly—the Martinican society I grew up in, which was made up of the black petite bourgeoisie. I can still see those people, and, at a young age, I was shocked by their deep-seated need to imitate Europeans."[11] He dreamed of leaving, and soon had the chance to do so when he was awarded an educational scholarship to study at the prestigious Lycée Louis-le-Grand in Paris.

France "offered the promise of freedom, of opportunities, of hope and self-discovery."[12] In the French capital, Césaire befriended two fellow students who would become the future co-founders of the Négritude movement with him—Léopold Sédar Senghor from Senegal and Léon Damas from Guyana. Indeed, Paris in the 1930s was a meeting place for many members of the African diaspora.[13] Césaire recalled the influence that Langston Hughes and Claude McKay had on him, for example, when for the first time he met Black writers whose work expressed pride in their culture, their difference, and their race. This was a revelation for Césaire, as it represented an approach so entirely contrary to that of French assimilationism.[14] Césaire's time in Paris was also shaped by the literary salon of the Nardal sisters and literary publications such as *L'Étudiant noir* and *Légitime défense.* Contributors to *L'Étudiant noir* expressed their resistance to colonialism and racism, emphasizing pride in their African heritage, while writers of *Légitime défense* were critical of both the colonial system and bourgeois values, which they viewed as perpetuating inequality and injustice. As Brent Hayes Edwards has demonstrated, these publications provided a platform for Black students and intellectuals to share their experiences and perspectives, thereby fostering a collective diasporic consciousness. This, in turn, laid the groundwork for future intellectual and political movements within the African diaspora and contributed to Césaire's transnationalism.[15]

Césaire's friendship with Senghor was equally formative, as it transformed his opinion of Africa. Before meeting Senghor, Césaire's knowledge of the continent was reduced to colonial stereotypes that circulated in Europe and the Caribbean, portraying Africa as backward and lacking civilization and culture, as a center of barbarism that could only be corrected through the lasting influence and involvement of Europe. The Martinican bourgeoisie felt they were culturally closer to Europeans, and thus saw themselves as superior to Africans, motivating them to erase any sign of African influence on the island. But through Senghor, Césaire saw that Africa was the birthplace of multiple civilizations and concluded that the cultural link between Africa and the Caribbean needed to be revalorized.

Yet, it is another friendship from Césaire's time in Paris, and one that is frequently forgotten, that anchors our story on the Croatian coast. Césaire would later say that Yugoslav Petar Guberina, who had arrived in Paris from his hometown in Dalmatia, was as important to him as Senghor. In the 1991 documentary *Martinska-Martinique*, Césaire noted that only a few essential encounters can change the course of one's life, and that he had enjoyed such encounters with both Senghor and Guberina. Césaire credited Guberina for having "contributed to orienting my vision of man and my vision of history."[16] Given Césaire's own acknowledgment of the formative nature of this relationship, it is surprising that it remains largely unexplored.

Césaire himself has offered two versions of how he met Guberina. In an interview he gave to *Le Monde* in 2006, Césaire claimed their vegetarianism had brought them together in a student canteen in Paris. The server had wondered out loud whether Césaire was eating only tomatoes for financial reasons, and when Césaire explained that it was a question of philosophy rather than finances, his comments were met with approval by Guberina, who was waiting in line.[17] But in *Martinska-Martinique*, Césaire told a slightly different story, recounting that he and Guberina were in fact unable to pay for a proper breakfast in the canteen, so they chose to hide out in the table-tennis room and share stories about the poverty and misery of Martinique and Yugoslavia. Eventually, he said a third student who was also in need of a hideout joined them in the ritual, and this was how he met Senghor.[18] This puts a twist on the Négritude trio we typically envision, of Césaire, Senghor, and Damas, and their shared experience with the legacy of French colonialism, and introduces a more unusual triangulation between Martinique, Senegal, and Yugoslavia.[19] Guberina may have been the odd man out, but he and Césaire became inseparable, despite their differences.

One of the rare scholars to have probed deeper into the relationship between Césaire and Guberina is Anja Jovic Humphrey who, without conflating the two men, uses their friendship to draw a parallel between the Black and Balkan experiences. Analyzing the three existing prefaces to Césaire's *Cahier*, written by Benjamin Peret, André Breton, and Guberina, she concludes that "Guberina…demonstrated that he knew how to listen to Césaire more carefully than the two French writers."[20] While the prefaces of Breton and Peret are imbued with exoticism, Jovic Humphrey finds that Guberina showed a greater sense of respect and solidarity with Césaire, attributing this to similarities between the Balkan and Black condition that led Guberina to better understand his Martinican friend.[21]

While this perspective is one that I have waited many years to hear, I believe there is more to be said on the topic, as the focus of Jovic Humphrey is ultimately on the Balkans and her proposal that Balkanitude, mirrored on the concept of Négritude, is a framework for understanding the region. It is my desire to approach this question from the other side: that of Césaire. For him, his friendship with Guberina was important in part because the Yugoslav introduced Césaire to the European periphery. As Jovic Humphrey has argued, this led him to conceive of two Europes. While most critics speak of *a* Europe in Césaire's work, he always insisted on the fact that there were both a Europe that colonized him and a Europe that experienced domination. This second Europe was the Europe Césaire encountered in the Balkans.

Discovering Europe's Periphery

It is precisely as a land of contradictions and transitions that Yugoslavia represented a fruitful detour for Césaire.[22] This does not mean that *Cahier* would never have been written had Césaire not come to Yugoslavia. Perhaps, if he had visited Senegal with Senghor that summer, he would have been even more inspired. There is no way to know, and it is of no matter. I simply want to suggest that Guberina and Senghor played complementary roles for Césaire. Senghor challenged Césaire's conception of Africa, and Guberina infused his understanding of Europe with new subtleties. In other words, Africa was no longer a cultureless tabula rasa, but Europe was also no longer its antithesis. The Balkans had become a crack in the European myth that rested on the superiority and stability of whiteness.

Césaire's friendship with Guberina and his attachment to Yugoslavia allowed him to challenge the binary logic of the colonial worldview and build interracial solidarities in its place. For he and others, Yugoslavia became a site for the construction of what Edward Said called "adversarial internationalizations," or transnational alliances striving to dismantle imperialism.[23] And Césaire's relationship with Guberina and Yugoslavia continued long after his first visit in 1935. Césaire attended Guberina's dissertation defense at the Sorbonne in 1939, for example, and found the work of his friend to be revolutionary, as he was the first to show the importance of extraverbal elements to human speech.[24] Then, when World War II separated them, Césaire followed events from afar as the

Yugoslav Partisans won the antifascist struggle and the Socialist Federal Republic of Yugoslavia was formed. Césaire keenly tracked the development of Yugoslav socialism and self-management, which departed from the Soviet model.

In the 1950s, the two friends met again in Paris. Césaire was the mayor of Fort-de-France and a deputy in the National Assembly, and Guberina, who had been involved in the Yugoslav antifascist resistance, frequently visited Paris in his role as a diplomat. The two attended meetings at Présence Africaine and collaborated on organizing the First Congress of Black Writers and Artists, which took place in Paris in 1956.[25] Césaire commented on this in *Martinska-Martinique*, explaining, "One can ask oneself, what is a Yugoslav, a Dalmatian, doing at the Congress of Black Writers and Artists? He was like a brother, one of us…"[26] That same year, Césaire asked Guberina to write the preface for a new version of *Cahier*, to be published by Présence Africaine.[27] By including Guberina's voice in what would become the defining version of his poem, Césaire reintroduced the Balkans into *Cahier*, in a nod toward one of his initial inspirations.

It was also in 1956 that Césaire wrote his famous letter to the leader of the French Communist Party Maurice Thorez, announcing his departure from the party over its unwillingness to deal with the question of race, which it had merely subsumed into the universal fight of the proletariat. Yet, in his critique of existing socialist regimes, Césaire explicitly excluded Yugoslavia:

> All of this authorizes the statement that, *with the exception of Yugoslavia*, in numerous European countries—in the name of socialism—usurping bureaucracies that are cut off from the people (bureaucracies from which it is now proven that nothing can be expected) have achieved the pitiable wonder of transforming into a nightmare what humanity has for so long cherished as a dream: socialism.[28]

Clearly, when this letter was written, Césaire still saw in Yugoslavia the possibility of a different socialism, one that did not follow in Stalin's footsteps. By mentioning Yugoslavia in this way, Césaire also underlined that he was not in fact parting with Marxism and socialism per se, but with the politics and ideology of the French Communist Party, and its alignment with Stalin. He wanted to see "Marxism and communism be placed in the service of black peoples, and not black peoples in the service of Marxism and communism."[29] He was not advocating that colonized peoples follow the Yugoslav model, and was in fact quite unambiguous that the problem of colonized people is unique. But he also envisioned "a movement that places us shoulder to shoulder with others,"[30] which Christopher T. Bonner has described as a form of "non-aligned communism."[31] Césaire's affinity to Yugoslavia was noticed by the German newspaper *Die Zeit,* which that same year described Césaire as the "Black Tito."[32]

It is not accidental that just as he split with the French Communist Party, Césaire asked his communist Yugoslav friend to write the preface to *Cahier.* The choice was a reflection of Césaire's continued belief in the potential for another kind of socialism, for interracial solidarity, and for a changed Europe; and a gesture toward the fact that this position was present in *Cahier.* Though Césaire and Guberina did not share historical circumstances and experiences, seeing Europe from its periphery had allowed both to see its heterogeneity and instability, making it easier for them to undo the myth of European superiority and imagine new possibilities. When Césaire visited Yugoslavia in 1935, he discovered similarities between the European periphery and the colonized world. Dalmatia, he said, reminded him of Martinique in some ways, except that it was less green.[33] Both places were "handicapped" from having been "colonized" and "underdeveloped."[34] These resemblances opened Césaire to the possibility of building interracial solidarity across peripheries, and in this sense, the Yugoslav trip was a crucial detour for him.

A Fortuitous Detour

For Martinican philosopher and writer Édouard Glissant, the detour is:

> [T]he ultimate resort of a population whose domination by an Other is concealed: it then must search elsewhere for the principle of domination, which is not evident in the country itself: because the system of domination (which is not only exploitation, which is not only misery, which is not only underdevelopment, but actually the complete eradication of an economic entity) is not directly tangible.[35]

The detour is preceded by reversion, a search for the place of origin, the root, and a single identity. Once the impossibility of return is acknowledged, reversion is supplanted by the detour. The detour is a tactic, a ruse, "an indirect mode of resistance that 'gets around' obstacles rather than confronting them head on, and it arises as a response to a situation of disguised rather than overt oppression and struggle."[36]

Glissant found the primary example of a detour to be Creole language. Creole evolved from French but turned the master's language into something he could no longer understand, through a "systemic process of derision" whereby "the slave takes possession of the language imposed by the master, a simplified language, adopted to the demands of this labor (a black pidgin) and makes this simplification even more extreme."[37] It is a kind of "camouflage" that "facilitates diversion"; meaning that Creole is a language "constituted around its strategy of trickery."[38] The Antillean Creole of Martinique remains marked by this "camouflage" despite having moved beyond the need for it.

Syncretic religions, marronage, and emigration are other examples of this detour, and Glissant describes emigration as similarly marked by "concealment," in this case "of alienation."[39] It is only once emigrants from the Caribbean arrive in France that they realize they are seen and treated differently, and only then do they discover the inescapability of racial capitalism. However, by the time they make this discovery, a return is no longer possible as they have already become too Europeanized. Emigration thus leaves one in a state of "psychic torture," making it the perfect example of a detour, as one needs to go "elsewhere" to uncover the source of their alienation.[40]

There is an ambiguity to the detour, which "is not a freely chosen, rationally planned autonomous act of opposition, but neither is it simply an evasion."[41] It may leave one in a wilderness of anguish, but also "does not in any sense mean an escape from reality." As Glissant explains, "[i]n the Caribbean, one of the traditional forces of opposition in complicated situations is the ruse."[42] A detour sometimes "leads nowhere" when the initial ruse "does not encounter any real potential for development."[43] Yet, it may "lead somewhere when the obstacle for which the detour was made tends to develop into concrete 'possibilities'."[44]

As Mireille Rosello has observed, authors from Caribbean islands imbue their texts with the ambiguity of endless detours. The place from which exile can be defined has been annihilated by the colonial reality. Hence, it is only retrospectively that Antillean intellectuals have been able to rediscover a homeland, by talking about people of the Antilles as already exiled.[45] For Césaire, two detours shaped the pages of *Cahier*; one French, one Yugoslav, serving different yet complementary purposes. As a student in France, where Césaire met other members of the African diaspora who were aware and proud of their histories and cultures, he realized he had still not fully embraced either of these things, and moreover that his scorn for the Martinican *petite bourgeoisie* had not kept him from internalizing their values. In Yugoslavia, when Martinique reappeared for him in Dalmatia—a place where the downtrodden of the world gathered—Césaire discovered a Europe with which he could be in solidarity. His homeland was no longer the island where Césaire felt claustrophobic and isolated; it had become part of a global archipelago. His Martinican-ness did not condemn him to global isolation once he saw that the peripheries of the world could be joined in their fight against European capitalism and imperialism.

The French and Yugoslav detours of Césaire worked in conjunction, each offering him new opportunities for solidarity. In this way, *Cahier* was never a product only of "the binary space France/Martinique";[46] it was always about a world in Relation. The famous streetcar scene in *Cahier* illustrates the importance of the French detour for Césaire. In a Parisian streetcar, the poet encounters a group of white women sneering at a Black man, and in a moment of weakness and with a smile of recognition, sides with the women:

> A comical and ugly nigger, with some women behind me sneering at him.
> He was COMICAL AND UGLY,
> COMICAL AND UGLY for sure.
> I displayed a big complicitous smile…
> My cowardice rediscovered!
> Hail to the three centuries which uphold my civil rights and
> my minimized blood.
> My heroism, what a farce![47]

The scene represents a moment of acknowledgment by Césaire of his own alienation. He becomes aware of his own bourgeois tendencies, the impulse to cast himself as an educated Black man, closer to whiteness than to "a gangly nigger without rhythm or measure."[48] As the poet "rediscovers" his cowardice, he suggests he has been in this situation before. His repetition of "comical and ugly"—a reference to Baudelaire's poem *L'Albatros*—superimposes the words of the sneering women and those of the poet, as he realizes his alienation from the language he speaks. His sojourn turns into exile as the poet experiences "a permanent gap...between the 'I' and the community within which that 'I' temporarily finds itself."[49]

Césaire left Martinique, but he didn't leave what he hated most about it: the impossible desire to identify with whiteness. Still, as this scene in *Cahier* unfolds, it is clear this is not the only way to identify, and the poet recognizes he does not have to be in solidarity with the white women; that he can choose to side with "a gangly nigger." This detour has opened the possibility of choice, allowing new solidarities to develop, and it is a first step toward subsequent verses in *Cahier*, such as:

> I accept...I accept...totally, without reservation...
> my race that no ablution of hyssop mixed with lilies could purify.[50]

All of *Cahier* can in fact be read as a movement from the streetcar scene to the moment of acceptance by the poet of his race and its vices. This is also a first step toward return. To fully accept "the hungry Antilles, the Antilles pitted with smallpox,", Césaire must return to Martinique.[51]

Yet, in the summer of 1935, Césaire was too poor to return to the Antilles, so Guberina suggested he come to Dalmatia, where Guberina's family had a small farm. This was the first trip Césaire had undertaken since his arrival in France, in 1931, and he later recounted the events of that summer as tinged with a sweet serendipity:

> On his return home, [Guberina] telegraphs me: "Aimé, what are you doing in Paris? You're bored, it's summer, come see me in Zagreb." I don't have a penny to go back to Martinique, and this madman invites me to Croatia. In short, I take the train. At the end, on the quay, his family gives me an extraordinary welcome. The landscapes, the cut of the coast, the exile, the sea, everything reminds me of Martinique. And from the third floor of the house, in front of a splendid landscape that reminded me of Le Carbet, I saw a multitude of islands: "Petar, look at this one; it's my favorite, what's its name?" "Martinska!" "Well then, it's Martinique, Pierrot!" In other words, for lack of money, I arrive in a country that is not mine, which I am told is called Martinique. "Pass me a sheet of paper!": Thus I began *Notebook of a Return to the Native Land*.[52]

Césaire, arriving in a country that is not his, which he is "told is called Martinique," echoes the arrival of slaves several centuries prior to an unfamiliar land they would have to make their own. I do not mean, of course, to equate Césaire's travel to Dalmatia to the Middle Passage, but to suggest that the initial displacement continues to be reenacted not merely in obvious places like France but also in unusual ones like Yugoslavia. Long exiled from the African homeland, Césaire escapes the Antilles to study in Paris, and then wanting to leave Paris, ends up in Dalmatia. While the three displacements are not equivalent (exile, emigration that becomes exile, and travel), they complement one another, each deepening Césaire's knowledge about Martinique and its relation to the rest of the world. When he finds Martinique in Dalmatia, when he picks it out from a group of islands, Césaire realizes that this home which is not fully his and which he tried to leave, follows him everywhere. In other words, he cannot escape being a "nègre" and he cannot escape the Antilles.

Still, enclosure into a particularity is not the only potential outcome, and in Yugoslavia Césaire experienced what Glissant has called errantry, by perceiving that "each and every identity is extended through a relationship with the Other."[53] Glissant links errantry to the concept put forth by Gilles Deleuze and Félix Guattari of the rhizome, which replaces the fixation on a single root with a network of Relations. The word of the errant poet, Glissant suggests, "leads from periphery to periphery", as it "abolishes the very notion of center and periphery."[54] For Césaire, experiences in Yugoslavia (along with those in Paris) led him to appreciate that he need not build his identity solely in connection with, or opposition to, metropolitan culture. It was also possible to be in Relation with other parts of the world, including the European periphery, and share in the (differential) experience of being positioned as Europe's Other.

According to Guberina, Césaire went to Martinska every day to write, and after some time, began reading verses to Guberina of what was to become *Cahier*.[55] Later, Césaire remarked about how "bizarre" it was to have found Martinique in Dalmatia:

> Martinique is so called because it was the island of St Martin. In other words, if I had to translate "Martinska" into French, I would say "Martinique." And so that set off something in me, I rediscovered my own country. And since I had in my mind a poem about my return to

> Martinique, I wrote whole pages, some of the most important pages of my book or poem, *Notebook of a Return to the Native Land*, in Dalmatia.[56]

Wherever Césaire went, he found Martinique, but not quite Martinique; and he found his way there because he lacked money. This was a historical positioning that allowed him solidarity with Dalmatian youth who, as Guberina explained, went to Martinska because they were too poor to go to more expensive beaches.[57] In this sense, Martinska performs in Dalmatia a similar function as the beach at the end of Paille street in *Cahier*, where "the village youth go astray."[58] Martinique and Martinska thus become connected as places people go when they are too poor to go anywhere else.

It is notable, too, that Césaire "rediscovered" his homeland in Dalmatia, whether by discovering it anew or by gaining a different perspective from which to understand it. From Martinska, Martinique had reappeared in Relation to Europe's periphery. Initially, though, Césaire did not find himself on Martinska, only across from it, separated by the sea, facing it but not physically there. A sea, yet again, separating him from his homeland. And, as Césaire wrote, this "wasn't a homecoming in a strict sense, but rather an evocation, on the Dalmatian coast of his own island."[59] He had reencountered Martinique at a distance and in translation, a haunting presence following him.

The idea for *Cahier* was not entirely born from Martinska, as Césaire had already been contemplating a poem about his return, but it *was* the inspiration for him to begin writing. Discovering the connection between Martinska and Martinique provoked feelings of familiarity and alienation, distance and proximity, inevitability and fortuity. It is not identification he felt exactly, though, as Martinska is not Martinique. He describes something similar in *Cahier* in the lines:

> As there are hyena-men and panther-men, I would be a jewman
> a Kaffir-man
> a Hindu-man-from-Calcutta.[60]

This does not depict identification as an absolute but rather as an attempt to fight the mutual isolation of various peripheries that result from a dichotomous world built through European colonialism, a way of thinking about marginalization across difference. Years later, in *Martinska-Martinique*, an example of how Césaire thought across difference is offered when he recalls an encounter with an old woman pushing a donkey cart in a place called Žirje, explaining through laughter that the woman dropped something from her hand when she saw him, crossed herself, and exclaimed, "Vrag!" [Devil]. Césaire understood her, laughed, and responded in Serbo-Croatian, "Draga, kako znaš?" [My dear, how do you know?], before the woman ran away frightened.[61]

According to Francoise Vergès, the reason Césaire could laugh in this instance was because he understood that, unlike in France, this woman "could have been dumbfounded by his apparition and that her terror was caused not by hostility but by sheer surprise."[62] A lack of historical weight behind the encounter allowed Césaire to accept his condition as the "vrag" in this scenario. Yet, I would argue that the situation was a bit more complicated. It made Yugoslavia a place both where he was accepted by Guberina's family as a son and had a racist encounter; and it is precisely the simultaneity of these experiences that makes Yugoslavia a productive detour for him. Indeed, Césaire experienced there what Europe *is* and what it *could* be. And when he wrote in *Cahier*, "I accept...I accept... ...my race pitted with blemishes,"[63] it was an echo of his, "My dear, how do you know?" from Žirje. Both moments mark his acceptance of his condition as "nègre" and his identification with all the "nègres" of the world. It is not the first time this has happened, but the Yugoslav detour underlines for Césaire the impossibility of escaping Martinique or the historically constructed experience of blackness.

Rather than deny her claim or explain himself to the dumbfounded woman in Žirje, Césaire had joyously accepted her designation of him as the devil. Still, in the next scene of *Martinska-Martinique*—after Guberina discusses how deeply beloved and appreciated Césaire was by the youth of Šibenik and presents the audience a picture of him and Césaire (whom he calls "Ljubo," the Serbo-Croatian translation of Aimé) with local friends—Césaire shows viewers another photograph, taken in Martinska, and points out the "great devil with disheveled hair" next to him, Guberina.[64] Given Césaire's deftness with the French language, his repetition of "devil" here is hardly a coincidence. He has transferred the interpellation attached to him in Žirje to his friend, embracing identification with the "devil" due to his race and applying it to his white Yugoslav friend. In doing so, he de-essentializes the condition and opens it to others, not merely reappropriating

Figure 2. Photograph, shown in *Martinska-Martinique*, of Césaire and Guberina in Martinska with friends.

this external designation but also redefining it, in an archipelagic manner, as an identity that allows solidarity and similarity with a young Yugoslav. Césaire also upends the situation: In a photo where he is surrounded by white, Dalmatian youth, it is not he who stands out but the local "devil with disheveled hair."

> Two lines in *Cahier* stand out here as especially relevant:
>
> and the determination of my biology, not a prisoner to a facial angle, to a type of hair, to a well-flattened nose, to a clearly Melanin coloring, and negritude, no longer a cephalic index, or plasma, or soma, but measured by the compass of suffering.[65]

And:

> And there are those who will never get over not being made in the likeness of God but of the devil...[66]

The devil Césaire is in France, he remains in Žirje. He accepts this condition, but he refuses it as an essence, the product of mere biology. Instead, Négritude is the product of historical suffering. And while the suffering of the African diaspora remains historically specific, Négritude is, from the beginning, open to the world and all its devils, including Césaire's friend Guberina.

In this way, the Yugoslav detour becomes a possibility, an overcoming of obstacles (the inability to travel to Martinique) that induces a more transnational vision of oppressions. The Yugoslav detour helps Césaire understand how the principle of Western European domination functions globally, in distinct yet connected ways. Michael Naas, writing about Jacques Derrida, claims the detour is always about giving and receiving, that one takes their time, hoping to get something in return. In his view, the detour is "always given with the expectation of some future taking or taking-back, the expectation of getting back on track—back on track further down the road or with a greater appreciation for the road already taken."[67] And this is true of Césaire's detour, taken as an intermission in Martinska until he can return to Martinique.

Yet, his detour does more than bring Césaire further down the road; it uncovers other paths altogether. The binary France-Antilles space (and even the triangular France-Africa-Antilles space) expands as Césaire experiences Europe's periphery. The Yugoslav detour encourages him to think about oppression comparatively, in relation to marginalized places that exist beyond that triangle, like the Balkans. When Césaire speaks in *Cahier* about "[t]hose who invented neither powder nor compass,"[68] he gestures toward this comparative understanding of race and oppression.

Thus, *Cahier* is the product of two detours. It was in France that Césaire realized that being in the metropole would not solve the feelings of boredom and isolation he felt in Martinique, as he found himself in exile, in relation to the community that was supposed to receive him. His need to return to Martinique grew from the need to fight his own alienation. But first, he would visit Yugoslavia, and this would change his relationship to the return, so that he would no longer be returning to the insularity he felt as a child. He could now build a transnational vision emanating from Martinique. Césaire's experiences of exile and errantry, of alienation and Relation, of the need to simultaneously accept one's historical positioning and build transnational connections in the fight against European imperialism, pervade the verses of *Cahier*.

Cahier as an Archipelagic Text

It is generally acknowledged that Césaire wrote *Cahier* in reaction to the "bovarysme" he experienced among the Antillean elite, with their tireless efforts to sound, speak, and write like Europeans. Still, the place to (and from) which the poet returns in *Cahier* remains a topic of debate. Many have asserted that the poem represents a move away from Europe toward Africa, the original "homeland." Raphaël Confiant, Jean Bernabé, and Patrick Chamoiseau—the founders of the *Créolité* movement—have argued for example that texts of the Négritude movement simply replace one externality (Europe) with another (Africa). These authors further assert that, despite seeing themselves as Césaire's literary progeny, they view his work as "anté-créole" if not necessarily "anti-créole," painting the picture of a linear and teleological Caribbean literary history in which Négritude was important but was merely a stage of development, and one that has been surpassed. They claim that Négritude was based in abstract generalizations more characteristic of Western than Caribbean culture, and that it proposed an essentialist vision of the world based on a white-black binary; whereas they view the Caribbean as a kaleidoscope, a space refracted and recomposed.[69]

This echoes the analysis of Sartre in "Black Orpheus," which was originally published in 1948 as an introduction to Senghor's *Anthologie de la nouvelle poésie nègre et malgache de langue française*.[70] Sartre contends that, since Black people have been oppressed due to their race, it is through their race that they first need to affirm themselves. But this "awakening of consciousness" can only happen by way of language, and more specifically, poetry. Sartre writes that "black poetry in the French language is, in our time, the only great revolutionary poetry."[71] Moreover, in his view, Négritude is primarily a poetics; its innovation and contribution lie in the language it brings into existence. The poets of the Négritude movement speak the colonial language to destroy it, they "de-Frenchize" the words, break their usual associations, expose them and imbue them with violence. And, according to Sartre, this act of aggression brings them in proximity to French modern poets, who are equally trying to destroy the French language. Therefore, Négritude is revolutionary solely as a poetics.

By insisting so much on the poetic value of Négritude, Sartre completely erased the political dimension of the movement, out of which he argued no social revolution could come because it represented only a mere moment in the dialectics that arose purely as a negation of the supremacy of the white world. This would be surpassed, he said, with the abolition of race differences and the merging of colonized peoples into a universal proletariat: "The unity which will come eventually, bringing all oppressed peoples together in the same struggle, must be preceded in the colonies by what I shall call the moment of separation or negativity: this anti-racist racism is the only road that will lead to the abolition of racial differences."[72] Négritude is but a poetic halt on the way to this proletarian revolution; a halt that should be brief, because its specificity represents a danger to the universality of the proletariat. In other words, the "real" revolution can only begin when Négritude ends.

Souleymane Bachir Diagne has characterized "Black Orpheus" as a "kiss of death" that helped popularize Négritude but also forced its founders to spend most of their lives disproving Sartre.[73] For his part, Césaire insisted throughout his life that Négritude was not essentialist and that its value extended beyond poetics. In a speech he gave in 1978 in Geneva, before the premiere of a Robert Cornman cantata based on *Cahier*, he explained his decision to write it in French rather than Creole. Black literature in French (including *Cahier*) can best be understood in relation to Kafka's (and subsequently Gilles Deleuze's) theorization of a minor literature: a literature written by a minority in a major language. Césaire offered an additional characterization, that of a pirate literature; a literature that (mis)appropriates, overturns, and redefines, but also dynamizes the language in question. This literature, particularly in the form of poetry, is both nostalgic and prophetic. It is "récupératrice de l'Être, et intensificatrice de vie"[74]—a redeemer of the self, an intensifier of life. In the same speech, Césaire responded to Sartre's description of Négritude as "anti-racist racism," arguing that Négritude does not promote regionalisms and particularisms, because on the other end of difference is a universal community of men. Yet, to reach it, one must first embrace their specificity: "The principle of particularity, precisely by the fact of developing for itself up to totality, passes into the universal."[75]

Since then, various critics have joined Césaire in challenging Sartre's understanding of Négritude. Christopher Miller has claimed for example that a close reading of *Cahier* reveals the return in question is to the Caribbean, not Africa, while also asserting that the poem encompasses but also supersedes the (French Atlantic) Triangle as it spins out in many possible directions rather than proposing a definite return to a single location.[76] Diagne has reframed Négritude as a philosophy of becoming that advocates for the advent of a civilization of the universal.[77] Similarly, Yohann Ripert has recently suggested that "one of the most critical legacies of the poets of Négritude is their invitation to rethink the relation between colonies and metropole, challenge an imposed choice between total assimilation or national independence, and theorize a globality radiating from a vindicated margin onto crumbling centers."[78]

Appreciating the origins of *Cahier* and understanding the text through its connection to Yugoslavia contributes further to a (re-)reading of Négritude as a movement with global aspirations, and one that moves both within and beyond the Triangle. Against the backdrop of Martinska, we can also read *Cahier* as an archipelagic text. Yolanda Martinez-San Miguel and Michelle Stephens position archipelagos as "spatial articulations that are based not necessarily on historico-political similarities but on the creative *rearticulations* promoted by connectivity and interactions."[79] Archipelagos, which are both connected and disconnected, result from human interactions, and archipelagic thinking thus "allows us to focus on comparative studies to make visible discontinuous and multifocal experiences that are sometimes historically connected but have been disconnected by national, international, transnational, hemispheric, and global frameworks."[80] Hence, reading *Cahier* as an archipelagic text allows us to identify its multiple departures and returns, movements inward and outward, and the ways historical fortuity and contingency are balanced out by an active attempt to build transnational connections with places like Yugoslavia.

Césaire first described Martinska as forming part of a "multitude of islands," and it is from within this multitude that Césaire chose "the island" he liked most.[81] Despite his description of his childhood in Martinique as boring, isolating, and confining, it is still this island to which he cannot and does not want to return, this island of Saint Martin, that he chooses as the most beautiful one in a series. And like Martinique, Martinska is part of an archipelago, so we are not merely in front of an island that repeats, but an archipelago that repeats. As Antonio Benítez Rojo writes, "Within the (dis)order that swarms around what we already know of as Nature, it is possible to observe dynamic states or regularities that repeat themselves globally."[82] In Dalmatia, Césaire discovers an archipelago that reaches beyond the Caribbean to reappear in the Adriatic; and there he finds the repeating rhythms of the marginal and the heterogeneous.

Césaire reflects in *Cahier* on his "non-fence island."[83] He wishes it was no longer peripheral and isolated but was joined in an archipelago, connecting it to the rest of the Caribbean, to the rest of the African diaspora, and beyond, to other marginalized islands like Martinska. Thinking across these peripheries reverses their peripheral-ness, placing them at the center of a new vision of humanity.

The repetition of the archipelago can be seen and heard in Césaire's poetry, which has been recognized for the irregularity of its rhythm, the originality of its syntax, its array of neologisms, and its creative reappropriations of archaic and specialized vocabulary.[84] He opens *Cahier* with the words, "At the end of daybreak..."[85] and repeats this across multiple pages, each time with a new qualification:

> At the end of daybreak burgeoning with frail coves, the hungry Antilles...
>
> ...
>
> At the end of daybreak, on this very fragile earth thickness exceeded in a humiliating way by its grandiose future—the volcanoes will explode...
>
> ...
>
> At the end of daybreak, this inert town and its beyond of lepers...
>
> ...
>
> At the end of daybreak, the morne in restless, docile hooves...[86]

This anaphora marks a repetition, but with a variance. The regularity of "At the end of daybreak" unravels into something as concrete as "the hungry Antilles" or as general as "this very fragile earth."[87] The Antilles are not always explicitly named, and more frequently than not, Césaire introduces designations such as "this town," "a street," "the famished morne." In this way, his repetition leaves room for indeterminacy; an uncertainty as to whether Césaire is referring to the Antilles or to somewhere else. Therefore, any movement is always a return *and* a departure, at the same time. His verses are both locally grounded and open to the world. Césaire is trying to reconfigure "the relationship between universality and particularity by fashioning an original Antillean modernism...simultaneously rooted and cosmopolitan."[88]

The verses of *Cahier* arise from the specificity of the Martinican condition but quickly travel to an elsewhere (which always exists in Relation to the Antilles), making a locally grounded transnationalism possible, and this transnationalism is the result of multiple departures and returns:

> To go away. My heart was pounding with emphatic generosities. To go away...I would arrive sleek and young in this land of mine and I would say to this land whose loam is part of my flesh: "I have wandered for a long time and I am coming back to the deserted hideousness of your sores."
> ...
> And again I would say:
> "My mouth shall be the mouth of those calamities that have no mouth, my voice the freedom of those who break down in the prison holes of despair."[89]

Back in Martinique, the poet reminisces in these verses about his initial departure from the island and the excitement he felt dreaming of his future return, when he would become the spokesperson for those who cannot speak. The goal, from the beginning, is an eventual homecoming, and a transnational vision of "those calamities that have no mouth." Yet achieving this transnational perspective will require several departures and returns, as well as a change in perspective. Hence, a few pages later, the poet is again in Paris, in the tramway, realizing his arrogance in imagining himself as the spokesperson for his people. He cannot speak for his people, he can only speak with them; and even this is not enough. He must speak with other marginalized people, like his Yugoslav friend Guberina.

That is to say, the returns and departures of the poet occur multiple times, in multiple places. This includes Martinska, which offers additional perspective to the transnational vision Césaire is trying to construct. These multiple movements are there from the start, with his use of the phrase, "At the end of daybreak"—evoking a moment that marks a rising, a renewal, and a regeneration. Here, in early dawn, where an ending meets a beginning, this departure, too, is a return.

The end means a new world can be born, and this one destroyed, as Guberina wrote in his preface to *Cahier*: "In this destruction the qualities of all the races will be manifested equally and a new world will be built with the help of all the races."[90] In fact it is crucial, in Césaire's view, that this new world be built with the help of all races, in order to move beyond the white/black dichotomy and the potential pitfalls of Black nationalism. This leads him not toward the enclosure of Martinican particularity but toward a global vision from the perspective of that particularity.[91] His experiences in Yugoslavia were among those that fostered the emergence of this global vision.

Nick Nesbitt has proposed that *Cahier* is more than "a mere celebration of victorious negritude," calling the poem, "at once the triumphant call to negritude it has always been seen as, and a measure of enormous difficulties facing its imminent realization."[92] The utopian impulse is thus balanced out by a dystopian prediction. Césaire understands both the importance of exploring Négritude as "the story of a community whose experience appears…singular with its deportations of populations, its transfers of men from one continent to another, the memories of distant beliefs, its remains of murdered cultures"[93] and the risk of a "degeneration of the promise of negritude into tyranny and violence."[94] I contend that Césaire made sure his Négritude remained open to the world in part through his lifelong friendship with Petar Guberina and his attachment to Yugoslavia.

In *Martinska-Martinique*, Césaire recites the following verses from *Cahier*, which he says are characteristic of the poem as a whole:

> do not make me into that man of hatred for whom I feel only hatred
> for entrenched as I am in this unique race
> you still know my tyrannical love
> you know that it is not from hatred of other races
> that I demand of myself to become a hoer for this unique race
> that what I want
> is for universal hunger
> for universal thirst [95]

In these lines, the poet acknowledges his own potential to feel both love and hatred, and in a 2008 interview, René Depestre recounted Césaire's struggle with hatred: "…do you know what Césaire said to me? 'You know, you will have been the best of us, because you kept the innocence of brotherhood. You, you have never known hatred'."[96] For Césaire, hatred was a simultaneously generative and destructive force, and in the verses above he has offered a prayer, a solemn request for help, an earnest wish, as if he himself did not have the agency to control this hatred. He addresses someone or something, yet who or what remains unknown. He has staged a dialectic between his own subjectivity and a collective, with which he pleads. It is only a collective effort, a collective fight, that can save him from the hatred he feels; yet the collective becomes a singular, and turns out to be the poet's heart.

Surely, Césaire chose to read these verses in *Martinska-Martinique* for a reason. Transnational solidarities and interracial friendships like the one he shared with Guberina saved him from being overcome by hatred. And they helped him transform hatred into freedom. Of course, the European periphery played an important role in this as well. When Césaire cites universal hunger and thirst in the lines above, he invites what Wilder describes as "a utopian commitment to political imagination and anticipatory politics," meant to "transcend the very idea of France, remake the world, and inaugurate a new epoch of human history."[97] By choosing to read those lines in *Martinska-Martinique*, Césaire incorporated his friend Guberina and Guberina's Yugoslavia into his vision of a new humanity. After all, Césaire's experience in Dalmatia, his relationship with Guberina, and his friend's research in linguistics had all contributed to his transnational perspective.

In fact, in *Martinska-Martinique*, Césaire brought attention to Guberina's 1939 dissertation defense, calling it a memorable battle. Guberina had shown that elements ordinarily associated with non-Western cultures (intonation, rhythm, body, emotion, cultural context) were crucial to the functioning of all human languages. In other words, these supposedly particular characteristics were in fact universal. It is only natural that Césaire would find this interesting, as it served as further proof that the particularity of his own experience was the path to universality.

Guberina, Linguistics, and Négritude

In 1951, Guberina became a professor at the University of Zagreb, where he established the Institute of Phonetics and the Department of Phonetics. His research resulted in the Global-Structural Audiovisual method, which transfigured the learning of modern languages, and the Verbotonal method, which revolutionized the pathology of hearing and speech. In developing the Verbotonal method, Guberina found that people with hearing impairments were unable to produce certain sounds in their mother tongue not because they lacked the physical ability to do so, but because they could not hear them. Based on his conviction that all language evolves from spoken language, and that speech is a social event, Guberina emphasized the importance of developing good rhythm, intonation, and voice quality in hearing-impaired children.

In *Sound and Movement in Language* (*Zvuk i pokret u jeziku*), Guberina argued that language should be studied in relation to the sociocultural context of the speaker, thus challenging the linguistic formalism that prioritizes grammar and disregards elements considered non-scientific such as intonation and rhythm.[98] According to Guberina, the spoken act, in all its complexity, is vital to the study of language, privileging the oral over the written. He explains that, in any linguistic expression, two tendencies collide: "the articulated word, which sought liberation from natural necessity, and natural sound and movement (values of spoken language), which were tied to natural reality."[99] Gestures and sounds mark the human connection to nature and represent the "imitation of...movements and changes of things in nature."[100]

By asserting that language still holds a direct relationship to the natural world, Guberina deconstructed binary oppositions between nature and culture, body and mind. To illustrate his theory, he employed various literary examples, including from Césaire's *Discourse on Colonialism*, writing: "All the words used by Aimé Césaire are movements, hand gestures, anger expressed through movements and sounds, as if we were listening to the rhythm of syncopated music."[101] Behind each of Césaire's words is a gesture and an emotion, notes Guberina, and not because "emotion is Negro, as reason is Hellenic" but because non-verbal elements are a part of all human language.[102]

I cannot entertain the validity of Guberina's propositions, as I am no linguist, but instead seek to show why his work was so important to Césaire. And it was not only *Sound and Movement in Language* that resonated with Césaire; Guberina's *Connection of Linguistic Elements* (*Povezanost jezičkih elemenata*) was also important vis-à-vis the Négritude movement. In it, Guberina argues for a holistic approach to language that is focused on the connections between different linguistic elements, as well as an interdisciplinary approach to the study of language that recognizes links to other disciplines like acoustics and experimental physics. He maintains that external reality, the reality of thought, and the reality of linguistic expression, while containing dialectical contradictions, are inevitably linked. And at the level of language itself, elements such as the predicate and the subject are connected and exist in mutual constitution.[103]

The relevance of *Connection of Linguistic Elements* to Négritude is twofold. First, Guberina's theory about the connectivity of linguistic elements challenged racist assumptions about non-European languages, which are rooted in suppositions about the inferiority of these languages based on a separation of linguistic elements and an analysis of certain verbal modes and tenses that ignores their connection to other parts of the sentence. As Guberina put it, "Looking at linguistic elements from the standpoint of form, regardless of their connection with other expressive elements, leads to extracting from the 'character,' which is assigned to individual isolated words, and forms, the 'character' and type of thinking of the people who speak that language."[104]

Second, Guberina rejects the classic argument that non-Europeans are more prone to concrete (as opposed to abstract) thinking, and questions the claims of linguists like Galichet, Bally, and Vendryes, who built on the work of Levy-Bruhl to conclude that "The savage…gives, for example, to spatial considerations a greater attention perhaps than our languages give to temporal considerations…. Now, time is of a higher degree of abstraction than space…"[105] But it is equally important *how* he counters this argument, including by citing Father Placide Tempels, whose influence on Négritude has been well documented.[106] Discussing Tempels' work *Bantu Philosophy*, Guberina explains: "The Bantu considers everything that exists, either as an influencing force, or on the contrary as an influenced force, foreign to his life or linked to his life…. In Europe, we conceive of things separately, without connection, independent from one another."[107] Yet, Guberina's argument is slightly different from that of Tempels, for the Yugoslav is not claiming that the European and Bantu conceptions of the world are diametrically opposite yet should be valued equally, he is claiming that the Bantu conception of interdependence exists within European languages, which do not reflect those vaunted European sensibilities of independence and separation. In other words, this Bantu particularity is in fact universal, and studying African languages reveals universal truths about all human language. Particularity is the path to universality; this is a position that Guberina and Césaire shared.

In the view of Césaire, Guberina and he led parallel lives. They were true contemporaries—he born in June 1913 and Guberina in May—and neither could contemplate his life without evoking the other. In *Martinska-Martinique*, Césaire claimed that both as a poet and a politician, he had always remained loyal to the values he and Guberina shared. These values had led them into the same fight, he said, for humanity at large.[108]

It had been both Yugoslavia and Guberina who had reminded Césaire that the ideas he fought for were indeed universal. His Yugoslav detour was among multiple displacements that shaped *Cahier*, but when Césaire arrived in Dalmatia only to encounter Martinique, the surprise of rediscovering this island, which reappeared for him in the most unusual places, inspired the poet to explore the (im)possibility of return and use this as the basis for a more global understanding of oppression and resistance. He saw that Négritude was open to the world and needed to remain so. He saw the possibility of a different socialism, of an interracial solidarity, of a different Europe. And he saw that he could only fully understand and fight European imperialism by thinking across and in Relation to the world's many peripheries. Even so, he knew he first needed to understand and embrace his own historical positioning. He needed to return.

CHAPTER TWO

A Tale of Poets and Politicians: Léopold Sédar Senghor, African Socialism, and Yugoslav Federalism

> Africa is a part of my life, both culturally and emotionally. When I first set foot on African soil in 1961, when Senghor invited me to celebrate Senegal's independence, that was the greatest experience of my life.[1]
>
> —Petar Guberina

The greatest experience of his life, Petar Guberina writes, was his trip to the African continent. It was with Aimé Césaire that Guberina had visited their mutual friend, Léopold Sédar Senghor, who had become the President of newly independent Senegal the year beforehand. In fact, Guberina is the bridge between the Yugoslav stories of Césaire and Senghor. During his visit to Yugoslavia in 1975, Senghor explained that his attachment to the country dated back to his student days in Paris: "I too had, as was the fashion in the Latin Quarter in the 1930s, my crisis of Slavophilia, favored, it is true, by the frequentation of a Yugoslav comrade, Petar Guberina, who has since become one of the greatest linguists of our time."[2]

Senghor's relationship with Yugoslavia and his friendship with Guberina continued beyond the 1930s, as he closely followed the development of Yugoslav federalism and self-management. In the Yugoslav system, Senghor saw an important method (and here, following Senghor, I make a distinction between method and model) vis-à-vis his own conceptualizations of socialism and federalism, which were intertwined in his thinking. Senghor's interest in Yugoslavia stretched from the time he met Guberina in the 1930s through to his vision of a democratic federal French Union (and later, the short-lived Mali Federation). His interest and proximity to Yugoslavia reemerged in the 1970s, when Senghor developed a friendship with Macedonian poet Aco Šopov, who served as the Yugoslav ambassador in Senegal from 1971 to 1975. Thus, when Senghor visited Yugoslavia in 1975, he hoped to expand economic, political, and cultural cooperation between the two countries. But this visit would also prove important to Senghor as he attempted, toward the end of his political career, to reinvigorate his theory and praxis of African socialism.

Criticisms of Senghor have emphasized both the essentialism of his thought and the neocolonialism of his policies. As Gary Wilder writes, "Images of him as a racial essentialist, servile Francophile, and neocolonial comprador informed scholarship long after the political conditions that generated them disappeared."[3] Among the sharpest critiques came from Frantz Fanon who characterized Senghor as a "colonial intellectual" and protector of the "Greco-Roman pedestal."[4] Recently, however, several studies have attempted "to revisit Senghor's political project from the perspective of the postwar opening and think with him about that openness."[5] This chapter builds upon those studies.

Though Yugoslavia was certainly not the primary influence on Senghor's political thinking, it did play an important role in shaping his views. This has not been analyzed in depth, despite the fact that Senghor's Yugoslav story contributes to our overall understanding of his version of African socialism as well as his interest in internationalism, which was an element of Négritude as he conceived it. From the beginning, Senghor's internationalism extended beyond the Francophone world or even that of the African diaspora. His was a vision of "social interdependence and cultural reciprocity as the basis for new forms of transcontinental solidarity and postnational democracy."[6] In this context, Yugoslavia was an influential example of a different type of socialism, one that did not follow the Soviet model. Hence, Yugoslavia was a part of Senghor's vision of an interconnected Global South and a more just international economic order. The Yugoslav story of Senghor is one of two originators of Négritude (he and Césaire) and two Yugoslav intellectuals (Guberina and Šopov), bound by friendship, solidarity, global perspectives, and local initiatives.

In the following section, I discuss the importance that the concepts of "balkanization" and "federation" held for Senghor. I then focus on two official visits to Yugoslavia, by Mamadou Dia (Senghor's prime minister) in 1961 and Senghor in 1975, that played an important role in Senegalese politics.

Balkanization, Federation, and African Socialism

Senghor was a man of many interests and talents. While he remains widely recognized as one of the founders of the Négritude movement, he was not only a poet, but a teacher, a statesman, and more. Indeed, after becoming the first African *agrégé* in France, Senghor worked as a teacher in Tours and then as a professor of African languages and civilizations at the École Nationale de la France d'Outre-Mer. He was then drafted at the beginning of World War II, and was captured by the Nazis in 1940, spending two years as a prisoner of war in Germany.[7]

Following the war, Senghor returned to Paris as one of Senegal's two deputies to the National Assembly in 1946, elected on the socialist ticket. In 1948, he founded the Senegalese Democratic Bloc and was reelected as that party's candidate in 1951. Senghor did not advocate independence for Francophone West Africa, calling instead for a democratic federation involving France and its former colonies. When it became clear that France was not moving in this direction, Senghor joined with the leaders of French Sudan, Dahomey, and Upper Volta to create the Mali Federation in 1959. Upon dissolution of the Federation the next year, Senghor became President of an independent Senegal; a position he would hold until the last day of 1980, when he voluntarily retired after two decades in power.

In Senghor's early political writings, he makes few references to Yugoslavia explicitly, but mentions "balkanization" rather prolifically. Though balkanization was originally used to refer to the processes of dissolution and disintegration that took place within the Ottoman and Habsburg empires during the nineteenth and twentieth centuries, the term was later adopted by many African political theorists. In fact, historian Benyamin Neuberger argues that it became "a basic part of the phraseology of modern African nationalism."[8]

It was Kwame Nkrumah, an anticolonialist who would later serve as President of Ghana, who was among the first to apply the term balkanization to postcolonial Africa. Nkrumah contended that balkanization has historically led to the creation of small, weak nation-states which remained politically and economically dependent on European imperial centers. But Neuberger highlights a contradiction in this negative view of the term from the perspective of African nationalists, noting that "the same arguments against the partition of Eastern Europe could have been—and, indeed, were—raised against the dissolution of the British and French Empires in Africa. It is fair to assume that their dislike of the concept of 'balkanisation' rests on a misreading of modern European history."[9]

According to Neuberger, Senghor in particular employed the term with some ambivalence. The first time he used it was in 1956, to express his opposition to legal changes that threatened the future of French West Africa.[10] Then, in 1958, when Guinea voted "non" in de Gaulle's plebiscite on the French Community, Senghor considered this an act of balkanization because it unraveled his hopes of reconstituting French West Africa.[11] After independence, he argued similarly that the separate states of Senegal, Guinea, Upper Volta, Ivory Coast, Benin, Mauritania, and Niger were the consequence of African balkanization. Neuberger posits that these postcolonial developments "led Senghor to confuse the concept of the nature of the status quo with the revisionist process designed to change it. He cannot decide whether balkanisation is a present condition or a future danger."[12] Yet, I propose there is no such contradiction in the thinking of Senghor, who vociferously defended federalism throughout his political career, both as an inter- and intra-continental project. As Senghor saw it, Africa faced different stages of balkanization at different points in time, making it both a present *and* a future threat.

In other words, Senghor's negative use of the word balkanization is not the result of a misreading of modern European history. Quite the contrary. Indeed, I suggest that Senghor did not view balkanization in a metaphorical way, as a term that refers to any process of fragmentation dissociated from the region where it originated. Senghor had a certain affinity for the Balkans and an interest in the region's history, and had concluded that "balkanization" may have delivered independence from colonial rule but it had not delivered freedom. And, if balkanization had been an impediment to freedom, Yugoslav-style federalism represented a possible solution. This is why Senghor followed the development of Yugoslav socialism so closely.

In the summer of 1955, at the request of then Prime Minister Edgar Faure, Senghor had organized a commission to propose modifications to the French Constitution of 1946. In the resulting report, he argued for a democratic federation between France and its former colonies "of the type of the Strasbourg Consultative Assembly, the Nordic Council or the Balkan Union."[13] The Balkans appear here not merely as a warning, but also as a positive model. In fact, every time Senghor mentions balkanization, he cites Yugoslavia as a counterpoint. This duality between balkanization as a threat and the Balkans (specifically Yugoslavia) as instructive continued to mark Senghor's political thought over time.

A year later, in the wake of passage of the *Loi Cadre*—which granted increased territorial autonomy to French colonies in Africa—Senghor published an article entitled "Balkanisation ou fédération" ("Balkanization or Federation"). He opposed the law, which made a democratic union between France and its former colonies unlikely.[14] As Senghor saw it, the Loi Cadre "was not a serious attempt to refigure France as a federal republic. Instead, it devolved power to discrete African territories in ways that reinforced the integrity of the sovereign metropolitan state."[15] Senghor positions balkanization and federation in opposition to one another and asserts that a federation is the only solution to balkanization.

He continued to develop this argument in a heated discourse against the Loi Cadre in the French National Assembly, suggesting that the dissolution of French West Africa and French Equatorial Africa (the two colonial-era federations of French territories) would lead to a centralization of the power of the metropole and the creation of balkanized African states in conflict with one another. By linking individual African territories directly to France, Senghor claimed the Loi Cadre made them dependent on the metropole and precluded the possibility of an African federation.[16] He insisted that the colonial-era federations were no more artificial inventions than the individual territories within them, as ethnic groups were spread across these territories; partitioned by borders that Senghor believed had been put in place to prevent "natural" solidarities across the African continent and separate people who were "linked by everything, not only economic structures, but also race, culture, administrative organization and political aspirations."[17] In his view, the goal of the Loi Cadre was to replace existing affiliations with "the powers of the High Commissioner, but exercised by the State, that is to say, in fact, by the metropole. As if we could make people happy without their active participation!"[18]

It was clear to Senghor that the people of Africa would do everything possible to maintain "these natural solidarities that they want to deprive us of." Meaning, Africans would oppose the balkanization of Africa.[19] Yet, here again, Yugoslavia appears, invoked by Senghor to remind the Assembly that balkanization can be reversed:

> [I]n 1957, in the 20th century...the strongest states and empires are federal in structure: the USA, the USSR, India, Canada, Brazil, West Germany, Yugoslavia and, closer to us, England who is about to grant independence to the Gold Coast within the Commonwealth, which has ceased to be British. The idea of a federation frightens some members of the Assembly. But, my dear colleagues, to federate is not to separate. To federate, in the etymological sense of the word, is to bind, but without suffocating; this is too often forgotten.[20]

As Senghor explained, to federate is to collaborate with others while maintaining one's own specificity. He was inspired by global examples of federalism, which he believed could be adapted to the conditions of the Francophone world. Nevertheless, and despite Senghor's objections, France dismantled French West Africa in April 1959. Individual African territories would be connected to France through a series of bilateral agreements instead.

Given this new context, Senghor moved pragmatically toward efforts to establish a socialist African federation. In January 1959, at a meeting in Bamako, representatives from Senegal, Sudan, Upper Volta, and Dahomey agreed to join a new federal state that would be an autonomous member of the French Community. When Dahomey and Upper Volta withdrew from the plan, Senghor and Sudanese leader Modibo Keïta stayed the course and co-founded the Mali Federation. They also co-led the Parti de la Fédération Africaine (Party of the African Federation, or PFA), which advocated "a Negro-African Nation, freely associated with France." At the Constitutive Congress of the PFA in July 1959, where Senghor pushed for a federation, he continued to warn of the risk of balkanization.[21] He framed balkanization in Africa as both a political and economic problem, emphasizing that "if the balkanization of French-speaking black Africa were to continue, [industrialists] would have to close the doors of their factories."[22]

As far as Senghor was concerned, the development of African economies was impossible without an influx of capital and an integrated market. If limited to their national territories, these economies would operate within the imposed constraints and highly uneven power dynamics of global capitalism, which would reduce them to exporting natural resources. And if France was no longer politically linked to its former colonies, it would have no incentive to uphold economic agreements benefiting African countries at its own expense. Senghor was convinced that only a strong regional market, and equitable trading and investment agreements with the former metropole, could save Africa from underdevelopment.

To fully understand Senghor's federalism and his fear of balkanization, it is important to examine the way that politics and economics were intertwined with culture in his thinking. Senghor viewed true independence as an independence of the mind and spirit. It was through art and culture, he believed, that the potential of people could be realized: "A people is not truly independent when, having acquired nominal independence, its leaders import…institutions—political, economic, social, cultural—which are, elsewhere, the natural fruits of geography, of history, of race."[23] In other words, the role of political independence is to create the conditions for cultural independence, not the other way around. Senghor envisioned a central role for culture in the postimperial world. His effort to use art and culture to cultivate a sense of community and solidarity among African nations and the global African diaspora is notably visible in the elaborate and costly First World Festival of Negro Arts, organized in 1966 in Dakar.[24]

However, from the time it became clear that decolonization was a possibility, Senghor feared that political independence would be merely nominal, and would not lead to economic and cultural independence. Colonial economies had long been concentrated on exports, and individually, they were neither large enough nor diverse enough to satisfy the needs of their populations. Newly independent African states would remain economically and politically dependent on the former colonial power, but this relationship would be restructured so that these nascent states had no means to demand accountability.

Senghor's argument in favor of a federalization resembles that of Césaire in support of departmentalization. They both believed France was indebted to its former colonies and that the only way it would be convinced to repay this debt was in the context of a democratic union in which former colonial subjects could exert equal rights. This was a practical and an ideological stance, grounded in the belief that the recognition of former subjects as equal fellow citizens would transform both France and its former colonies. To borrow from Gary Wilder again, Senghor was sure that Africans could "decolonize France;"[25] and in the context of a federation, that the metropole would be obliged to engage in resource distribution and invest in the economic development of its former colonies. Senghor felt this political structure would best protect Senegal from economic obligations that may detract from a focus on cultural revitalization. In this way, political independence was not an end for Senghor, but a path toward cultural and spiritual freedom.

Négritude, which Senghor has described as "the sum of the cultural values of the black world as they are expressed in the life, the institutions and the work of black men," thus appears as an antidote to balkanization.[26] Politics, economics, and culture are mutually reliant, and a federation is simply the political confirmation of already existing connections. In the case of the African continent, it is these links that Senghor believes can counter neocolonial attempts to maintain its dependence. And in much the same way that he understood balkanization, he considered Négritude to reflect an existing reality as well as an attempt to build that reality.

Scholarly discussions of Senghor's federalism are frequently separated from those of his socialism, mostly because "his commitment to African socialism is often regarded as a superficial or opportunistic state ideology rather than a considered engagement with Marx's writings."[27] Yet federalism and socialism were inseparable for Senghor, and he considered them two of the three pillars—along with democracy—of an ideal political arrangement. He envisioned a federation that included France and its former colonies but did not cater to the interests of investors and corporations. In fact, the socialist policies he supported could not be implemented outside a federation, as it was only a larger internal market that could safeguard against the instabilities of the global economy. In his 1959 report to the Constitutive Congress of the PFA, he cited Yugoslavia as a model:

> The federal structure—decentralization and deconcentration—will be extended, within the framework of the federated state, to regional and communal entities, including in the economic and social domains. The Yugoslav structures, adapted to our realities, will serve us, in this case, as a model. Thus, we will fill the void that currently exists between the federated state and the village.[28]

To be clear, it is not my goal to list every reference Senghor made to balkanization and Yugoslavia, but to show that Senghor's interest in the region was historically and ideologically informed. He did not conceive of balkanization as a term "detached from the context of international relations."[29] In fact, Senghor saw similarities between historical events that had taken place in the Balkans and those he anticipated on the African continent. When Senghor wrote his report to the PFA in 1959, the Yugoslav federation encompassed six republics, and multiple languages, religions, and ethnicities. Tito's government was also developing the politics of non-alignment and offering support to struggles for decolonization across Africa. Both Senghor and Mamadou Dia (a protégé of Senghor who became Vice-premier of the Mali Federation and then Prime Minister of Senegal) were keenly interested in this combination of federalism and self-managed socialism.

While Senghor believed that any model would need to be adapted to local realities, his interest in Yugoslavia was concrete and specific in terms of its workers' cooperatives, its large rural population, and its efforts to build its own socialism. In Senghor's view, socialism is a method, a manner of organizing society that inevitably varies from context to context. What he drew from the Yugoslav experience were ideas about how to adapt Marx to local circumstances. It mattered little that the circumstances in Yugoslavia and Senegal were so different, as it was the method of adapting socialism to meet local needs that interested Senghor.

In this manner, Yugoslavia became the paradigm of method for the Senegalese President. This is important for two reasons. First, it demonstrates the importance of the Yugoslav model to emerging postcolonial countries that were looking to pave their own socialist futures. And second, it points to transnationalities in Senghor's African socialism that remain to be explored. The specificity of his African experience did not preclude Senghor from looking outward, which is why one of Dia's first official trips as Prime Minister of newly independent Senegal was to Yugoslavia.

Mamadou Dia, Senegalese "*animation rurale*," and Yugoslav Self-management

Dia's trip took place soon after independence, before his split with Senghor and subsequent imprisonment. Senghor's later visit was partly inspired by his friendship with the Macedonian poet Aco Šopov, who had arrived in Senegal in 1971 as the Yugoslav ambassador. These two journeys were bookends of a sort. Dia and Senghor had turned toward Yugoslavia as their government took shape in the early 1960s and they attempted to formulate and implement African socialism. And in 1975, as Senghor was nearing the end of his political career, having released Dia from prison one year prior, he was rethinking the direction of the country and turned back to one of his early inspirations.

Dia's 1961 visit was initiated in June of that year, when the Yugoslav State Secretariat for Foreign Affairs sent an urgent memo to President Tito, informing him that Prime Minister Mamadou Dia was requesting a visit of a private nature, primarily in order to visit industrial and agricultural cooperatives. Dia had already expressed his desire to visit Yugoslavia the year before, as the Senegalese ambassador in Paris conveyed to his Yugoslav counterpart.[30] Yugoslav officials were initially reluctant to consent to a meeting; they found Senghor to be more conservative than some other African allies, like the Guinean Sékou Touré, as Senghor remained too attached to France and continued to defend certain French neocolonial interests in Senegal. Yet, the Senghor-Dia government appeared to be stable, and since both Senegalese leaders had expressed an interest in Yugoslav self-management, the Yugoslav government extended a "semi-official" invitation to Dia.[31] He was to be welcomed by Slovenian economist and father of Yugoslav self-management Edvard Kardelj.

Dia's main objective was to replace Senegal's export-based economy with a more equitable alternative. He and Senghor wanted "to link a socialist program for local self-management and humane economic development to the transformation of imperial France into a federal democracy."[32] Central to Dia's understanding of African socialism was a policy of "*animation rurale*," whereby rural schools would be opened, and local teachers would also act as local leaders, encouraging people to take charge of their communities and join peasant cooperatives. These cooperatives were "simultaneously to be the site of educational activities, the liberation of the peasantry, and the realization of development."[33]

In a series of interviews later given by Dia's former chief of staff Roland Colin to commemorate sixty years of African independence, Colin explained that Senghor and Dia had envisioned the transformation of the economy taking place over four years, building from the establishment of 750 cooperatives in the first year. Colin also claimed that this had been at the heart of the conflict between Senghor and Dia, which ended with

Dia's imprisonment in 1962. According to Colin, their falling out had been manipulated by opponents of Dia, who sought to remove him from power before three-quarters of peanut production—which constituted Senegal's biggest export—was placed under the control of agricultural cooperatives.[34] They did so largely by playing the two leaders off each other, portraying Dia as increasingly radical and Senghor as a more reasonable moderate.

When Dia turned toward the east in the second year of Senegal's planned economic transformation, seeking inspiration and support most notably from Yugoslavia, his visit to the Balkans occurred within the context of increased criticism of his supposed radicalism. This was matched by growing pressure on Senghor to adopt a more moderate approach.[35] As Colin saw it, Dia believed Yugoslavia was his biggest ally against both internal opponents and the Soviet bloc, which advocated for stronger centralization.

It should be noted that Senghor and Dia saw an important difference between Senegal and Yugoslavia, in that they considered traditional rural communities in Senegal already organized according to socialist principles.[36] Historian Mamadou Diouf characterizes this as a problematic preconception, however, because it ignored the hierarchies inherent in those communities.[37] In any case, Dia visited various rural cooperatives and self-managed factories in Yugoslavia. Upon returning to Senegal in August 1961, he sent an official telegram to the Yugoslav government confirming that a Senegalese mission would arrive in October to sign economic and technical cooperation agreements. Unfortunately, it was not long after this that Dia was accused of staging a coup against Senghor and sentenced to life imprisonment. And, while various Senegalese delegations visited Yugoslavia after his 1961 trip, bilateral cooperation remained underdeveloped until Senghor's visit in 1975; and was reignited at that time in part by his friendship with the poet Aco Šopov.

Between Poetry and Politics: Senghor and Šopov

Thanks mostly to Šopov, Senghor remains a "household name in Macedonia" to this day, according to Ljubica Spaskovska.[38] In fact, while serving as the ambassador in Senegal, he translated a selection of Senghor's poetry into Macedonian, which was released in 1975, the year Senghor visited Yugoslavia. Šopov also published a collection of his own poetry, *The Song of the Black Woman* (*Pesna na crnata žena*) in 1976, inspired by his stay in Senegal.[39] The fact that the two men became friends is not entirely surprising, as there are many similarities between them: both grew up in small villages, fought in World War II, and were proponents of socialism and federalism, and both had taken the path from poet to politician.

Šopov, who was born in the Macedonian village of Štip in 1923, joined the antifascist struggle of the Yugoslav Partisans at the age of nineteen. Much of his poetry deals with experiences he had in World War II, especially the death of his lover and fellow Partisan, Vera Jocić. After the war, Šopov became active in Yugoslav cultural and political life, in the fields of journalism and publishing. He co-founded the Macedonian Academy of Sciences and Arts in 1967, and was awarded the prestigious AVNOJ prize three years later.[40]

In 1961, Šopov was involved in establishing the Struga Poetry Evenings, an international poetry festival held annually in Macedonia. Over the years, the festival has honored a diverse group of poets with its "Golden Wreath," including Pablo Neruda, Mahmoud Darwish, Allen Ginsberg, and, in 1975, Léopold Sédar Senghor. It is easy to draw parallels between the way Šopov and Senghor thought about both poetry and politics. In one of his many interviews, for example, Šopov defined the role of the poet in the following terms:

> The poet is an explorer. But an explorer of a particular kind. He searches for something there, something that does not exist in the natural order of things, uncovering their deeper and lasting meaning. A poem exists precisely because it does not exist in that order. Otherwise, it becomes a bare fact with no artistic value.[41]

This overlaps with Senghor's distinction between the "*raison-étreinte*" (reason-embrace) and the "*raison-oeil*" (reason-eye), wherein the *raison-oeil* is the discursive and analytic reasoning that underlies Aristotelianism and Cartesianism, and the *raison-étreinte* is rooted in intuition.

Such a perspective erases the line between subject and object, intelligence and emotion, so that we experience, in Senghor's words, "the lived identity of knowledge and the known, the lived and the thought, the lived and the real."[42] Whereas discursive reason places the object at a distance and analyzes it as a function of its parts, intuitive reason considers the object in its totality; whereas discursive reason fixes an object in a moment and strips it from its internal movement, intuitive reason espouses a reality of constant and dynamic change. Facts and matter—objects of discursive reason—are superficial, and only intuition can grasp reality in all its depth. This grasping at an ever-changing reality was central to Šopov's writing as well: "The poem is not only the consciousness of existence," he noted, "it is also the consciousness of itself, and that is why it affirms and realizes itself in a constant collision—with reality and with itself. In other words, it is the awareness of an ever-changing human reality and of one's own being."[43]

Šopov also emphasized the difference between a superficial, static reality and a world in constant movement, much as Senghor did, arguing that the role of poetry is to capture the movement of the poet and his world. Šopov's understanding of poetry was deeply influenced by his time in Senegal and by Senghor himself, who helped the Macedonian better appreciate the rest of the world and his own origins. In 1976, he explained:

> Africa—for example—had a huge impact on me: it was, above all, an incredible discovery. I went there with completely misguided notions, even though I had prepared in order to make the encounter as painless as possible. For my "discovery" of black Africa, I owe the most to the rich poetry of Leopold Senghor. He taught me more about Africa than the countless books I read! From beliefs, legends, stories, he managed to create poetry that is a true poetic universe. He viewed the whole world through one small, unknown Senegalese place—his birthplace.
>
> For me, Senghor is one of the greatest poets of the modern world and a great example of what poetry means: how much it has to say to a man, no matter how much he is, at first glance, a foreigner and a stranger. I learned a valuable lesson from that: if a person wants to better understand themselves, their country, and their people, they must also understand others. And secondly: when you view yourself and your environment from a different perspective, say from an African one, many surroundings that oppress you at home become much more understandable, some completely different. And poetry, in both cases, plays an unimaginably significant role![44]

Senghor played a similar role for Šopov as he did for Césaire, introducing them both to the cultural and social complexities of the African continent. Šopov admired Senghor's ability to conceptualize at a global level from a local vantage point, and became convinced that gaining self-knowledge required seeing oneself through the eyes of others. In this sense, the two poets shared the belief that local specificities were not an impediment but a precondition to transnational solidarity, and that learning and interacting with others did not mean losing oneself in a faceless universality. The influence of Senghor (and Senegal) on Šopov can be clearly seen in *The Song of the Black Woman*, which includes "In the Dream of the Black Woman"—a rather explicit homage to Senghor's "Femme Noire":

> Your body a black olive,
> The darkest bronze, the deepest sound,
> The sound of your ancestors' tam-tam, from their
> Ancient bark.[45]

Still, even if Šopov's Senegal-inspired poetry was meant to offer a deeper understanding of the continent, it mobilized many stereotypically exotic elements, evoking the sensuality of the Black woman, the sounds of the tam-tam, and the wilderness of the African landscape (as did some of Senghor's poetry). This speaks in some ways to the liminal position of Yugoslavia vis-à-vis the Global South. Indeed, like many other Yugoslav intellectuals and politicians, Šopov proclaimed an affinity with postcolonial nations around the world but reproduced stereotypes that reflected the gaze of the colonizer. Yugoslavia was, after all, a part of Europe, and Yugoslavs were influenced by European discourses and ideologies. In this context, Šopov's thinking wavered, between the exoticism seen in some of his poetry and efforts to legitimize and convey the universality of Négritude as both a philosophy and an aesthetic. At times, he described Senghor and the Négritude movement with reverence:

> A spiritual world, located in a small geographical area such as the land of the Serer in Senegal, grows before our eyes in a world of universal dimensions and universal significance. With the magic of the poetic language, Senghor transforms this world into a singular poetic universe, close and accessible to everyone.[46]

Only poets like Senghor, Šopov contended, "can dive into the immense depths of the soul and the spiritual world of their homeland, and emerge from it with messages for all humanity."[47] He considered Senghor's poetry to be powerful not because he had forsaken the specificity of Senegal but because he had conveyed that specificity in universal terms.

Šopov's deep attachment to Senegal, and to the thinking and poetry of Senghor, is perhaps most evident in his own writing. Here, he conjures his own hometown in Macedonia and Senghor's in Senegal:

> Štip and Joal,
> One under the Isar,
> the other by the ocean.
> Same loves,
> same stirrings
> same poetic dreams and torments.[48]

In Šopov's mind, there was a parallel between these two remote villages on opposite sides of the globe, and this led him to play a crucial role in organizing Senghor's visit to Yugoslavia.[49] It is worth analyzing several speeches Senghor gave while he was there, as well as a project that was realized as a result of his visit: the founding in Senegal of a school for hearing-impaired people, with instruction based on Petar Guberina's verbotonal method. These speeches and this project reflect Senghor's understanding of internationalism, solidarity, and perhaps surprisingly, even Négritude. In fact, Senghor's embrace of both Négritude and African socialism were no impediment at all to his commitment to internationalism, because he believed that it was only through cooperation across the Global South that either could be realized.

Diplomacy, Culture, and Rhythm: Senghor in Yugoslavia

In June 1975, Ambassador Šopov sent an official memo from the Yugoslav Embassy in Senegal, informing the Secretariat for Foreign Affairs that President Senghor had enthusiastically accepted an official invitation to visit Yugoslavia in August, to meet with President Tito and be honored with the Struga Poetry Evenings Golden Wreath.[50] A subsequent telegram conveyed Senghor's request to receive the French translations of Tito's works in advance of his visit, particularly those in which "the thoughts of Marx and Lenin are elucidated and applied to Yugoslav conditions."[51] Senghor's travel to Yugoslavia had in fact been in the works for quite some time, as the Secretariat for Foreign Affairs had suggested in February 1974 that Tito officially invite the Senegalese President, who had repeatedly expressed an interest in visiting.[52] Thus, while he was in the country in August 1975, an exhibit at the Belgrade National Library featured sixty of Senghor's own works, thirty photos of life in Senegal, and three films—depicting Senghor's private life, his public life in Senegal, and the First World Festival of Negro Arts.[53] Šopov's translation of Senghor's poetry was also released for the occasion.[54]

It is not entirely surprising that Senghor's interest in Yugoslavia had been renewed in 1974, which was quite an eventful year; first and foremost because Mamadou Dia had been pardoned and released from prison. After Dia's imprisonment in 1962, Senghor had turned to prioritizing the construction of infrastructure, funded mostly by French capital, no longer burdened by concerns that Dia's economic radicalism and African socialism would alienate the French business class and the local Muslim brotherhood, leaving Senegal without the capital it desperately needed to fund development. Hence, Senghor limited African socialism mostly to "the use of advanced European-style technology by Africans who respected their own traditional culture."[55]

The Senegalese economy remained focused on the export of groundnuts in the early 1970s, which kept it dependent on fluctuating prices within the global market. As a result, Senghor relied heavily on French development aid, technical expertise, and private investment, so that there was "a division of labor whereby the French ran the economy and the Senegalese the government."[56] The government had adopted policies favored by French companies, making it a trusted ally of the French state, but most of the French profit made in Senegal was repatriated, only marginally benefiting the local economy or population. By the 1970s, these dynamics combined with a series of droughts that negatively affected groundnut production, significantly slowing the country's economic growth. Student protests in 1972 and 1973 elevated demands for more transparency from the government, better educational opportunities, and an end to the privileges enjoyed by the French business elite.[57]

Support for Senghor and his vision of African socialism began to decline. To people concerned with trying to make ends meet, "and particularly to the leaders of the towns who felt they did not get the power and respect they deserved, Senghor's continued emphasis on the arts and culture and an African socialism that seemed in reality to favor French business sounded increasingly hollow."[58] Senghor responded to his obviously waning popularity by making policy changes, in an effort to "rehabilitate himself through democratic reforms."[59] He ratified a new constitution, reinstituted the post of prime minister, legalized trade unions, and held open elections.[60] According to Senghor's biographer Janet G. Vaillant, "Senghor's final political wish was to commit Senegal firmly to representative democracy...[and] reestablish his position as a democratic socialist."[61] It was in this context that Senghor developed his friendship with Šopov and expressed his desire to visit Yugoslavia.

Without overstating the role played by Yugoslavia in Senghor's thinking, it does seem that Senghor returned in the 1970s to some of his earlier inspirations, as the limits of his economic program become clear. His renewed interest in Yugoslavia at this time suggests an attempt on his part to reinvigorate and salvage his vision of African socialism. Indeed, associating it with Yugoslavia, which Senghor admiringly characterized as an "experimental polygon," was a means of distancing his brand of socialism from identification with the Soviet Union.[62]

During their official encounter, Senghor and Tito broached various topics, including the Second General Conference of the United Nations Industrial Development Organization held in Lima, the Arab-Israeli conflict, and the decolonization struggles in Angola, Rhodesia, Namibia, and Spanish Sahara. Senghor expressed his satisfaction that Yugoslav companies would be building a dam on the Guinean side of the Senegal River, because the Senegalese government didn't want it to affect the country's water access. Deputy Federal Secretary for Foreign Affairs Lazar Mojsov confirmed to Senghor that Yugoslavia would not be involved in any project that harmed original members of the Organization of Senegal River States (OERS)—Guinea, Senegal, Mauritania, and Mali.[63] The OERS was an attempt to de-balkanize Africa and encourage federalism, and Yugoslav officials were happy to support it.

Senghor explained that he welcomed cooperation between the Socialist Alliance of the Working People of Yugoslavia (SSRNJ) and the Progressive Union of Senegal (UPS), because Africans had started to see socialism as inefficient as they looked around and saw little success in the socialist countries in their neighborhood. Senghor believed this was the result of a sort of catechism in those countries, an insistence on a single way toward socialism. Yugoslavia, on the other hand, offered a useful example to Africans by encouraging other countries to examine their socialist model but also to adapt it to local realities. As Senegalese youth had very limited access to socialist literature and most had never read Mao or Tito,

Senghor suggested to Tito that Yugoslavia should send French translations of these texts to Senegal, for distribution at universities and other educational institutions.[64]

Later, in his toast to Tito, Senghor further elaborated on his interest in Yugoslavia and its importance to African socialism. In this relatively brief tribute, Senghor found a way to bind together all the concepts that shaped his thinking—socialism, federalism, Négritude, *métissage*, and the Civilization of the Universal—which are often analyzed separately and attributed either to different (temporal) stages of his life or to his separate interests in aesthetics and politics; yet, here, these concepts are very much connected. Senghor noted that Yugoslavia's rapid development since World War II had positioned it "among the countries of Europe that are, for us in the Third World, not precisely a model, but a significant example."[65] This distinction between a model and an example, which had already appeared in Senghor's 1959 report to the PFA, is fundamental to Senghor's understanding of African socialism, in that a model is a norm which should be applied and imitated and an example is a variation on a theme. Thus, while the model is static, the example is fluid, allowing for permutation and adaptation.

It was the view of Senghor that "socialisms exist as the many translations of socialism without an original text to be considered the normative model," as Souleymane Bachir Diagne has put it.[66] Yet, the problem of translation does not render examples irrelevant. On the contrary, the very existence of examples helps position socialism as a dynamic process of translation. In fact, Senghor wanted to introduce Yugoslav socialist writing into the universities of Senegal not only because these texts described practical socialist policies but because they also offered a method of translation. He was just as interested in the process by which Yugoslavia translated socialism to meet its own specific needs as he was in the concrete workings of Yugoslav self-management. As he saw it, it was the method of translation that could be shared among countries.

In his 1959 report, Senghor had stated that the most important aspect of socialism was its dialectic methodology, explained most poignantly in Marx's 1844 manuscripts. Dialectics allows us to capture reality in movement, marked by a continuous becoming. As opposed to classical logic, it allows for contradiction, reciprocal action, and change. Senghor believed social reality can be comprehended only through a dialectical method, explaining:

> Things, like living beings, are in perpetual becoming. They contain within themselves their own negation—not to mention the reciprocal action of one upon the other—internal contradictions that, by developing their natural movement, will lead to the destruction of these things, or more precisely, their transformation into new syntheses or symbioses, into new realities.[67]

A socialism based on dialectics must therefore remain flexible enough to accommodate a constantly changing reality. Instead of seeking to abolish contradictions, such a system should aim to synthesize them; though, this will result in outcomes that contain their own contradictions.

Ultimately, to borrow yet again from Diagne, Senghor's conception of socialism places it "in the cosmogenetic order of the movement of the world, so to speak." For Senghor, this made socialism "more than a choice of ideology or an economic system in which the course of things is not left to the free play of market forces," as he equated it with "the ethical choice to proceed in the direction of the push of life toward 'more being', always toward more humanism."[68] Still, methods need applications, and while Senghor's spiritual socialism manifested more as an overarching ethic in the end than as a concrete economic plan, he was concerned by the mid-1970s that Africans had come to associate socialism with Soviet authoritarianism and were unfamiliar with the multiplicity of ways that socialist dialectics had materialized in practice. His turn back toward Yugoslavia and his appeal to distribute Yugoslav socialist writings across Senegalese universities stemmed from a desire to position socialism once again as thought and practice in movement.

In his 1975 toast, Senghor linked his particular interest in Yugoslav self-management to the fact that it entailed replacing Soviet-style national property and "authoritarian planning" with the concept of social property. "It is thanks to self-management that the Yugoslav worker was able to escape the constraints that hindered the development of his person," he noted, "all the while respecting the principles of individual freedom and community development."[69] Senghor did not see it as problematic that self-management had changed since it was first implemented in 1948, contending that this is precisely what has made the "experience conscious and dynamic."[70]

In the Yugoslav experience, Senghor had identified dialectics in action. And he saw proof of this in the fact that self-management was not stultified into a model to be followed blindly but was continually adapted to changing local and global circumstances. In other words, the Yugoslavs conceived of socialism as a method:

> Starting from the very texts of Marx and Engels, you have made a lucid rereading in light of your national realities and those of our 20th century. Therefore, synthesis—more exactly symbiosis—that is to say living work, between the Plan and the Market, the constraint of discipline, imposed by realities, and the freedom of creative thought, which is the conquest of man.[71]

Yugoslavia represented for Senghor what his own theoretical understanding of socialism could look like in practice. Yet, Senghor redefines the third stage of dialectical thinking—the synthesis—as a symbiosis, thereby equating the economic and political system of Yugoslavia (and any country) to a living organism. This was indicative of Senghor's rejection of pure materialism in favor of a more vitalist understanding of socialism.

In fact, Senghor saw the universe as a web of forces that exist in a certain equilibrium. For Descartes, nature had no inner qualities; but for Senghor, the sub-reality of objects, which can be accessed only through intuition, was akin to a network of life forces.[72] God has endowed all beings with this life force—minerals, plants, animals, and humans—and these collective life forces are always influencing each other, which means they can be either de-forced or re-inforced. Senghor envisioned a hierarchy of forces, and believed God had given man the role of a demiurge who can contribute to the creation of the universe by acting to reinforce those life forces.[73] Thus, man's becoming, development, and freedom are not only for his own benefit.

While this ontology of life forces is a founding principle of African religions, Senghor was also influenced by Henri Bergson and by Father Pierre Teilhard de Chardin.[74] In Teilhard, Senghor found the coexistence of spiritualism and socialism, something absent from Marx. Senghor appreciated the "neo-humanism" of early Marx, but also believed that in his later writing, Marx had betrayed this humanism by turning toward rigid materialism and determinism. Teilhard, on the other hand, took up the dialectics of Marx and combined it with the latest scientific findings, extending it from humankind to the entirety of the universe. This set the stage for thinking about humankind as a "*phénomène cosmique*" (cosmic phenomenon).[75] While Marx was unable to adequately explain the transition from matter to spirit, Teilhard had found a solution: the mind-matter is organized in the universe by two forces—outer and inner gravity. Outer gravity works by compression, organizing particles in such a way that they don't crush each other; and inner gravity "attracts toward the most improbable, the most complex combinations."[76]

It was in Teilhard's cosmology that Senghor discovered his own philosophy of life forces, alongside the evolutionary, dialectic method he so appreciated in Marx. From atom to humankind, all life moves in the direction of complexification. The biosphere thus becomes the "nous-sphere" (noosphere), the domain of the human and of thought; a space divided into three stages: reflection, co-reflection, and ultra-reflection. In this sense, reflection is not associated only with the ability of humans to think, but also with the ability to be aware of themselves as thinking beings. As various thoughts in various places across the earth interconnect and overlap, they create a web that envelops the totality of the globe.[77] This activates the stage of co-reflection, in which a "compressive convergence of socialization"—involving human cooperation in the process of inventing new thoughts, techniques, and instruments—organizes humanity so that it can co-habit the earth without self-destructing. The intensification of socialization (i.e., of co-reflection) enables movement toward the final stage of ultra-reflection. Here, humankind nears the Omega point, the "personalized center that attracts all human centers in order to develop them by organizing them."[78]

Senghor also associated the ultra-reflection stage with the creation of the Civilization of the Universal—a symbiosis of all civilizations. In this conceptualization, symbiosis does not imply a loss of particularity within a larger whole, nor is the Civilization of the Universal equivalent to a Universal Civilization. In fact, Senghor has quoted Teilhard on numerous occasions to stress that "true union (or synthesis) does not confuse; it differentiates."[79] This is an important distinction, as Senghor considers a true union one that preserves the characteristics and specificities of its constituent elements, or even makes them *more* personalized. From this perspective, every civilization contributes necessary elements to the formation of a planetary civilization, but without dissolving into a set of universal values. For both Teilhard and Senghor, it was socialism that offered "the meta-physical significance of being the driving force of Love in the direction of that cosmo-genetic convergence; in contrast, the nature of capitalism is to separate, fragment, and pull in the direction opposite to the cosmic push of life"[80]

When, in 1975, Senghor used the term symbiosis in his toast to Tito, he was rejecting a materialistic separation of live beings from inert things. Furthermore, where a synthesis points toward an overcoming of contradictions within a newly created reality, a symbiosis foreshadows a mutually beneficial relationship. In other words, Senghor was proposing a model in which the market and state planning could influence one another in a way that would lead to more life. With this gesture, Senghor was inviting Yugoslavia to join him in this movement toward the Civilization of the Universal.

Cooperation with Yugoslavia was also important in the context of Senghor's (and Yugoslavia's) support for a New International Economic Order (NIEO).[81] In his toast to Tito, Senghor explained that while developed countries have reduced the prices of Senegal's main exports, oil and groundnut cake, by 40 percent, the prices of goods imported from these developed countries have simultaneously increased by 40 percent. If a lack of foreign capital was dangerous, so too was the dependence of the Global South on monocultures and on fluctuations of the international market.[82] Throughout his presidency, Senghor continued to support the NIEO. In July 1980, a few months before retiring, he wrote a text about the New International Economic Order, in which he reiterated that even though the current economic order has significantly increased global GDP, it has not been able to solve the problem of economic inequality. Countries of the Global South provide most of the natural and mineral resources used by the Global North yet continue to struggle with poverty and underdevelopment. Senghor appealed here once again for greater economic cooperation and connectivity. In this text, as in Senghor's thinking at large, respect for local difference and specificity are supplanted by regional integration and global cooperation.[83]

We should not forget of course that Senghor's toast to Tito was given during a diplomatic exchange, and it fit a specific political format. This was an official visit to Yugoslavia and Senghor sought to strengthen diplomacy between the two countries, so it was certainly not the occasion to criticize Yugoslav self-management. Yet, whether Yugoslav socialism corresponded exactly to Senghor's description of it is of little importance here (clearly, the system contained various internal contradictions that the country was ultimately unable to resolve); just as there is little likelihood that Yugoslav socialists would have had much interest in Senghor's vitalist and spiritual interpretation of their system, as they practiced a strict separation of church and state. Generally speaking, the Yugoslav understanding of socialism was significantly more materialistic than Senghor's, and Senghor knew this. Still, this did not prevent him from seeing Yugoslavia as a valuable example, even if he had not given up on the specificity of African socialism.

His use of the term symbiosis in describing Yugoslav socialism gestured toward Senghor's own translation of the Yugoslav experience. He understood the Yugoslav system, and he wanted to make it useful to Africans by adapting it to African socialism. For Senghor, both Négritude and African socialism were simultaneously open to the world and specific to each locality. And he saw the process of exchange, translation, and cooperation that occurred across the Global South as the route from Négritude to the Civilization of the Universal.

Examining Senghor's political and economic thinking in the context of international diplomacy allows us to shed a different light on his conceptualization of Négritude. The cultural specificity of any people cannot be realized in political and economic isolation. Even more, it requires cooperation and connection, not only with regional neighbors but also with those far away, like Yugoslavia. And in fact, Négritude made an explicit appearance in the second part of Senghor's toast to Tito. As culture is the ultimate purpose of human existence, Senghor noted, the search for a national identity—which is, above all, a cultural identity—is of primary importance. Here Senghor saw a useful parallel with the Yugoslav experience, as he related Négritude to Slavitude:

> For us Senegalese, neither Islam nor Christianity, and even less the Colonizer, have succeeded in fundamentally altering our cultural values, those of Negritude, which are expressed with such strength by each of the six ethnic groups that make up our nation. The values of Islam and Christianity, as well as European values in general, we have simply integrated them into our cultural heritage.
>
> I am pleased to note that, for you too, despite centuries of domination, whether under the Ottoman Empire or the Habsburg Empire, the Yugoslav popular soul has remained faithful to its cultural traits: to the eternal values of Slavitude...
>
> It is in this spirit that, since 1948, you have developed—and practiced—a federalism of republics and regions, with the ultimate goal of fostering the original, popular values of each ethnic group, values whose symbiosis will allow the Yugoslav people to achieve, in the cultural domain,

> maximum development. It is Marx, once again, who spoke of the 'eternal charm' of Greek art because it is the product of 'popular imagination'...
>
> The Yugoslav-Senegalese cooperation was established following our national independence. I hope that during this trip and our discussions, we will adopt a number of measures that will strengthen this cooperation, not only in socialist construction but also in the building of the Civilization of the Universal.[84]

Notably, Senghor places Yugoslavia within the dominated world, due to its history of Ottoman and Habsburg rule, and compares these empires to Islamic and Christian influences in Senegal. Furthermore, he represents both Yugoslavia and Senegal as mixed states, composed of various ethnic groups. But it is particularly interesting that Senghor juxtaposes Négritude and Slavitude, as Slavitude is not a concept in widespread use locally. If Négritude is understood as "the sum total of the values of the Black world," however, then Slavitude, by extension, is "the sum total of the values of the Slavic world." The parallel between these concepts transforms both of them, from static sets of values into methods (just like socialism). Négritude is represented as a concept in movement, capable of integrating Islamic, Christian, and European values without being fundamentally altered. It is thus more flexible than is often assumed, and is in this sense a method of being open to the world while preserving local values; a method that can be shared. This serves to shift relations between civilizations and regions of the world so that they are not based merely on shared values but on a shared method of building and preserving culture.

By turning a negative external designation (Nègre or Slav) into a means of "becoming," Senghor sees the grounds for new relations between Senegal and Yugoslavia. And interestingly, though communist Yugoslavia was established in 1945, Senghor alludes in his speech to 1948 instead—the year Yugoslav self-management was implemented—as the true beginning of Yugoslav federalism. He positions the country's economic (socialism) and political (federalism) systems as essential to the free cultural expression of its people, contending that the combination of these systems in Yugoslavia has allowed for the expression of Slavitude.

Senghor's dialectical thinking here moves in two directions. On the one hand, he points to the need for preserving original, popular values, specific to each civilization. On the other, he emphasizes the importance of federalism and symbiosis. Slavitude, according to Senghor, was realized only when the values of different ethnic groups came into contact under a federal system. These two directional movements are not contradictory in Senghor's view, as they in fact necessitate one another to maintain the universe in constant flux.

During his visit to Yugoslavia, Senghor received quite a bit of media attention, and in numerous television, radio, and newspaper interviews, conveyed his perspectives both as an official statesman and as a poet to be honored at the Struga Poetry Evenings. In Struga, at a press conference, Senghor discussed parallels between Senegalese and Macedonian poetry; marking a shift toward more specificity, away from the focus he had placed on Yugoslavia writ large during official government meetings, and pointing to his political and oratory prowess. Within Yugoslavia, he argued, the cultural production of Macedonians bore a specific resemblance to that of Senegalese creators, owing in part to the fact that both countries had been colonized for several centuries, one by the Ottomans and the other by the French. French colonization had strangled the originality of Senegalese poetry, he explained, which had found refuge in popular art, and he pointed to similar work done by Macedonian poets who had turned toward popular poetry in order to reinvigorate the Macedonian language. Senghor said he had followed the same path, initially inspired by French poets until he ultimately turned toward "his people," particularly the female poets of his home village.[85]

Senghor also suggested that, as a consequence of the imperialism of the world's superpowers, alienation characterized the Global South, noting that the Senegalese believed themselves to be culturally independent while speaking French and living in a technical and technological world built by Europe. Similarly, Yugoslavia had been inundated with information and products from those same superpowers. But here, he spoke as a poet, and this is where poetry enters the picture; for, Senghor saw poetry as the primary vehicle toward dis-alienation and cultural independence. Poetry, according to Senghor, should reflect "*notre sentir profond, notre vouloir profond*" (our deep feeling, our deep wanting), as the role of the poet is to express what is "*essentiel chez nous*" (essential for us). In the case of his Yugoslav hosts, Senghor imagined that would be a "*sensibilité yougoslave au milieu de la sensibilité slave*" (Yugoslav sensibility in the middle of the Slavic sensibility); and for Macedonians, a "*sensibilité macédonienne dans la sensibilité yougoslave*" (Macedonian sensibility in the Yugoslav sensibility).

In much the same way, he explained, the role of Black poetry is to translate "*l'âme négro-africaine*" (the Negro-African soul) through images, music, and rhythm. Statements like this have led critics to accuse Senghor of cultural essentialism. Yet, as he continued, Senghor softened this absolute understanding of culture by invoking *métissage*. All great civilizations, he claimed, result from "*métissage biologique et culturel*" (biological and cultural mixing). Yugoslavia, too, has been formed by the migrations of Slavic people and their mixing with other people, and he considered this mixing to be the basis of Yugoslavia's cultural richness and critical spirit.[86]

Within Europe, Senghor cited the Yugoslav and Romanian experiences as most useful to Africans. Yugoslav self-management in particular, he felt, had responded to Marx's argument about the withering of the state. Yet, self-management requires an evolved working class, aware of its social positioning, and that did not yet exist in Africa. In a somewhat problematic manner, Senghor embraced here developmentalist thinking, arguing that the first task of Africans was co-management, to prepare workers for self-management. Nonetheless, he said, Africans had much to learn from both Yugoslav self-management and its poetry, which Senghor described as "*poésie exemplaire*" (exemplary poetry).[87]

Though Senghor made a distinction between Slavic and Black civilizations, he included Yugoslavia in his vision of "a global postcoloniality" in which countries on the periphery are linked through their parallel fights for dis-alienation.[88] Once again, method and process are at the basis of Senghor's internationalism. As in his other speeches, Senghor left room here for local differences, including the different conditions of the Yugoslav and African working classes. He was clear that African socialism cannot and should not look exactly like Yugoslav socialism, but also drew parallels between the two experiences. It was his perspective, as he later wrote, that man is "a composition of mobile life forces which interlock: a world of solidarities that seek to knit themselves together;"[89] and that the same was true for cultures and nations, particularly those on the global periphery.

Senghor's understanding of local conditions and his capacity to draw these parallels speaks to his sophisticated understanding of politics and diplomacy, which had developed over his fifteen years as president by the time of his visit to Yugoslavia. Yet the speeches he gave there represent more than mere political rhetoric. They are a product of Senghor's long-term interest in Yugoslavia as well as his elaborate philosophy of relationality and internationalism. Senghor did not avoid talking about Négritude just because he found himself in a white, European country. In fact, it was precisely his understanding of Négritude that had facilitated his relationship with Yugoslavia. In the context of shifting global superpowers, widespread economic crisis, and rising postcolonial disappointments, Senghor sought support from one of the few countries that remained socialist.

In a short documentary by Macedonian director Kiril Cenevski, made in honor of Senghor's recognition in Struga, Senghor is shown in conversation with his friend Aco Šopov, challenging the reading of Négritude as a form of reverse racism that is incompatible with Marxism. Marx himself, Senghor claims, spoke to the ethnic character of the Greek civilization, and it was precisely this expression of popular spirit that Marx valued in Greek art. Négritude is a similar ensemble of values that explain African civilization, political organization, and art, Senghor explained. He proposed that the primary problem for socialism in the nineteenth century had been class inequality *within* nations, but that the imperial rise of capitalism had made the economic gap *between* developed and developing nations the most pressing issue for socialist movements. Only a new Global South consciousness (and Senghor included Yugoslavia in this category), and a new socialism emanating from this consciousness, would address these inequalities.

Senghor insisted that socialism could not be reduced to a reframing of economic relations, though, as the ultimate struggle of man is for dignity and cultural expression. Fights for national languages, art, and culture are therefore socialist; and this, he noted, was a struggle shared by Yugoslavs and the Senegalese.[90] In other words, this was a struggle Senghor shared with his friends Šopov and Guberina. And as it would turn out, Senghor's Yugoslav visit became an opportunity to revive his friendship with Guberina, which had marked his Parisian youth.

Petar Guberina in Senegal

It had been agreed during Senghor's visit to Yugoslavia that Guberina's verbotonal method would be introduced in Senegal. The relevance of Guberina's work in linguistics to the founders of the Négritude movement, as discussed in the previous chapter, had to do with his findings that rhythm, intonation, and gesture were universally important to human speech. While the introduction of the verbotonal method may seem like a minor project given the volume of political and economic cooperation between Senegal and Yugoslavia, and was in many ways, Senghor insisted that it be put into practice as quickly as possible. Working with Guberina to implement the method was yet another way that Senghor returned to ideas and connections from his earlier life, toward the end of his political career. Guberina had been a part of Senghor's formative years in Paris, and here he was again, several decades later, having developed a globally renowned method for working with hearing-impaired people.

Guberina's verbotonal method was grounded in Senghor's understanding of rhythm: "the movement of attraction or repulsion that expresses the life of the cosmic forces; symmetry and asymmetry, repetition or opposition."[91] In fact, Senghor's influence is highly visible in Guberina's writing. In addition to his work on linguistics, Guberina founded the Institute for African Studies in Zagreb and wrote extensively on African poetry and art. In the postface to the Serbo-Croatian translation of Basil Davidson's *The Africans*, Guberina cites Senghor extensively, and concludes:

> Language, individual vowels and consonants, emerge from the Black artist as architectural or plastic material that constructs a linguistic whole in which tone, voice, word, and sentence resonate with a common sound. And this is not because African languages would be primitive or impoverished, or because they would be at the stage of blindly imitating natural sounds... but because the rhythmic element of music is present at every moment, and it combines the sounds of words into a harmonious whole.[92]

Senghor's understanding of rhythm thus found its way into Guberina's linguistic work, and by extension into his verbotonal method, which emphasizes the importance of developing good rhythm, intonation, and voice quality in hearing-impaired children. Senghor's ideas, rooted in the specificity of African ontology, took a Yugoslav detour and acquired a global, therapeutic, component. It only made sense that the verbotonal method would find its way (back) to Senegal.

It was January 1976 when Guberina traveled to Dakar to oversee the implementation of the verbotonal method. He had agreed to begin by working with fifty children in November of that year, not in a designated institute but in their regular schools. Senghor's plan was to repatriate all of Senegal's deaf children from France, to be rehabilitated in Senegal in an African language. The verbotonal method was to be introduced into the University of Dakar as well, in its Center for Applied Linguistics, the Linguistics Department, and the Institute for the Study of African Languages.[93] Introduction of the method was another sign that Senghor was turning away from France and toward the rest of the Global South in these later years of his career; and it was not only used to provide therapy to hearing-impaired children, but also to teach and research African languages. In this way, the verbotonal method was another means by which Négritude extended beyond the world of the African diaspora and found innovative applications in unexpected global encounters and connections.

In 1980, five years after his visit to Yugoslavia, Senghor stepped down as President of Senegal. That same year, Tito died, and the unraveling of Yugoslavia began. By exploring Senghor's long-lasting attachment to Yugoslavia and the deep impact of his friendships with Petar Guberina and Aco Šopov, however, we have been able here to reevaluate his politics, ethics, and poetics from an internationalist perspective. Though Senghor was often criticized for espousing an "anti-racist racism" and for his essentialist depiction of both European and African civilizations, he was deeply committed to both learning from and collaborating with oppressed people around the globe. He certainly made significant political compromises in order to avoid alienating French capitalists or Senegalese religious leaders after his falling out with Mamadou Dia, but he continued to see socialism as a comparative method, one that needed to be accepted globally and practiced locally. Indeed, Senghor believed that realizing the values of Négritude and the autonomous cultural development of African countries depended on instituting a different global economic system, and one that could be achieved only with cooperation from the Global South.

For Senghor, Yugoslavia was such a significant influence because it was a socialist federation that did not follow the Soviet Union but had adapted socialism to its local conditions. Any differences between Négritude and Slavitude did not prevent solidarity between his country and Yugoslavia; quite the contrary, as it was only by interacting with other civilizations that Senghor believed Négritude could contribute to manifesting the Civilization of the Universal. Thus, during Senghor's visit to Yugoslavia, the weekly newspaper *Ilustrovana Politika* published an interview with him that opened with the following description:

> Léopold Sédar Senghor suddenly stopped. He stood by the ancient walls of the medieval church of St. Panteleimon, on the hill, exactly at noon, admiring the greenish line of the lake that merged with the horizon. Earlier, we were told that the President of the Republic of Senegal, a politician and the greatest living poet of Africa, laureate of the 'Golden Wreath of the Struga Poetry Evenings for 1975,' and our dear guest, customarily reflects on his true experiences by the waters, whether in Senegal on the Atlantic, on the shores of the Senegal River, or, as now, in Ohrid, both as a man and as a poet.[94]

I end this chapter with this image of Senghor atop a Macedonian hill, with this juxtaposition of the Atlantic, the Seine, and Lake Ohrid, as a metaphor for the intertwining friendships of Aimé Césaire, Léopold Sédar Senghor, Petar Guberina, and an ethics of solidarity and exchange across the Global South.

CHAPTER THREE

Laying Tracks, Crafting Narratives: René Depestre's Yugoslav Journey and Its Literary Echoes

I had been reading and teaching René Depestre for many years when I stumbled upon an interesting detail in one of his biographies: in 1947, Depestre had joined a communist youth brigade in Yugoslavia that was building the Šamac-Sarajevo railroad. Nothing about this was further elaborated, and when I set about researching Depestre's connection to Yugoslavia myself, I could find no mention of it. Yet, my curiosity was piqued; why had one of Haiti's most renowned authors been in Yugoslavia? What was his experience? And why has he never written about it?

As I could not find the answers I sought in the critical literature on Depestre, I decided to write him, though I hardly expected a response. Indeed, how many letters must René Depestre receive each day? And on topics significantly more important than travel he undertook seven decades ago. Still, to my surprise, he responded in a very enthusiastic letter several months later, recalling his trip to Yugoslavia fondly. Yugoslavia has meant a lot to him as a writer and an intellectual, he said, and he invited me to his house in Lézignan-Corbières, in the South of France, to discuss it in person. This is how it was that I visited Depestre in his home in the summer of 2017 and had a fascinating conversation with him about his Yugoslav experience which, however brief, has deeply impacted his relationship to politics. While there, he fell in love with a member of the antifascist resistance, Kostadinka Crnojević, and, throughout his life, he remained attached to the values embodied by Yugoslav youth. Depestre never wrote about his Yugoslav experience, in part due to his close affiliations with the French and the Cuban communist parties, which were aligned with the Soviet Union and unconvinced by Yugoslav socialism. Until 1990, when he published the collection *Éros dans un train chinois* (*Eros on a Chinese Train*), which includes a story set in Yugoslavia.

Understanding Depestre's Yugoslav experience adds nuance to existing narratives about his relationship to communism, wherein his youthful enthusiasm turns into disappointment as he withdraws to the South of France. Literary critic Charles Forsdick has argued, for example, that Depestre "emphatically eschewed the revolutionary politics of his youth in favor of exoticist métissage and apologies for la francophonie."[1] This "emphatic rejection of revolutionary politics" by Depestre has also been raised by Chris Bongie, who has characterized Depestre as "a fully disenchanted modernist."[2] Yet, Depestre's relationship to different communisms over time must be historicized and contextualized. Throughout his life, he participated in multiple (and very different) communist experiments and had complex and conflicting relationships with them, which move beyond a mere rejection of communism's supposedly inevitable authoritarianism. While he was critical of specific outcomes of communist projects, Depestre remained committed to the values of early communist revolutions, including those promoted by the youth brigade that built the Šamac-Sarajevo railroad.

Through a close reading of Depestre's short story "The Skirt," as well as the interview I conducted with him, I show that his later turn toward individual eroticism was not entirely apolitical, as various critics have suggested.[3] While the story is marked by his mixed feelings toward the outcome of communist experiments, I argue that it remains a homage to Yugoslavia, and to the commitment, force, and dedication of post–World War II communist youth. The tale of love recounted in "The Skirt" is one between comrades, and theirs is a highly political *eros*, inseparable from the collective work of railroad building. Given that the story is based on the trip Depestre took to Yugoslavia, which he recounted to me in our interview, there is some extent to which it reads as autobiographical; though it certainly remains fiction. My concern here is not with the veracity of the story, however, but with how lived experience, memory, and fiction intersect within the space of a love story.

The format of this chapter is slightly unusual as a result, combining Depestre's own account of his Yugoslav experience with an analysis of a fictional story based on this experience.[4] The reason that I include excerpts from our interview is twofold. First, Depestre stated that he wished he had written more about Yugoslavia and I wanted to offer him space to do just that. Furthermore, the background information offered in the interview allows me to highlight the political dimensions of the story. Yet it is important to note that I do not take the interview to be entirely factual. In this sense, I consider Depestre as the type of interviewee which John Rodden has described as a "raconteur," a "storyteller whose main unit of discourse is the anecdote." This type of interviewee is a performer, whose "anecdotes are closer to legend than lived history;" they care less about the accuracy of their account than "the poetics of literary performance."[5] In his fictional work, Depestre often plays with multiple "I"s, frequently confounding authorial and narratorial positions. The interview becomes another space where an "I" is constructed on the border between reality and fiction. Subsequently, the "I" of the interview does not correspond to the "I" of the story, yet in both cases Depestre narrates into being a political subject shaped by his Yugoslav experience. The interview and the story, I thus read as two (semi)-fictional accounts of Depestre's Yugoslav experience.[6] Through the superposition of these two accounts, I also want to demonstrate how Yugoslavia becomes a shifting signifier, as the memory and depiction of the place changes according to the setting and medium of expression. Thus, the excitement that Depestre expressed about Yugoslavia in the interview, is modulated by the ending of "The Skirt."

Depestre's Yugoslav story is important for another reason. In fact, this link represents a point of intersection with his fellow Caribbean writer, Aimé Césaire, with whom he is often contrasted. In Chapter One, I analyzed the Yugoslav origins of Césaire's *Cahier*. In this one, I will show that the "*nomadisme enraciné*" (rooted nomadism) of Depestre was similarly tied to the Yugoslav experience. In the rest of the chapter, I first explain how the shared Yugoslav connection allows us to read Césaire and Depestre differently in relation to each other. I then discuss the place of Yugoslavia in Depestre's political and literary careers. Finally, I offer a close reading of "The Skirt," as I argue that understanding the historical setting of the story allows us to better understand its political dimensions.

A Point of Intersection

Césaire and Depestre are frequently mentioned in concert with a third literary figure, Louis Aragon, in relation to a series of articles published in the communist literary journal *Les lettres françaises*, starting in 1954. Aragon, its editor in chief and a former surrealist poet, had embraced the sonnet as the only poetic form capable of capturing the complexity of the post–World War II era.[7] From his exile in Brazil, Depestre read Aragon's essays and wrote an excited letter to his French friend, the poet and journalist Charles Dobzynski, noting that "thanks to Aragon," he was "in the process of resolving...the conflict around" his own formal individualism.[8] At the time, it had been nearly ten years since Depestre had left Haiti, and he worried he was losing his connection to the struggles of his people; that his writing had become little more than an expression of cosmopolitan individualism.[9] But in Aragon's defense of the sonnet, Depestre found a solution to this problem: he could remain far from Haiti and still mobilize his experiences and his writing in the service of his people. The revolutionary politics and poetics of Aragon, he believed, could both clarify and transform the Haitian reality.

Depestre had no intention of airing his excitement about the sonnet in a public debate, but Dobzynski shared the letter with Aragon, who published it in *Les lettres françaises* without Depestre's knowledge, sparking a year-long "Debate concerning the conditions of national poetry among black peoples" in the pages of *Présence Africaine*.[10] Various Black writers voiced their opinion on the subject, and Aimé Césaire accused Depestre of "detestable assimilationism."[11] In his poem written in the guise of a response, Césaire directly addressed Depestre, asking: "is it true that you doubt the native forest /.../ can it be / that the rains of exile / have slackened the drum-skin of your voice."[12] In this way, Césaire reproached Depestre for having reneged his African-ness, for having forgotten his origins. Exile, Césaire contends, has led Depestre to forget the cultural specificity of the African diaspora, which can never be expressed through European socialist realism.

This dialogue continued when Depestre's response was also published in *Présence Africaine*. He acknowledged that, in his attempt to rid Haitian poetry of its "formal individualism," he may have represented Haiti's "cultural duality" in a manner too binary and static. While Depestre was reconciliatory, his response also outlined what would become his long-standing critique of Négritude: that Black artistic expressions inevitably vary according to the historical conditions and class organization of each country. "[I]t is not the community of language or race that determines the national character of a culture, but in the final analysis, the conditions of life, the conditions of historical development specific to each country."[13] Here, Depestre expresses his Marxist perspective, and the specific concern he had about the oppressive role of the black bourgeoisie in Haiti. Any theory of Black art, he argues, is at risk of cultural essentialism.

Kaiama Glover is right to suggest that the divergent positions of Depestre and Césaire stemmed in part from their differing national situations and experiences of immigration. Depestre, in perpetual movement due to a series of exiles, was trying to inscribe himself and his work in an international socialist community. Césaire, on the other hand, aware of the failures of the departmentalization he had supported, was focused on "the crafting of a creative post-imperial political relationship with France," and the creation of an African diasporic poetic language.[14] As time went by, Depestre began to see things more as Césaire did, perhaps due to the criticism he endured for his initial embrace of Aragon. Still, his critique of Négritude persisted.

To be fair, Depestre always differentiated between cultural and political Négritude, defending Césaire as an advocate of the former and excoriating Haitian dictator François Duvalier as representative of the latter.[15] However, when Césaire and Depestre are analyzed in tandem, it is their differences that are often emphasized; with Césaire, as one of the founders of the Négritude movement, presented as interested primarily in the shared values of the African diaspora, and Depestre characterized as a devout communist and internationalist.[16] And, in fact, as Christopher T. Bonner has suggested, their debate raised conceptual challenges related to the politics of literature within the global Cold War context, positioning literary form as "the battleground upon which radical thinkers of contrary tendencies hash out their differences in a context of shifting ideological alignments."[17] However, Césaire and Depestre did not always have differing alignments, particularly regarding Yugoslavia.

Before Depestre and Césaire split ways over the question of national poetics, their paths had crossed in the Balkans. In the previous chapters, I discussed the ways that Négritude was open to the world from its beginnings, including to connections beyond the African diaspora, and this reaching beyond is where Césaire and Depestre came together. They may have disagreed over aesthetic forms for Black writers, but their points of intersection included a shared interest in emerging socialist experiments. This is important, because the positions of these two authors clearly weren't diametrically opposed. Césaire certainly felt more strongly than Depestre that a common historical heritage produced shared values within the Black world, and believed that it was only by embracing one's own historical and cultural particularity that one could be in relation with others. Yet, their debate didn't necessarily pit cosmopolitanism and cultural particularism against each other, rather it sought to reconcile the two. The fact is that both Césaire and Depestre explored various forms of interracial solidarity, and both thought within and beyond the context of the African diaspora.

René Depestre's Yugoslav Adventure

AP: In 1947, with a brigade of young people, you helped to build the Šamac-Sarajevo railway in Bosnia. Could you tell me a little bit about this experience?

RD: In the summer of 1947, I decided to participate in the World Youth Festival in Prague. On the train on the way there, I met some guys from Lézignan-Corbières. Some members of the Yugoslav delegation invited us to come to Yugoslavia. We went there as part of a work brigade. We stayed for almost two months in Šamac and Sarajevo to build the railway. It was an extraordinary experience: In '47, the air was full of democracy in Yugoslavia. For me, it was the first time that I met young people, of my generation, who had so much enthusiasm and such an impressive vision for the future. We really thought that we were going to make socialism a decisive reality in human history. There were Bulgarians there, Russians, Poles, young people from all around the Balkans. We talked a lot, we danced like crazy. It was a transformative experience, and not just in terms of politics and joyful camaraderie. As students, we were curious about everything, we talked about all the issues of our time. I had already been studying at the University of Paris for a year and was buzzing with intellectual curiosity. And I already had some political experience behind me in Haiti. In April 1945, I published my first book of poems, *Étincelles*, which was very successful. In collaboration with the young intellectuals Jacques-Stephen Alexis, Gérald

> Bloncourt, and Théo Baker, I launched a weekly paper, *La Ruche*. Our newspaper caused public opinion in Haiti to turn against the dictatorship of then-president Élie Lescot. Our movement hoped to overthrow his government. I was one of the main organizers behind the successful general strike in Haiti. So, I was really on the same wavelength as the young revolutionary Yugoslavs I met. Aside from Cuba, I have never met young people that were so motivated and so enthusiastic about political action. So, my stay in Yugoslavia really changed me. That's why after Marshal Tito broke with the socialist camp, I kept supporting Yugoslavia, while being a member of the French Communist Party.

Depestre was born in the Haitian city of Jacmel, in 1926. By the age of 19, he had received critical acclaim for his first collection of poems, *Étincelles* (*Sparks*). Inspired by this success, as he explains above, he went on to establish a left-leaning political and cultural review, *La Ruche* (*Beehive*), with Jacques-Stephen Alexis, Gérald Bloncourt, and Théodore Baker. Depestre built influential friendships with Haitian and foreign intellectuals, including Jean Price-Mars, Léon Laleau, Clément Magloire-Saint-Aude, Aimé Césaire, Wifredo Lam, and André Breton. In fact, when Breton visited Haiti in 1945, *La Ruche* dedicated an issue to him; a choice that had lasting consequences. The publication "had the effect of a bomb as it had placed itself in direct line with the spirit of protest which had been that of surrealism, at its beginnings, in the Paris of the 1920s."[18] When President Lescot retaliated by banning *La Ruche* and arresting Depestre and Baker, a student protest demanding their release turned into a general strike that overturned the government in 1946: "The whole country was on our side," Depestre wrote of the moment, "[o]ne can imagine the joy of André Breton in front of the kind of 'May 68'… that the young people of Haiti offered him, in homage to the libertarian values of surrealism."[19] Depestre's first exile to France followed soon after.

While this was his first exile, it would certainly not be his last. Several years later, Depestre was expelled from France due to his participation in decolonization struggles, and settled for a time in Czechoslovakia with his Jewish partner Edith Gombos. However, they were forced to leave in 1952 as antisemitism began to intensify. After a brief foray into Cuba, where they were not welcomed by the Batista government, the couple spent eight months in Chile and two years in Brazil. Then, in 1957, after eleven years away, Depestre returned to Haiti, which was already under the Black nationalist and increasingly totalitarian regime of François Duvalier.

During those years, Depestre listened to *Radio Rebelde*, to tune into the words of Fidel Castro and Che Guevara. His first reflex was to join them, but Haitian communists had convinced him that their bourgeois revolution and its "mulatto rebels" were not to be trusted. The Cuban revolution, they told him, was likely to fail.[20] Nevertheless, in 1959, after publishing an analysis of the Cuban revolution in a Haitian newspaper, Depestre made his way back to Cuba. Both Castro and Guevara read his article, and his arrival did not go unnoticed.

Though he was politically and ethically closer to Che than to Fidel, Depestre remained in Cuba for nearly two decades, serving its socialist revolution through his work in the ministry of foreign affairs, the Cuban National Press, the National Cultural Council, and Radio-Havana-Cuba. And for a long time, Depestre identified with Cuba and its revolution: "Haiti has taken away my Haitian nationality, so I was stateless. The Cubans told me I was just another Cuban—'un Cubano más'."[21] But Depestre would eventually break with Cuba. While earlier events played a role, his point of no return came in 1971, when poet Heberto Juan Padilla was imprisoned for criticizing the Castro government. Depestre's public defense of Padilla at the meeting of the Writer's Union marked the beginning of his rupture with Cuba. Later, he explained that he didn't just speak to defend Padilla but "to defend the honor of the communist movement."[22]

After this public outburst, Depestre was marginalized from Cuban affairs. Though he would remain in the country for another eight years, he was no longer at the heart of the revolution. So, in 1979, he moved to France to take a post at UNESCO, and in 1986 he retired and relocated to the South, settling in the quaint village of Lézignan-Corbières, where he resides to this day.

The work of Depestre is often categorized into two distinct phases—pre-Cuba and post-Cuba—which are thought to correspond to his two personalities: that of a young man of action who believed in the possibility of revolution and the promise of communism, and the older realist who has become disappointed in Cuba and has given up political action to spend the rest of his life writing.[23] Indeed, his earlier works deal with dictators, revolutions, and rebels, as in his 1953 *Le mât de cocagne* (*The Festival of the Greasy Pole*); while his later texts are more individualist, focused on what Depestre called "*érotisme solaire*" (solar eroticism). The Cuban experience thus represents a crossroads in his work.[24]

And yet, before Cuba, there was Yugoslavia. This is something about which Depestre and his critics have both talked very little. And to be fair, his trip to the Balkans was brief, a mere summer long. But Depestre has written and spoken about Cuba, while rarely mentioning his experience in Yugoslavia, despite telling me that this is where his "nomadic travels" really began.

AP: ...why did you never write about Yugoslavia?

RD: I had a bit of a romantic adventure with a young Serbian woman, which was forbidden on the construction site. The authorities prohibited any kind of sexual relations between foreigners and native young women. Dinka took huge risks to come meet me every evening. I will never forget the wonderful acts of love that we shared. It was the first time that I experienced so much happiness in the arms of a European woman. As a result, for my whole life, the idea of Yugoslavia has always remained closely tied to my secret love affair with Kostadinka Crnojević. If I had revealed this magnificent secret, I would have been expelled from the French Communist Party. A long time later, I experienced the same fate in Cuba. I was deeply invested in the communist experiment. For a year, I was the Cuban press correspondent in Moscow. I learned how to speak Czech, and a little bit of Russian too. The collapse of the socialist utopia was a personal tragedy for me.

...

Depestre did not keep all of his Yugoslav experience secret, however, as it was the setting for one story, which received little critical attention. "The Skirt" was published in the 1990 collection *Eros on a Chinese Train*, the third installment of Depestre's erotic trilogy, which also includes *Alléluia pour une femme-jardin* (*Hallelujah for a Garden-Woman*) and *Hadriana dans tous mes rêves* (*Hadriana in All My Dreams*). The trilogy was met with some ambivalence, as many scholars condemned his turn from explicitly revolutionary politics, as well as the objectification and exoticization of women.

Joan Dayan wrote that Depestre's "celebration of a glorious composite muse...both idealizes and disempowers the real flesh-and-blood woman."[25] This refers particularly to the section of *Hallelujah for a Garden-Woman* entitled "memories of geolibertinage," in which Depestre describes various sexual encounters he had during his time at the Cité Universitaire in

Paris, where he met women from around the world whose bodies allowed him to traverse the planet, becoming his "Northern and Southern hemispheres."[26] And, it is true that Depestre reiterates many stereotypes of the female body as a conduit for the male imagination. Women themselves are not developed as characters, they have no names or characteristics, they are not full subjects; they are simply objects in the writer's possession, sources of inspiration.

The same has been said of the Creole woman Hadriana, who is turned into a zombie on the night of her wedding. Published in 1988, *Hadriana* won Depestre the prestigious Prix Renaudot and sold 200,000 copies. Yet critics also disparaged the novel, arguing that Depestre had exoticized Haiti, with its colorful Carnival, beautiful women, and vodou.[27] But Kaiama Glover has recently proposed a different reading of the novel "as a highly sophisticated work of social criticism." Glover analyzes "gender clichés in the novel…as the springboards from which Depestre dismantles—or at the very least meaningfully pokes fun at—the very stereotypes he has been accused of promoting."[28]

Eros on a Chinese Train, the third in the solar eroticism series, did not receive good reviews either. Hal Wylie expected that "most readers" would find it disappointing, and called *Eros* "essentially apolitical, although it can be read as a disavowal of the author's past work."[29] Robert Hartwig, referring to the first three stories of the collection, all of which take place in communist countries (China and Yugoslavia), concluded that "these stories are tightly constructed, but their settings are depressing, and we begin to lose sympathy for a narrator whose exploits lead to tragic consequences for his naïve and innocent partners."[30] Through a close reading of "The Skirt," I want to push back on this by showing that the setting is not depressing, and the partner is neither innocent nor naive.

First, the settings in the stories mentioned by Hartwig are hardly all the same, as the first two take place in China and the third in Yugoslavia. The impulse to lump them together points to a critical blind spot. For, communism is not a singular, homogeneous system that has functioned in the same manner in all countries. And, in the same way that China and Yugoslavia are considerably different, so, too, are Xiluan, Baozhu, and Kostadinka Crnojévitch, the protagonists of these three stories.

The way Depestre engaged with the communist projects in which he participated was also marked by some important subtleties. Wylie lamented in his review of *Eros* that no story within it takes place in Cuba;

and yet, no story takes place in Cuba because these are the stories of "other communisms" that broke away from Stalinism. In fact, Depestre's biggest disagreement with Castro was over Cuba's rapprochement to the Soviet Union and the importation of Stalinism into the Caribbean:

> The Americans were simply not going to permit such a small country to stake out a sovereign position, to impose its own point of view, and even less nationalize the sugar industry and the American interests on the island—that was something sacred, and it was shocking. And when the hammer started coming down, the Cubans panicked, because if the Americans had decided to impose their full might against them from the very beginning, Cuba would have been incapable of resisting.[31]

This shift in the ideology of the Cuban revolution was a function of a specific international context, according to Depestre, in which "Cuba was in the wrong place at the wrong time and simply couldn't fight back against the pressure of American embargo."[32]

My intention here is not to enter a debate over whether Cuba did or did not make the right decision and over whether it had another choice. Instead, I want to note that Depestre believed the failure of the Cuban revolution resulted from a combination of local choices and ideologies on the one hand, and global forces and pressures on the other. Like his engagement with Cuba, his engagement with China and Yugoslavia was nuanced, and he remained aware of the significant heterogeneity within the communist world. Furthermore, the first three stories of *Eros*, which combine his interest in individual eroticism with his communist past, don't fit neatly into the dichotomy that splits Depestre into a younger man engaged with political questions and an older one whose gaze has turned from Cuba toward France and Haiti.

Notably, Eros had already played an important role in the work of Depestre, having made an appearance in early texts like *Le mât de cocagne*. And in later works like *Eros*, Depestre returns to his communist youth. The relationship between sexuality and politics thus goes beyond the mere opposition of *eros* and revolution. Indeed, in "The Skirt," the collective work of communist youth and lovemaking are part of the same effort to rebuild a different world in the aftermath of World War II.

"The Skirt" begins on a train. The narrator, Marc Zénon, is traveling with his girlfriend Chantal and other young Europeans to Bosnia, to build the Šamac-Sarajevo railroad. At the construction site, having joined an international volunteer brigade, Zénon meets a Montenegrin girl, Kostadinka Crnojévitch, who becomes his lover. Love affairs between local women and foreign volunteers are forbidden on the work sites, however, so these lovers must meet secretly in the hills above the Bosna River; and even still, Kostadinka is ultimately arrested and her head is shaved in public as punishment.

In our interview, Depestre described the story as one of his best:

AP: Did your love affair continue after those two months?

RD: We exchanged some letters, I proposed to her. I had returned to Paris to continue my studies, and I asked her to come and meet me in Paris. But it wasn't easy for Yugoslavs to leave the country at the time. So we grew apart and eventually I lost track of her. When I went back to Belgrade years later, I couldn't find her. When the memory of a country and its people are tied to a great love story, that has a huge impact on the life of a poet.

AP: In *Éros dans un train chinois*, you did, however, write a story that took place in Yugoslavia.

RD: That's one of my best short stories. Critics said it was excellent. I also managed to express my loyalty to Yugoslavia by sharing a brilliant moment of my nights!

In Yugoslavia, politics and sexuality are intertwined. In fact, the setting for the love story is the Šamac-Sarajevo railroad, an important socialist project that Yugoslavia embarked on in the aftermath of WWII.

The Youth Railway

Yugoslavia had emerged victorious from WWII but had suffered a huge loss of population and was materially and economically devastated. Out of some fifteen million people, nearly two million had died in the war. The construction of the Šamac-Sarajevo railroad, also known as the "*pruga bratstva i jedinstva*" (the brotherhood and unity railway), was meant to unite Yugoslavia's diverse ethnic communities and represent the new socialist federation to the world.

Some called the route "*Omladinska pruga*" (the Youth Railway) because it was built by volunteer youth who had embarked on the project to reconstruct the country. It took them less than eight months to build the 242 km-long stretch of rail, working from the beginning of April to mid-November 1947, a record time for a project of such scale. The project, and railway, is famous to this day, due to the involvement of so many (887) voluntary youth brigades, totaling 211,381 volunteers from across social strata. They included 55,812 workers, 112,277 peasants, 34,613 students, and 8,669 intellectuals, but also 5,842 international volunteers from forty-two countries who were divided among fifty-six work brigades.[33] Volunteers came from Poland, Czechoslovakia, East Germany, Bulgaria, Greece, Romania, Hungary, England, Italy, France, Denmark, Sweden, and more.[34] The project promoted collectivism and internationalism in the aftermath of the brutality of war. The collaborative, voluntary nature of both the local and foreign brigades signaled a better future ahead; one of unity and solidarity, not ethnic and racial hatred. The work was democratically organized by the volunteers themselves, with existing brigades distributing tasks to new brigades. The project was one of Yugoslavia's first experiments in horizontalism and radical democracy, one capable of proving that self-organized youth could build a railroad faster than any capitalist corporation. And indeed, they did.

Though mostly forgotten now, there were many narratives written of life and work along the railroad. For example, prominent British historian Edward Palmer Thompson edited a booklet in 1948, which recounts the experience of British youth volunteers. The text has remained in the public eye (and was recently reprinted) primarily due to Thompson's association with it.[35] In his lengthy introduction to the book, Thompson characterized the railway workers as "the natural inheritors of the spirit of the partisans." Through projects like the railway, qualities promoted by the Partisans like "comradeship, self-abnegation and conscious unity" were "carried forward intact into the days of peace."[36]

The railway thus represented the continuation of the antifascist struggle, as organizational models were borrowed from the Partisans. One of the many chants that accompanied its construction—"*mi gradimo prugu, pruga gradi nas*" ("we build the railway, the railway builds us")—reflected the dialectic core of socialism, wherein the industrialization and rebuilding of the country were also educational endeavors aimed at shaping new citizens. The collectivism, internationalism, and solidarity of the project were supposed to reflect existing values but also instill them as the foundations of a radically different society. Chants and songs, art, newspapers and pamphlets, and dances were all part of this popular education. On the one hand, theater troops, actors, and musicians were sent from the cities to entertain the brigadiers. On the other, brigades organized various forms of entertainment in the evenings.[37]

The Šamac-Sarajevo railroad was clearly as dialectical as it was infrastructural. In this context, collective work was prefigurative; it was meant to create a new social configuration, to liberate individuals from old values and prepare them to embrace new ones. Nika Autor's cinematic homage to the Šamac-Sarajevo youth emphasizes the emotional dimension of the project: "Out of the ruins of war, out of the ruins of their own emotions, out of the pain and sadness due to their fallen loved ones, out of the underdevelopment of the country, they built the railway line, and it built them."[38] In our interview, Depestre similarly emphasized how the collective work turned postwar pain into joy.

AP: At UNESCO, you had many Yugoslav friends.

RD: In our conversations, I would always talk about my trip to their country with so much joy. Sometimes, I would even break into song: "*Šamac-Sarajevo, to je naša meta, izgraditi prugu još ovoga ljeta. Jedan, dva, jedan, dva, omladina Titova radi na pruzi ovog leta*" (Šamac-Sarajevo, that is our target, to build a railroad this very summer. One, two, one, two, Tito's youth is working on the railroad this summer).

AP: You have an incredible memory!

RD: I've never forgotten the songs we used to sing while we worked on the railway. We were always singing. We had a lot of fun. Many years later, I would have the same feeling of youthful exuberance while doing voluntary work in Cuba. In my mind, throughout my whole life, these two revolutions infected me with their joyfulness, despite the defamation campaigns engineered by Stalinists of all stripes against Tito's regime!

AP: And what were the reactions of your friends at UNESCO when you sang to them in Serbo-Croatian?

RD: I would sing: "*Tito je maršal, Tito je genije, Tito je komandant slavne armije*!" (Tito is marshal, Tito is a genius, Tito is the commander of a famous army). A Haitian singing in their language, they couldn't believe their ears. I also remembered a handful of Russian songs, having lived

> for a year in Moscow as a press correspondent for *Revolución*, Fidel Castro's newspaper. I had travelled all across the Soviet Union where people also sang a lot. For that reason as well, the rupture with Tito left a gaping wound in my life.

Ivo Andrić, the Nobel Prize-winning Yugoslav author, framed the construction of the Šamac-Sarajevo railway as an overcoming of both the past and natural obstacles, where the youth engages in "the fight with the forces of nature, the fight with the errors of the past, fight with prejudice and rusty legacies in ourselves."[39] As Andrić noted, the fighting may have ended but the fight did not. The future in the making would require that the mistakes, violence, and hatreds of the past were defeated. That was the burden of the new generation, the one building the railway. But this was also a fight with nature. Through the lens of Marxism and materialism, the construction of the railway represented a reshaping of nature according to the needs of new men and women. That this was to occur on the shores of the Bosna, on this river that symbolizes life, rebirth, and regeneration, did not seem accidental.

In "The Skirt," Depestre discusses how labor was divided on the railway construction site, how thirty-nine international brigades were each charged with building a different segment. His description includes an elaborate numerical breakdown of the project and its participants where "two hundred and nine thousand boys and girls proposed in 199 days of labor to build a railway. They had to lay 300 kilometers of rails, 429,000 crossties, 289 switching devices. They would also have drilled 9 tunnels and built 803 concrete structures, including 9 bridges with a total length of 2,469 meters."[40] Depestre also provides an exacting enumeration of the volunteers by ethnic and other identities, as proportions of the entire youth brigade: 45.5 percent Serb, 25.1 percent Croat, 2 percent Slovenian, 4.7 percent Macedonian, 2.9 percent Montenegrin, 2.2 percent Muslim, and 1.6 percent Albanian; 55 percent peasants, 25 percent workers, 15 percent students, and 3.5 percent intellectuals.

The engineers required figures to map the advancement of the project, while brigades and headquarters relied on them to assess both individual and group performances. The consensus was that optimal results could only be attained when every worker was thoroughly briefed on the project's progress and understood the impact of their contributions to the overall effort.[41] Slovenian scholar Martin Pogačar interprets this fixation on statistics as arising from both the desire to shape and control nature, and the need to motivate, plan, and measure results. These were a measurement of progress, a numerical turn toward the future and away from the past.[42] The train thus became a symbol of new networks of communication and solidarity. Within Yugoslavia, it was meant to connect ethnic communities that had not necessarily been on the same side during the war, as a newly built rail network would link the different Yugoslav republics into one large federation. But it would also connect Yugoslavia to the rest of the world. In this way, the railroad was meant to achieve the unachievable, to bring people in proximity to faraway landscapes and places that, until then, seemed unreachable. It promised to democratize access to these places, allowing those who had only dreamed of exploring beyond their hometowns to see the entire world. This connectivity changed perceptions of time and space. A more connected world was synchronized to the trains, to their arrival and departure, promising solidarity, engagement, modernization, reconstruction, and prosperity.[43]

These glowing descriptions of the Šamac-Sarajevo rail project raise some inevitable questions: How widespread was the enthusiasm exhibited in these narratives? Was the vision of a better tomorrow reflected in these accounts born from the grassroots or from the state apparatus? Did the railway fulfill its promise? And, are these memories simply a rose-colored indicator of what is now known as "Yugonostalgia"?[44] The answer to all these questions is probably both yes *and* no. Still, I agree with William Mazzarella that our compulsion in the present to doubt any genuine possibility for change has more to do with an internalized neoliberal cynicism than the actual experience of the youth volunteers who built the Šamac-Sarajevo railroad in 1947.[45] In any case, in our interview and in "The Skirt," Depestre portrayed an atmosphere of joy and optimism, one that inspired him for many years to come.

Eros, Politics, and Trains

As the early chapters of "The Skirt" are set on a train, carrying international youth to Yugoslavia to build a railway, the symbolism of the train in this story is twofold. Another story in the collection, "Faisane dorée" ("Golden Pheasant"), also features a train as an important setting, as the narrator traverses communist China. In "The Skirt," the first train, connecting Paris to Zenica on one railway, and carrying youth volunteers to the site where they will build another, becomes a space of encounters:

> On the train at Gare du Nord [in Paris], when we arrived at the compartment, two boys were keeping two young ladies company. During the first two hundred kilometers, there were no more than nineteen words exchanged between the six of us. Chantal and I were seated in the direction of the train, corridor side. We were all hungry to live. In front of us, the two beauties, visibly Parisian from the sixteenth arrondissement, were not letting go of the aloofness of their beautiful neighborhood. By the window, the young men, cheerful lads from the South, all words and skin, mocked them freely, in flamboyant Occitan. They were from Lézignan-Corbières.[46]

The trip begins in this way with distinctions made based on race and class and geography. It quickly becomes clear that the joy of renewal and a lust for life will not come from the French bourgeoisie of the 16th arrondissement, but rather from those on the margins, those from Haiti, Lézignan-Corbières, or Yugoslavia; who will bring their enthusiasm and collectivism to the stuffy Parisians. Indeed, it is youth from the South—be it the South of France or the Global South—that are leading the postwar transformation at the center of this story. The silence and distance they initially encounter in the train compartment is contrasted with the joy and exhilaration they later encounter at Yugoslav construction sites.

During our conversation, Depestre explained that he had ultimately settled in Lézignan-Corbières himself precisely because he had never forgotten the joy he observed in the young people he met on that train. His decision to live in Lézignan-Corbières can thus be understood as more than a return to France and an embrace of Francophonie. In fact, this return also brought him closer to Yugoslavia. And in the story, it is the train, as a space of connection, that ultimately brings the six youth closer. Though, not without considerable effort from our Haitian narrator:

> Listen, I said, speaking to the crowd, the world is just recovering from a deadly conflict. This is the first summer that the borders of Europe have reopened to youth. Surely, the young Yugoslavs who invited us would be sorry to see a tribe of killjoys disembark looking like they came from a funeral.[47]

This is followed by the narrator quoting Blaise Cendrars, who wrote that, in the aftermath of a war, the mere fact of being alive was a reason for true joy, prompting the six youth in the compartment to engage both in conversation and numerous sexual encounters.

As noted above, Depestre has been criticized for his focus on individual eroticism, which is often framed as frivolous and apolitical. While it is true that the endless proliferation of names for male and female genitalia, as well as the accompanying *glossaire* at the end of *Eros*, do become tiresome, Depestre has countered this view that eroticism is apolitical, explaining: "The pagan and solar side of my temperament as a man from the Caribbean immediately places my vision of love at the opposite of the painful experience that marked the historical adventure of Western Eros."[48] Depestre contends that sex and sexuality are accompanied by feelings of shame and guilt in the West but are freely experienced in the Caribbean; an assertion that could reasonably be questioned for its cultural essentialism.[49] Perhaps this is why Depestre quickly embeds his views on eroticism in a historical context, linking them to the specific material conditions of the Caribbean. On the plantation, he writes, sexuality was the only domain of freedom for enslaved people.[50]

Notably, this historical particularity differentiates the sexuality of the Creole slave from that of people from both Africa and the West. In the Caribbean, sexuality is not associated with sin, as men and women "make love, as free and sovereign beings who reinvent the four seasons, the carnival of stars, the magic wheel of beauty, in a state of poetry and wildly mutual wonder."[51] The freedom of the Caribbean sexual encounter stands in opposition to the shame of Christian sexual sin, which even the "*amour fou*" of the surrealists couldn't fully transcend. According to Depestre, a sexuality devoid of vice or reproach is prevalent in Haitian oral culture, though still not in its written culture; his own eroticism thus aims to counter the puritan love of the European and allow for the possibility of enjoyment for no other reason than enjoyment itself.

Some contradictions remain within the solar eroticism of Depestre, however. For instance, he mentions only in passing that sexuality was often a means of violence on the plantation, as Black female slaves were raped by their white masters. There is also a lack of analysis of the ways in which sexism and imposed heterosexuality function to limit the enjoyment of women, in both Europe and the Caribbean. After all, power relations persist even "at the time of the rooster and the enchanted garden."[52]

Nonetheless, I introduce his reflections on "*érotisme solaire*" because Depestre himself has never considered his eroticism to be apolitical. Particularly so in "The Skirt," which takes place after and against the ravages of World War II. The exuberance of the youth, and their victory over the forces of death, are expressed in the story both through their construction of the railway and their free expression of sexuality.

The prudishness of the two girls on the train from the 16th arrondissement is contrasted with the joyful sexuality of our narrator from the Global South. Yet, by also describing Chantal and the youth from Lézignan-Corbières as cheerful and filled with joy, Depestre complicates the simple opposition between a puritan North and a sexually liberated South. Puritanism and indifference are associated with the wealthiest neighborhood in Paris, drawing a line to class and not merely to cultural belonging. Still, the sexual encounters between these six youths are little more than a prelude to the love affair between Marc Zénon and Kostadinka Crnojévitch.

A Love Story Between Comrades

> "Can I ask you for another favor?"
> "Which is?", She said.
> "What is your name?"
> "Kostadinka Crnojevitch. And you?"
> "Marc Zénon."[53]

Thus begins "The Skirt" *in media res*, with the narrator asking for "another" favor, implying that there has already been a favor to which the reader is not privy. In this way, the atmosphere of secrecy that permeates the story is introduced from the very beginning. The start of this dialogue is withheld from the reader as something private, shared only between the narrator and this woman he has just met.

We soon learn, too, that this moment took place forty years ago. This missing piece of the conversation may in fact be missing because memory fragments, because this was a fleeting encounter, even if it has marked the narrator deeply. That the story begins with this exchange of names is notable, for the narrator's name is fictional but his would-be lover's name is autobiographical. Kostadinka Crnojévitch (spelled Crnojević in

Serbo-Croatian) is the name of the woman Depestre met during his own time in Yugoslavia; which is not to say that the fictional Dinka resembles the real one, nor that I am concerned with the extent to which the narrative corresponds to Depestre's real experience in Yugoslavia. In fact, I argue that the stories in *Eros* are deliberately set on the border of reality and fiction, on the line between what is remembered and what is imagined. In each, the name of the narrator changes: René Depestre in China becomes Marc Zénon in Yugoslavia and then Jacques Agoué in France. This is meant to remind us that these tales are of course fiction, but also that they are not told by the same narrator. The "rooted nomad" travels throughout the volume to different places at different times, encountering different women. And with each encounter, he changes.

Depestre is "well aware of the dangers of using the 'I' in ways that encourage the conflation of his authorial position with that of his narrators. 'The writer's "I" is a plural "I", an imaginary "I",' he insists."[54] So, why is Dinka's name unchanged? Perhaps to ground the story in historical reality, or perhaps because the decades that have passed between the event and its recounting have rendered her fictional, or perhaps because Dinka's name carries a historical weight of its own. Indeed, the significance of Kostadinka's name makes the narrator feel irrelevant: "I didn't know that her first name was also famous: in 1943, at the time of the offensives of the Yugoslav guerilla, she was the legendary commander Dinka from the BBC reports."[55] Kostadinka, it turns out, played an important role in the Yugoslav antifascist struggle, making her the more experienced revolutionary.

Kostadinka Crnojévitch thus contains many dimensions. She is the Dinka of the BBC reports, the Dinka that Depestre met in 1947, and the Dinka who becomes the lover of Marc Zénon in a story published in 1990. In "The Skirt," after the reader learns the origins of Dinka's name and that the story's initial encounter took place so long ago, the narrator continues to wonder about Kostadinka and her whereabouts: is she still in Titograd,[56] has she married, does she have children? Then, in the past conditional, he imagines a visit to Kostadinka and her husband, one he wishes he had made.[57] He envisions drinking *rakija* (a traditional Yugoslav spirit) with Kostadinka's husband, and discussing the good and bad sides of Yugoslav socialism. This imagined encounter that never occurred brings the first, brief, chapter of the story to an end with a deep sense of longing:

> The fact is this: I will never set foot again in the land of my magnificent Southern Slav. The age of manhood—so heavy to bear in my native country—has wedged my days and humble labors thousands of kilometers away from Kostadinka. The fire in her fireplace will not welcome me like an old friend on a tender winter evening.[58]

This same sense of a fleeting experience, both personal and collective, appeared in our interview.

AP: And you never returned to Yugoslavia?

RD: In fact, yes I did, on an official mission during a UNESCO General Conference in Belgrade (1980) that lasted a month. I was then able to reconnect with my contacts in Yugoslavia. Once I was there, it renewed my solar attachment to Kostadinka's native land. In Cuba, I continued to reflect upon her beauty; my feelings never changed.

AP: What was the atmosphere like in Belgrade in 1980, compared to 1947?

RD: The atmosphere was different, of course. The contagious euphoria of youth that had existed during the postwar period was gone. In 1947, we had the impression that young people were in power. That was no longer the case in 1980. The regime had become dogmatic.

"The Skirt" is the only story in *Eros on a Chinese Train* that begins with this mixture of encounter, memory, longing, and regret. Many of the other stories are written of the past, and are also memories, but the particular combination of present, past, and conditional used in "The Skirt" is unique to that story. A dialogue written in the present tense is revealed to have happened forty years before, on the shores of the Bosna, before the narrative shifts into what could have been, only to end by acknowledging that Kostadinka, Yugoslavia, and the Šamac-Sarajevo railway are all lost to the past. The story is permeated by a sense of regret, a "what if," a "what might have been."

This is a "what if" that likely relates not only to a love affair lost but also to communisms that could have been. Depestre thought he had ended his nomadic ways in Cuba, only to part ways with Castro in the end, over his rapprochement with the Soviet Union. There are parallels to Yugoslavia here, as it broke from the Soviet Union as well, to forge its own path and its own communism. The "what if" of "The Skirt" gestures toward these various communist experiments, and what they could have been if local decisions and global pressures had been different.

The unambiguous "what if" of the first chapter is tempered by the romance of a "once upon a time" in the second: "Once upon a time, there was a young Yugoslav girl and a Haitian student. I was twenty-two then. For me, it truly was, 'the most beautiful age of life'."[59] We are now back at the beginning, before Zénon arrives in Yugoslavia and encounters Kostadinka. The fairytale-like beginning of their story echoes the euphoria and sense of utopia that accompanies the building of a new world. The role played by youth in building this world is immediately emphasized, when the narrator mentions his age, and expresses his jubilation at having survived the war and at being able to participate in the future.

And then the encounter with Kostadinka takes place on the shores of the Bosna. "She was then, totally, totally naked in my arms," writes Depestre.[60] He has presented us with an image of a woman being reborn on the banks of a river. Of course, one could problematize this depiction, wherein this woman is reborn in the arms of a man; a man, who as the narrator, is ultimately responsible for her rebirth. But I propose this moment should be interpreted slightly differently, by considering both the Bosna underneath and the railway above. Individual transformation is derived from the collective work of building the railway in which the narrator and Kostadinka are both participating, as it is through the love affair that unravels between them on the riverbanks. This construction work and this lovemaking are both powerful, each anchored by an undeniable physicality and each a form of solidary connection.

In a later description of the first encounter between Zénon and Kostadinka, the reader is offered more details, including what preceded the scene with which the story opens. Kostadinka is in the river washing clothes, and the narrator decides upon seeing her that she is the most beautiful woman in the world. He asks her whether she speaks French, and she responds that she is studying it at the University of Zagreb. An expanded and slightly modified dialogue follows:

> "Could we talk for a moment?" I asked
> "It's time to head in," she said. "Maybe another day, if it matters to you, comrade?"
> "Tomorrow?"
> She paused to think.

"Yes, tomorrow, why not?"
"Can I obtain another favor?"
"Which one?"
"What is your name?"
"Kostadinka Crnojévitch. And you?"
"Marc Zénon."[61]

It is worth noting several things from this passage. First, the latter half of this dialogue is nearly identical to that recounted at the beginning of the story, but with one small difference. "Can I ask you for another favor?" has become "Can I obtain another favor." This is a subtle change, but it reminds us once again that we are in the domain of memory, and fiction. The narrator's memory of Kostadinka is firm but also fleeting, shape-shifting with each re-remembering; not unlike memory of the Yugoslav project itself—which, despite being continuously swept under the rug by contemporary nationalist elites in the region, keeps rematerializing, each time slightly different. The second detail I would like to highlight is Kostadinka's use of "comrade" with the narrator, even after just having met. This corresponds to the historical context in which it was typical on communist work sites for all volunteers to greet each other this way, but it is also Kostadinka's way of taking charge in this moment by defining her relationship to the narrator.

Let us compare this scene to a moment depicted in the first story in *Eros*, "Golden Pheasant," set in China. The narrator receives a call from his interpreter, Xiluan, who is the only woman in the collection to refuse the narrator's advances:

"Listen, comrade Xiluan, do me a favor, will you?"
"Which [one], illustrious guest?"
"Don't call me that."[62]

Here, the narrator refers to the interpreter as a comrade in an attempt to forge a relationship based on equality, but Xiluan refuses, continuing to refer to the narrator as "illustrious guest" in order to clearly communicate the hierarchy they occupy. In "The Skirt," this relationship is reversed as it is Kostadinka who immediately places the two future lovers on an equal playing field. As such, their love affair is highly political; it is a love affair between comrades.

Jodi Dean offers a much-needed history and analysis of the term comrade, arguing that it "indexes a political relation, a set of expectations for action toward a common goal. It highlights the sameness of those on the same side—no matter their differences, comrades stand together."[63] Comrades share a vision, and labor together to realize it. The term is of course associated with communism, but it has a much longer history. In Spanish, *camaradas* were historically two people sharing an apartment or room; and similarly, in French, *camarade* initially referred to soldiers sharing barracks. The word comrade thus implies an intimacy, a shared space, an ability to cohabitate in a specific environment, an experience of uniting in pursuit of a common purpose. It suggests trustworthiness and accountability; someone on whom you can rely.

Dean resuscitates camaraderie within the contemporary frame of allies and allyship. Without dismissing allyship as such, Dean questions its predominance within contemporary social organizing, noting that "allyship is a symptom of the displacement of politics into the individualist self-help techniques and social media moralism of communicative capitalism."[64] In contrast to the individualist approach of the ally, the comrade is part of a utopian and collective politics in the making. In other words, comradeship is a mode of collective belonging that opposes the isolation, individualism, and hierarchies of the capitalist order, and in striving for equality challenges its inherent divisions. Anyone can become a comrade, but this requires a shared leftist politics; and while the invitation for collaboration is open, no one is predisposed to being a comrade due to their identity or position. Comrade thus designates a relationship between two people who find themselves on the same side of the political truth, but not the individual identity of either of them, as it is an inherently relational concept.[65]

While incredibly important in this age of rising nationalisms and right-wing politics. Dean's essay too quickly dismisses the complexities of race, gender, and sexuality in building leftist social movements and organizations. Dean does acknowledge that comradeship requires hard work, but it is unclear how comrades can overcome histories of racism, sexism, and heteronormativity that are so deeply internalized. At the same time, when Kostadinka uses the term "comrade" with the narrator in "The Skirt," she invites a prefigurative bond based on a common understanding and a common struggle. The construction of the railroad was in fact an exercise in strengthening comradeship and overcoming differences, and also in collectively building a better future. By insisting on sharing statistics about the ethnicities, nationalities, and identities of these comrades in "The Skirt," Depestre shined a light on the diversity of this collective.

Kostadinka's reference to her lover as "comrade" acknowledges that love and eroticism are always political. It also sends a signal about the kind of relationship she is willing to engage in; one based in equality, in which she makes her own decisions. She is neither innocent nor naive, and she embodies the values of the Yugoslav antifascist fight, including its vision of a more egalitarian future.

But then, there is the end of the story. After returning from their encounter by the river, the narrator discovers that a girl's head was shaved in public as punishment for engaging in a relationship with a student from Marseille:

> This scandal confirmed what had been whispered in hushed tones for the four weeks that we had been there: any romantic relationship between young Yugoslav girls and foreign volunteers was severely repressed. Every night, the militia patrols that circled the camps, supposedly to protect us from potential incursions by the 'Ustaše,' were actually guarding the virginity of the local girls.[66]

Here, the individualist *eros* opposes any collectivist projects, which inevitably try to suppress it, and yet can never do so fully. Any possible liberation is thus individual and occurs within the space of the bed, as the power of *eros* escapes any institutional and systemic containment.

Yet, Kostadinka cannot escape it; even if the narrator does initially formulate a solution for the two lovers: He will borrow a tent from his Egyptian friend Abdel Zifaat, and pitch it on a remote hill, far from the scrutiny of work camp officers. Kostadinka and the narrator meet at the tent, where Depestre describes their night of lovemaking in euphemism, adroitly deploying synonyms for the sexual organs. In the morning, when Kostadinka discovers that her skirt is stained with blood, the narrator runs to the camp of the French brigade to borrow a similar one from Chantal. Nevertheless, Kostadinka is later stopped by two police officers: "they found her 'more charming than ever the fairies.' It was so true, it was said, that the two soldiers who had come to arrest her nevertheless let her finish her bright August morning ballet."[67] Her dancing body is constrained, but not contained, by the forces of order, the power of her *eros* such that it impresses even them.

This ending to "The Skirt" contributes to a stereotypical portrayal of communism, in which the evil regime prevents expressions of individual freedom and tramples human rights. E. P. Thompson, for instance, offers an alternative explanation of the prohibition of sexual encounters, suggesting that it stemmed from a widely accepted moral code among the brigadiers. He argues that this code was necessary, because without it, parents would not have allowed their young daughters to participate in the project.[68] Depestre does not include this perspective and his depiction is somewhat at odds with his own description of "The Skirt" as a homage to Yugoslavia, and it has led to problematic readings such as that of Milan Kundera, which Depestre himself embraced as praise of his solar eroticism:

> Then I read other short stories by him, from the collection entitled *Eros on a Chinese Train*, and I dwell on a few stories that take place in communist countries which, to this revolutionary driven from his homeland, opened their arms. With astonishment and tenderness, I imagine today this Haitian poet, his head filled with crazy erotic fantasies, crossing the Stalinist desert in his worst years, where an incredible puritanism then reigned and where the slightest erotic freedom was paid for dearly.[69]

Kundera's use of "the communist world" homogenizes all socialist and communist experiments into one. The desert imagery he employs positions communist countries as a collectivity of emptiness, as a tabula rasa that is only worthy once it renounces its communist past and embraces neoliberalism. Implicitly, this desert is compared to the non-desert of Western Europe, of course, where sexual freedoms and individual rights prevail. Indeed, by evoking the desert, Kundera's analysis also conjures strains of Orientalist discourse. And this is a "Stalinist desert" at that, inevitably littered with the victims of his many crimes, committed in the name of communism.

It is against this backdrop that the brave Western (and here, Depestre stands in for the Western) poet ventures into barbaric, authoritarian lands, prepared to teach its oppressed population about sexual freedom. A string of generalizations is emphasized by Kundera through his use of hyperbole. For example, the puritanism of the communists is so "incredible" that a Western reader can hardly imagine it. Kundera thus fosters the idea of a faraway place with cruel customs aimed at snuffing out any "erotic freedoms." According to Nataša Kovačević, this type of portrayal has contributed to "the demonization of communist regimes and Eastern European cultures as a totalitarian, barbarian and Orientalist 'other'." Furthermore, such binary views of West versus East have been used "to justify transitions of Eastern European societies to market capitalism and liberal democracy, suppressing Eastern Europe's communist histories and legacies, whilst perpetuating its dependence on the West as a source of its own sense of identity."[70]

Why would Depestre claim on one hand that "The Skirt" is a homage to Yugoslavia, and yet embrace Kundera's reading of it on the other? I propose that this contradiction points to the ambivalent (but also very complex) relationship Depestre has had with the various communisms with which he has engaged over his lifetime. Furthermore, Kundera focuses on the ending of the story, essentially erasing everything that came before it, including the multilayered ways the text interacts with both Yugoslavia and Kostadinka Crnojević. This lack of contextualization in Kundera's reading of the story, and his choice to situate it so squarely in "the communist world," disregards the unique dynamics of Yugoslav socialism and of the Šamac-Sarajevo project—both of which are highlighted in the text. Yet, one may read Depestre's choice to emphasize the secrecy of the love affair in "The Skirt" as one that reverberates on more than one level: there is a secret affair not only between the narrator and his Montenegrin lover, but also between Depestre and Yugoslavia; a place he was no longer able to express his admiration for (at least publicly), once he opted to settle in Cuba. Still, one cannot help but notice that, to some degree, Depestre caters to a Western audience in his fictional works, in a way he does not in interviews. In my interview with him and in the interview Paul Miller conducted with him about Cuba, Depestre's analysis of the communisms he has experienced was significantly more complex and nuanced than he put forth in *Le métier à métisser*, for instance.

There is also a sentence, spoken by Chantal, that complicates readings of the end of "The Skirt." It appears during the conversation about the Yugoslav girl whose head was shaved, when Chantal says: "Calm down, guys…after all, it's their business. Our French 'spirals' are half a century ahead of the morals of the time."[71] If one reads this comment explicitly, it is another celebration of solar eroticism, in light of its systemic repression. Yet, there is also some sarcasm in this comment. Chantal designates an "us and them," where the "us" is the more evolved Westerner and the "them" has questionable morals, very much mirroring a decontextualized Western reading of communist experiences that may be used to establish Western superiority. This foreshadows readings of the story itself. In other words, while Depestre engages in criticisms of communisms, he also understands that his critiques will be taken out of context and used to justify the superiority of the West and the inevitability of global neoliberalism; just as Kundera has done. He thus problematizes the very critique he outlines.

For Depestre, his experience in Yugoslavia marked one of his first encounters with collectivism and with post–World War II communism. And as he himself has acknowledged, it shaped his subsequent adventures and stayed with him throughout his life, even if he almost never wrote about it. His Yugoslav stories confuse his (dis)attachment to communism, as this cannot be reduced merely to his relationship with Cuba. In fact, though Depestre is critical of the directions communist projects ultimately followed, he remains attached to the values manifested through early collectivist projects like the Šamac-Sarajevo railroad. Both this attachment and this critique are visible in "The Skirt," and yet it is only with the proper historical contextualization that it is possible to avoid a flat and apolitical reading of the story, and of Kostadinka. For, even where the story gestures toward some of the underlying problems in Yugoslav state organization, it remains a homage to the Yugoslav and international youth that fought against fascism and for a more egalitarian future. Hence, it is a homage to friendship, love, and most importantly, comradeship.

CHAPTER FOUR

Non-Aligned Networks: Aoua Kéita, Yugoslav Women, and Global Socialist Feminisms

Ljubljana, October 7th, 1971

Dear friend,

Your letter, which you sent to me through our comrade Veda Zagorac, gave me great pleasure.... Even though we are so far from one another, we are working on similar issues—above all, how to develop society so that women, too, can become subjects with equal rights. Of course, this does not depend only on women's organizations, but also on general development and progress.[1]

Vida Tomšič

Brazzaville, November 3rd, 1971

Dear friend,

I acknowledge receipt of your letter from October 7, which made me very happy. Since I did not have your address, I sent my last letter through our friend Veda Zagorac, knowing that she would deliver it to you. You know, my dear Vida, that I am in Brazzaville only incidentally—and not in any official capacity. Since January 1967, I have no longer held any position. When

> the Politburo and the National Assembly were dissolved, in August 1967 and January 1968 respectively, I was arbitrarily removed from all national and international responsibilities. My national functions were assigned to Mariam Travélé, the wife of the former President of the Republic of Mali, my cousin Modibo Keïta. Veda, who lived there for some time, must have told you about this. But I am not at all discouraged, because for me, the struggle continues—and will continue—until the complete liberation of the Continent and the economic as well as truly social development of all sectors of African society.[3]
>
> Aoua Kéita

These letters, exchanged between Aoua Kéita, a Malian midwife and anti-colonial activist, and Vida Tomšič, a former Yugoslav-Slovenian Partisan and member of the Central Committee of the Yugoslav Communist Party, offer a window into international socialist feminism as it emerged.[4] When Tomšič wrote her letter, she had recently spent all of March in New York City as the Yugoslav representative to the Commission for Social Development of the United Nations Economic and Social Council, and explains in the letter that she had undertaken a study for the Commission on the role of women in the economic and social development of Yugoslavia. Having heard through Veda Zagorac that Kéita may come to Yugoslavia the following year, Tomšič sincerely hoped they could meet. She sent her letter with Mara Radić, a comrade from the Conference for the Social Activity of Women (Konferencija za društvenu aktivnost žena, KDAŽ), who was traveling to Brazzaville for a seminar on women's issues.[5]

In her response, Kéita confirmed that she planned to visit Yugoslavia the following year, and congratulated Tomšič on her new work. She was living in Brazzaville, she said, because her husband, a specialist in education and culture, had obtained a job at l'Ecole Normale Supérieure d'Afrique Centrale. Kéita described Brazzaville as a pleasant if overpopulated city, with agreeable people, and said Congolese leaders were young, capable, and fully supported African unity; noting, "their socialist slogans are not empty words."[6] The Congolese Labor Party, Kéita added, was trusted by the working masses, an essential element of successful socialist politics.

Throughout her life, and particularly after 1962—when she became Secretary-General of the Women's Social Commission (Commission Sociale des Femmes, CSF) in the Sudanese Union-African Democratic Rally (Union

Soudanaise-Rassemblement Démocratique Africain, US-RDA), following Mali's independence[7]—Kéita maintained connections with Yugoslav activists like Tomšič and Zagorac. In their private correspondence, these women referred to each other as friends, and in official exchanges, as comrades. All were committed socialists who believed women's liberation can be achieved only through the wholesale transformation of society.

Tomšič, like many Yugoslav socialists, insisted that women's issues should not be delegated solely to "women's organizations," as if they do not concern society at large. This marked a key distinction between socialist women's activists and liberal feminists. According to Tomšič, women's emancipation required more than equal opportunity within the existing system. Society had to be transformed entirely, and reproductive labor collectivized, through the creation of new social institutions.[8] In fact, Tomšič rejected the term feminist, which she associated with women of the bourgeoisie.

Similarly, for Kéita, who vowed in her letter to continue the fight "until the complete liberation of the Continent and the economic as well as truly social development of all sectors of African society," women's liberation was inseparable from the liberation of the African continent. This was a liberation from imperialism, but as her letter suggests, Kéita became progressively convinced that only socialist development could lead to equality, meaning there could be no anti-imperial and socialist struggle without women's liberation and no women's liberation without anti-imperial and socialist struggle. On this, Tomšič and Kéita agreed.

Yet, the two women were confronting very different local circumstances and did not always appreciate the extent of these differences. Socialism and women's emancipation sometimes meant very different things to each of them. For Kéita, socialism was a "broader ideology for defending the right to self-determination of peoples, first of all, and women's rights, secondly."[9] Meanwhile, Tomšič supported Yugoslav self-management. Yet, these women were willing to learn from one another, and they believed this learning process to be fundamental to women's internationalism.

Aoua Kéita is generally studied vis-à-vis her 1975 autobiography, in which she describes her work as a midwife and her political involvement with the US-RDA, up until Malian independence.[10] Her political work continued beyond independence, though, and as the US-RDA gained power, Kéita rose through its ranks. In September 1958, she was elected to the Bureau Politique National, the party's executive body, and the next year she became the parliamentary representative of Sikasso and was appointed to the committee charged with drafting a new constitution. When Mali gained independence in 1960, she was the only woman in the National Assembly.[11]

In newly independent Mali, Kéita's work moved beyond national borders as she participated in building international women's networks, both within and outside of Africa. There is continuity between the work she described in her autobiography, from before independence, and her work in its aftermath, for Kéita had long challenged the social roles assigned to women and had sought to involve women in revolutionary struggle. As a midwife, she pushed back against the idea that the domestic sphere is apolitical, encouraging women to take part in decision-making affecting their local communities, and in building the new nation. Through a close reading of Kéita's autobiography, as well as archival materials that document her collaboration with Yugoslav women activists, I trace the progressive expansion of Kéita's involvement in politics, from the local, to the national, to an international network of women from socialist states. In this sense, the narrative that emerges from her collaboration with Yugoslav women activists, complements Kéita's autobiography.

These materials allow us to place Kéita's work, like that of Tomšič and Zagorac, "within a global web of antifascist, anti-colonial, and internationalist postwar networks."[12] The collaboration among these women (and with other members of the KDAŽ, as we will see) therefore enables us to further advance debates on transnational feminism. Breny Mendoza has outlined the genealogy of this concept, explaining that it has supplanted the term "global sisterhood"—which was put forth in the 1970s and 1980s by white, middle-class feminists and is now recognized as ethnocentrically biased. The notion of global sisterhood was based on the assumption of "a universal patriarchy and a common experience of oppression of women around the globe," ignoring divisions among women based on nationality, race, class, and sexual orientation.[13] Transnational feminist theories (particularly those working within the framework of postcolonial studies), on the other hand, question whether a universal feminism can exist and dispute the view of women as a homogeneous subject. Instead of disregarding women's differences, these theories depart *from* these differences.[14] Thus, according to Mendoza, the term transnational feminism "points simultaneously to the position feminists worldwide have taken against the processes of globalization of the economy, the demise of the nation state and the development of a global mass culture."[15]

Chandra Talpade Mohanty's concept of a "feminism without borders" has also been crucial in theorizing transnational feminist solidarity; and importantly, Mohanty distinguishes between "border-less" feminism and feminism without borders. Whereas border-less feminism envisions the possibility of a singular feminist position, feminism without borders embraces the reality of feminist multi-positionality and seeks to "envision change and social justice work across these lines of demarcation and division," grounded in doctrines of "decolonization, anticapitalist critique, and solidarity."[16] Here, solidarity is not a given, it is a result of "mutuality, accountability, and a recognition of common interests as the basis for relationships among diverse communities."[17] Both Mendoza and Mohanty associate transnational feminism primarily with the latest stage of globalization and the commonalities of oppression under neoliberal capitalism. Feminist scholars Inderpal Grewal and Caren Kaplan similarly emphasize multilocal feminist practices that have emerged in response to contemporary "transnational economic links and cultural asymmetries."[18]

It is the type of solidarity described by Mohanty that was practiced by activists like Kéita, Tomšič, and Zagorac, all three of whom believed women would only truly become subjects of rights through socialist transformations in their respective states, but who also realized that their activism had to move beyond national borders. Newly emerging socialist countries that wanted autonomy from the USSR needed each other, as a matter of survival in a bipolar world, and the same was true when it came to women and their rights. Hence, the friendships between and among these women developed in the context of non-alignment, which was the path of both Yugoslavia and Mali. Mendoza observed that "we are still left with a theoretical and political void to understand the transnational linkages between Third and First World women."[19] Yet, I argue that this void can be (partially) filled if we look to Cold War collaborations between activists in Eastern Europe and the Global South, and would point out that Chiara Bonfiglioli and Kristen Ghodsee have recently highlighted the intentional effacing of a past internationalist women's activism that united the Global South with Eastern Europe's socialist states.[20]

Bonfiglioli and Ghodsee agree that postsocialist feminisms tend to be overlooked within transnational feminist theories, but also assert that "continued equation between Western and socialist colonialities—and the assumption of a long-lasting missed encounter between (post)colonial and (post)socialist subjects—silences the existence of past socialist anti-colonial networks."[21] In fact, the parallel between postsocialism and postcolonialism often does not take into account the socialist experiments of newly decolonized countries. As Ghodsee notes, this has framed the way contributions of Eastern European socialist women are portrayed, even in feminist historiographies, which often downplay the role of women because it is assumed they merely carried out the orders of male socialists in power.[22]

This chapter is rooted in what Bonfiglioli has described as "the emergence of a new field of studies, namely global socialist feminism," which analyzes collaborations between Eastern European socialist women and their counterparts in the Global South.[23] While these women indeed worked within their parties, they did not follow orders blindly, nor were they victims of dogmatism. On the contrary, they thought deeply about and worked actively to realize women's emancipation, sometimes in very subtle and very innovative ways. Their collaborations did not always go smoothly and involved a fair bit of misunderstanding about their respective local contexts, but were based on the shared belief that women's responsibility was both local and transnational and that national movements had important lessons to learn from each other. And they did.

In doing so, these women offer an example of what it means to think and act across borders without falling into the trap of a universal feminism. They managed to build "forms of alliance, subversion and complicity operating in a privileged in-between space where asymmetries and inequalities between women can be acknowledged."[24] For Aoua Kéita, the transnational consciousness that eventually facilitated this alliance-building and solidary action began with her local work as a midwife. In the rest of this chapter, I first offer an analysis of Kéita's autobiography, as her local political work served as the basis for her developing internationalism. I also demonstrate how certain aspects of Kéita's early work already aligned with that of Vida Tomšič. In the second part, I focus on Kéita's collaboration with the Yugoslav KDAŽ (Conference for the Social Activity of Women). I read across various types of documents including personal correspondences, official memos, and conference papers, in order to outline a theory (and practice) of female emancipation that was based on dialogue, exchange, and friendship.

Midwifery as Activism: The Path of Aoua Kéita

Présence Africaine published Kéita's autobiography, *Femme d'Afrique: La vie d'Aoua Kéita racontée par elle-même* (*An African Woman: The Autobiography of Aoua Kéita Told in Her Own Words*), in 1975.[25] As the title implies, this is the story of a specific woman, but she could not be any woman from anywhere; it matters that she is an African woman. The individual does not stand in for the collective, as Kéita does not represent African women in the plural. This is a story about how being a woman in Africa has shaped her life, about the political activism of an African woman, about her participation in events that led to the independence of her country.

On the title page of *Femme d'Afrique*, just below the title itself, Kéita is described as a "Retired midwife / Former member of parliament / Former member of the National Political Bureau / the U.S.R.D.A."[26] These are the three designations with which Kéita also signed her personal letters to Veda Zagorac. And, appropriately, Kéita's autobiography deals with the intersection of her work as a midwife and as a member of the US-RDA. It was through her work as a midwife that she was able to mobilize women for the party, and because she was a member of the party, she was able to politicize her work as a midwife.

As other scholars have noted, in nearly 400 pages, Kéita dedicates a mere thirty to her childhood and family.[27] Still, in this brief interlude, we learn that Kéita's father once served in the French Army, that he received a small pension, and that he was assigned to the post of hygiene officer ("agent d'hygiène") by the French government. She recounts that her mother frequently told cautionary tales about women who wanted to marry for love and ended up either miserable or murdered by their husbands. In fact, Kéita begins her autobiography with one of these stories, of Diadiaratou, who insisted on marrying Zoumana—a beautiful young man who showed up one day at her doorstep but turned out to be a *djin*, an evil spirit sent to teach Diadiaratou the lesson that she should not contradict her parents. It is fitting that Kéita opens her autobiography by telling this tale, as *Femme d'Afrique* is, in many ways, its counterpoint, though not merely its opposite. *Femme d'Afrique* is not the story of a woman who defies her traditional mother and marries out of love. Rather, it is the story of a woman who dedicates her life neither to love nor to her parents, but to politics.

So, while Kéita's mother did not support her daughter's education or political work, this is not a simple story of tradition versus modernity. After all, it is precisely Kéita's knowledge of and embeddedness in local structures and modes of living that enabled her to so successfully mobilize women in the anticolonial struggle. And though she frequently disregarded her mother's opinion, sometimes Kéita heeded it, as in her choice to avoid writing sentimentally about her life in *Femme d'Afrique*, and thus practicing discretion, which her mother advised.

Annette Joseph-Gabriel has produced a poignant analysis of *Femme d'Afrique*, in which she explained that Kéita challenges the conventions of an autobiographical narrative by placing a collective at its center, rather than an individual subject. In the original French, "the singular 'je' is often expressed either as an integral part of a collective 'nous' or defined to that collectivity but never independently from it."[28] I agree, but would like to push this argument even further by suggesting that the collective subject which emerges from Kéita's narrative does not pre-exist, as "women" do not exist as a political subject absent political organizing. In fact, in the book, Kéita describes the many divisions that exist among women, first recalling disagreements with her own mother. Later, she relates an experience in Niono (a town in Mali) when, as she was discussing politics with a local woman, the woman's husband yelled that she should return to the kitchen as politics was a male affair, and the woman reacted by looking at Kéita with disdain, as if she had cursed her. Toward the end of the book, Kéita also remembers being chased away from a village by angry women throwing rocks at her vehicle, because while women are connected through their social positioning, they diverge greatly in their opinions and actions.

Women's shared oppression does not automatically unite them, in other words, which means the construction of a collective female subject requires difficult and time-consuming political organizing. This means that the collective female "nous" results from the collective political actions of women, including debates, protests, and votes. Organizing may be local, but different communities can become models for one another, as was the case when Kéita arrived in the Sudanese town of Nara in 1953 and politics was considered a male domain. To convince the women of Nara to join the US-RDA, Kéita used the example of the women from Gao (another town in Mali), whose collaborative activity had yielded results. According to Kéita, the political power of these women was derived from the very fact that they had been dismissed as political actors. Colonialists had disregarded and disparaged the impact of women, and had certainly never viewed illiterate rural women as a threat, as they believed they had no political potential at all. This is precisely why this potential, once activated, posed such a threat to existing power structures.

Bollo Yattara, Vice President of the Women's Committee in Gao, put it this way: "Our position is unique and well known...why would we be afraid?

We are not civil servants. We cannot be transferred, demoted, or dismissed. We are our own commander; we are our own governor."[29] Yattara's point was that, at the bottom of the social hierarchy, given everything women had suffered, even being sent to jail did not scare them. Women were thus the revolutionary anticolonial subject because, unlike men, they had nothing to lose. And this made Malian liberation a function of women's emancipation. In the Yugoslav context, Vida Tomšič similarly argued that women positioned themselves as the revolutionary subject during WWII. Their involvement in the antifascist struggle marked a significant shift in the perception of their role in society; it provided a broad platform for the affirmation of women, facilitating the dismantling of patriarchal and conservative views regarding their roles in marriage, family, and society.[30] In other words, female involvement in both the anticolonial and antifascist struggles was the conduit to their post-independence/post-WWII emancipation.

In *Femme d'Afrique*, Kéita questions the exclusion of women from the public sphere as well as the view that the private/domestic sphere is apolitical. Her first husband, a doctor, was also her political comrade, so that the intimate space of the couple also became a space of political discussion, political exchange, and organizing. Indeed, Kéita attributed her initial interest in politics and international affairs to her first husband, who talked with her about events like the Italian invasion of Ethiopia, or local elections and his preferences for specific candidates. The private sphere was thus her point of introduction into politics, rather than its impediment, and her first marriage represented a place where the boundary between the private and the public, the domestic and the political, was broken.

It was then that she joined the US-RDA, and their home was frequented by local party organizers, again positioning this intimate space as one of political organizing. Of course, the domestic sphere is not without its conflicts, nonetheless. In Niono, for instance, during visits by party members, her husband advised Kéita to remain quiet, as the men were not accustomed to discussing politics with a woman. In this way, the private and public were filled with contradictions as Kéita attempted to navigate both.

Kéita began her career as a Colonial Health Services Worker, a functionary of the colonial government tasked with promoting and establishing the conditions for Western birthing norms. She was a proponent of Western medicine, but subverted her colonial assignment by turning midwifery into a tool of anticolonial organizing in part because when she arrived in Gao, the situation she encountered was dire as "there was no maternity ward or obstetrical equipment."[31] She thus endeavored to set up a proper maternity ward in which women could give birth in sanitary conditions, and her political work with women thus emerged in a struggle for reproductive justice. At the end of 1931, Kéita submitted a request to the Governor for the construction of a maternity ward, and three years later, the ward would become "one of the first permanent buildings in Gao."[32]

Femme d'Afrique places reproductive work at the center of political organizing, as it is the bonds and trust between Kéita and the mothers and babies for whom she has cared in Gao that enabled her to mobilize women. Kéita shared this belief in the importance of reproductive justice with Tomšič, who became involved with the International Planned Parenthood Federation (IPPF) after 1967. Yet the contexts were also quite different and whereas in pre- and post-independence Mali, Kéita focused notably on prenatal and postpartum healthcare, in socialist Yugoslavia, Tomšič advocated for abortion and the availability of contraceptives.[33]

In Niono, Kéita organized clandestine political gatherings, once again challenging the division between spaces considered male, public, and political on the one hand, and those considered female, domestic, and apolitical on the other. She was advised multiple times not to pursue politics, including by her husband, who warned her: "You observe, you take care of the comrades...you represent us at the bureau and you vote.... Above all, avoid talking about politics."[34] And he wasn't alone. While working in Senegal, Kéita was visited by a health inspector who pleaded with her to stop engaging in politics. While visiting Portuguese Guinea, Kéita conversed with a Black postal worker who offered "advice from an elder: withdraw from politics, it is not good for men and it can be fatal for a woman."[35] Kéita responded that she would "do politics until the very end."[36]

This serves as a refrain that punctuates the narrative of *Femme d'Afrique*, repeating from community to community, from country to country, as men ranging from colonial officials to local elders (to her own husband) offer Kéita this same advice, underlining the complex social positioning and simultaneous marginalization of African women due to race and gender. Her response, over and over, is to extend the sphere of women's political action, with organizing that begins in Gao but subsequently takes hold in every other local community to which she is posted. Her time in Senegal, a result of a disciplinary action, brings Kéita closer to the condition of women in other African countries, helping her understand the situation of the continent overall and compelling her to participate in "the political and trade union activities...of the whole of Africa."[37] Her work thus became progressively internationalized.

In 1957, Kéita traveled as part of the delegation from the General Union of Workers of Black Africa to participate in the 4th Congress of the World Federation of Trade Unions (WFTU) in Leipzig. This visit to Leipzig represented an important moment in the internationalization of Kéita's work. Initially taken aback by the cold and what she described as "an unbreathable atmosphere for the poor bush midwife," as she started to see the value of internationalism, her perspective of Germany started to shift.[38] In fact, she was later embarrassed by her earlier views, which she felt had been influenced by the horrors of World War II, and German disdain toward the *tirailleurs sénégalais* that she had learned about as an adolescent.[39]

At the WFTU Congress, Kéita discovered the existence of an international workers' movement and its engagement with female workers. In *Femme d'Afrique*, she quoted the organization's secretary-general, who emphasized "the need to consolidate the results obtained following the first World Conference of Working Women and the decision of the Executive Bureau...regarding the organization of an international seminar for female trade union activists."[40] Kéita noted that her comrade Sow Aissata had participated in this conference (held in Budapest), and that "...this participation greatly contributed to raising awareness among working women in Sudan. It also played a decisive role in the creation of the inter-union organization of Sudanese working women."[41]

Kéita admired female delegates at the Congress who did not hesitate to debate issues with men, and who had launched an urgent appeal to the working women of the world to build a vast women's movement. While most of her autobiography is focused on anticolonial organizing, it is clear toward the end that Kéita's political vision has embedded itself in the global struggle of workers (and particularly female workers) within a capitalist system. Until the WFTU Congress, she had never seen so many people assembled for a solidary cause:

> In the second capital of the German Democratic Republic, representatives of hundreds of millions of workers from all countries and all continents gathered. They had come to this part of Europe to study their problems and find satisfactory solutions for all, without distinction of race, color, ideology, or religion. This meeting of the colonized and the colonizers...was very revealing to me.[42]

This depiction of the WFTU as unaffected by differences of race, ideology, or religion is of course idealistic, but this passage shows Kéita's political vision moving beyond independence, her focus shifting toward the class divisions her newly independent country will have to confront. The binary between the colonizer and colonized has broken down, as Kéita realizes she shares certain interests with European workers. The category of the colonized had already been complexified in her autobiography by gender divisions, and in a similar manner, the category of the colonizer is complicated here by questions of class and gender. Kéita begins to think beyond the Manichean world of colonial relations, and places the women of French Sudan (later, Mali) in a global context. Recalling the things she learned in school and from her family, she realizes, "there was a whole world between what I had learned and what I was experiencing."[43] This recognition will form the foundation for Kéita's future collaborations with European socialist organizations, including KDAŽ.

After her return from Leipzig, Kéita continued her international work, and in 1958, she was invited to the 2nd Congress of the Democratic Party of Guinea. There, she watched as female Guinean participants debated the issues with men, already embodying a post-independence woman, "liberated both from the colonial yoke and all other retrograde prejudices."[44] That same year, Kéita traveled to France to accompany a sick child, stayed for four months in Paris, and completed an internship at the Hôpital des Enfants-Malades. She thus lived the historic events of 13 May 1958, which led to General de Gaulle's ascension to power.

It was also in 1958 that she was elected to the Bureau Politique National, where she served first as commissioner of the women's wing of the US-RDA and then as a member of the constitutional committee. In those roles, Kéita witnessed the proclamation of Malian independence on 22 September 1960. And with independence, her autobiographical narrative ends. Her post-independence political work is not part of the narrative, and *Femme d'Afrique* closes with the following lines: "Political independence was the great culmination of our efforts and the sacrifices of our martyrs. But the struggle was not over yet. It continues and will continue for a long time for freedom, democracy, and universal peace."[45]

This ending stands in stark contrast to the beginning. "When I became aware, around the age of six or seven," the book starts, "Bamako was a small town of barely eight thousand inhabitants."[46] This narrative voice is locationally grounded, Kéita's subjecthood is linked to her geographical positioning in a small community. But at the end of the book, she offers an opening, inviting the question of universal peace; the frame has shifted from locally grounded political organizing to transnational justice. This does not mean that local context no longer matters, as *Femme d'Afrique* recounts a fight for national independence, first and foremost. That fight is progressively internationalized, however, first at the continental level, and then beyond. Its final lines gesture toward a space and time of post-independence, where local action unfolds into transnational solidarity. And this unfolding is what Kéita continued to concentrate on after independence. She continued to organize locally, and act transnationally, and in this transnational work, her connections and collaborations with Yugoslav women played an important role.

Kéita's Socialist Internationalism and Yugoslav-Malian Connections

In June 1962, Latinka Perović, then president of the KDAŽ, wrote an official letter to the Executive Committee of the Women of Mali, of which Aoua Kéita was secretary-general. Perović wanted to establish more regular cooperation between the two organizations and begin a dialogue with Malian representatives.[47] The following month, the Executive Committee responded, praising the KDAŽ for its work toward women's emancipation, and proposing a joint exploration of issues affecting girls and young women. Specifically, Malian women hoped to discuss female education, employment, and youth participation in social and political activities with their Yugoslav counterparts.[48]

In March of the following year, Mali's Ambassador to Yugoslavia Alidou Touré asked to be received by the KDAŽ. Before his post in Yugoslavia, Touré's work had been focused on women and children and he wanted to familiarize KDAŽ members with activities taking place in Mali to promote women's liberation. He was also interested in learning more from members about the role women were playing in Yugoslav development, and about the work of the KDAŽ. He highlighted that there had already been close cooperation between Yugoslav and Malian women, including through the networking of unions and youth organizations, and hoped this would continue. Members of KDAŽ believed that the views of the ambassador on women's emancipation very much reflected those of the organization, and that collaboration should thus be pursued.[49] Following the meeting, Ambassador Touré wrote the KDAŽ, indicating that he had transmitted the organization's messages of friendship to the National Organization of the Women of Mali, and that in return, the women of Mali sent their warm regards to the women and people of Yugoslavia, "who have constantly and firmly supported the people of Mali in their struggle for liberation and national development."[50]

The KDAŽ requested another meeting with Touré in May 1965, regarding a potential visit by Kéita to Yugoslavia. Members of the organization had aspired for quite some time to invite Kéita to the country, but thought it best the trip be combined with other European travel due to the cost. They had heard she was traveling in Bulgaria and Albania, and wanted to extend an official invitation. The Ambassador told them that Kéita herself had asked whether any such invitation to Yugoslavia had been offered, when she spent two hours in Belgrade at the airport on her way to Albania in April. And once in Albania, she had apparently inquired yet again about the possibility of visiting Yugoslavia. The Ambassador transmitted the invitation to Kéita, who was by then in Paris.[51]

Kéita thus visited Yugoslavia from 27 May to 15 June 1965, where she divided her time between Belgrade, Kosovo, and Croatia. Accompanied by Savica Hočevar, then vice president of the KDAŽ, Kéita met with KDAŽ members as well as representatives of the Yugoslav Red Cross. In Kosovo, she learned more about efforts to mobilize women politically to improve their education and medical and social protections, as well as the important role played by teachers, midwives, and doctors in rural areas. In Zagreb, she was introduced to institutions focused on the welfare of children.

According to a summary report by the KDAŽ, the primary purpose of Kéita's visit had been to seek assistance for her own organization. But she had spoken positively about Yugoslavia as well, and had extolled the fact that Yugoslav aid to African countries came with no strings attached. She opposed Yugoslavia to the USSR, which donated faulty machines to newly independent African countries and discriminated against African students. Despite this critique of the USSR, which the report describes as "intolerance," Kéita continued to collaborate with Soviet women's organizations throughout her career.[52] She thus either exaggerated her criticism to align with Yugoslav interests or worked with Soviet organizations despite her reservations to further her own goals. Either way, this inconsistency highlights Kéita's pragmatism and diplomatic acumen.

In the report, Kéita is portrayed as bright, energetic, and enthusiastic but immodest; she had presented herself as the first woman of Mali and as superior to the Malian masses, and was said to be very demanding. This depiction of Kéita marks a notable contrast from the way she represented herself in *Femme d'Afrique* as a woman most comfortable when engaged in grassroots organizing with rural populations. Importantly, though, the KDAŽ report does acknowledge that Kéita's "demandingness" may be a consequence of difficulties she encountered both in Mali and in Europe, as a woman in politics and as a representative of a newly independent African country, and it is clear that KDAŽ members understood Kéita's behavior through the prism of global race relations. At the same time, the report describes her relationship to the Malian population as demagogic, perhaps revealing a lack of knowledge on the part of the KDAŽ about Kéita's organizing history. In any case, the report concludes by noting the desire of the organization to continue working with her.[53]

For Kéita, her visit to Yugoslavia resulted in valuable material aid, including sugar, blankets, school supplies, first aid and midwifery kits, and sewing machines, donated by the KDAŽ and Yugoslav Red Cross to the women of Mali.[54] Once home in Bamako, Kéita sent a letter to the KDAŽ in which she thanked the organization and also mentioned how impressed she had been by Mara Rupena of the Yugoslav Red Cross. Human connections are of utmost importance, she noted. Kéita was confident that the connections she had made with Yugoslav women would contribute to strengthening relations between Yugoslavia and Mali.[55]

Moreover, she said, the trip had helped her "get to know the Yugoslav people and to truly admire them" and she had learned "from your experiences, which will be incredibly useful to me...in my country."[56] Here, Kéita links deeper knowledge of a country and its people with the ability to translate experiences and make use of them across borders. As the ability to learn from others is not simply about reproducing models, it is therefore unimpeded by diverging local circumstances. A common vision of the future, based on the emancipation of women within a socialist society, is enough to create opportunities for this learning, while still leaving room for variations in implementation.

In July 1965, the Yugoslav magazine *Žena* (*Woman*), published an interview with Kéita, subtitled, "A Malian Woman's Place in Freedom."[57] Kéita's narrative of her country's anticolonial struggle is characterized in the article as "teeming with many examples of courage, heroism and enthusiasm by Malian women, who, even in the most difficult moments, would take up arms—sometimes the most primitive, like poisoned arrows—or use cunning strategies to strike decisive blows against the colonizer."[58] The description of the armed struggle of Malian women is compared to that of Yugoslav women in the fight against fascism, a parallel often mobilized by the magazine when describing women's movements in the Global South.[59] On the other hand, the use of "primitive" reflects a developmentalist discourse and evokes an exoticized image of Africa as technologically backward. Hence, the account in *Žena* operates simultaneously to reconcile and divide Yugoslav and Malian women, pointing to the ambivalence of racial discourses circulating in Yugoslavia at the time.

In the interview, Kéita explains that Mali inherited poverty and underdevelopment with its independence. Her party, which chose the socialist path, had been able to improve education by opening new schools, and was prioritizing the education and emancipation of women, "the first cell in the development of humanity."[60] Women, Kéita argues, need and deserve an education that allows them to take on the same responsibilities as men.[61]

In September of that same year, two members of the KDAŽ, Nevenka Petrić and Jelica Marić, traveled to Bamako to participate in a seminar on health protections for mothers and children in Africa. Upon returning home, Marić wrote to Kéita that she and Petrić had been very impressed in Mali by "the care devoted not only to women's emancipation, but also to economic development and the elevation of the people's cultural and educational standards, clearly represents one of the key prerequisites for genuine progress and for women's complete liberation."[62] In line with the position of the KDAŽ, Marić correlated the emancipation of women and society as a whole, much as Vida Tomšič had in her letter to Kéita, when she insisted that women's emancipation cannot be treated as a separate social issue.

The personal note Marić sent to Kéita had been preceded by a more official letter from KDAŽ Vice President Savica Hočevar, who confirmed the Yugoslav Red Cross had prepared the aid discussed during Kéita's visit to Yugoslavia.[63] Two months later, Kéita wrote to Marić, Hočevar, and Mara Rupena (of the Red Cross) from a sanatorium in the Soviet Union where she was being treated, to relay that a plane flying from Moscow to Bamako would land in Belgrade on December 15th to collect the aid. The next month, having returned to Bamako, Kéita confirmed she had received the delivery, in a letter to Hočevar. The aid, she wrote, represented

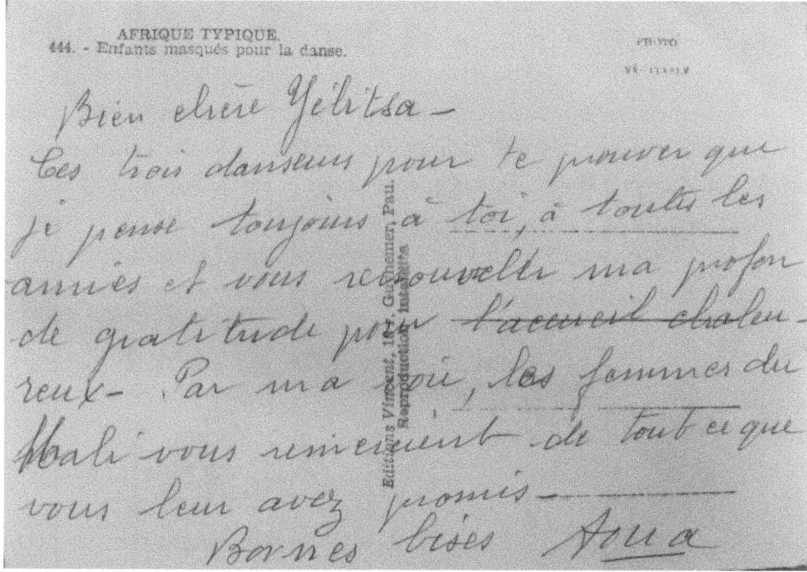

AFRIQUE TYPIQUE.
444. - Enfants masqués pour la danse.

PHOTO

Éditions Vincent, 18, Guemener, Pau. Reproduction interdite

Bien chère Yelitsa —
Ces trois danseurs pour te prouver que
je pense toujours à toi, à toutes les
années et vous renouveler ma profon-
de gratitude pour ~~l'accueil chaleu-~~
~~reux~~ — Par ma voix, les femmes du
Mali vous remercient de tout ce que
vous leur avez promis —
Bonnes bises Aoua

Figure 3. A postcard sent to Jelica Marić by Aoua Kéita.
AJ 142 (SSRNJ), A-631

a gesture "which forms part of the international solidarity so dear to all women of goodwill—yourself included."[64]

Kéita also continued her private correspondence with Marić. "My dear Jelica," she wrote on a postcard (above), "the three dancers to show you that I am always thinking of you, of all the friends, and to renew my deep gratitude for the warm welcome. Through me, the women of Mali thank you for all that you have promised them."[65]

In this short message, Kéita first recognizes her individual friendship with Marić, and then extends this frame to members of the KDAŽ, and finally to Malian and Yugoslav women as a whole. The individual friendship becomes a precondition and conduit for collective political action. The bonds of solidarity are both individual and collective, personal and political.

The Struggle Continues

> January 8th, 1966, to the President of the Conference of Yugoslav Women
>
> Dearest friend,
>
> The women of Mali place great hope in the year 1966 and ardently wish that it will bring the fulfillment of our legitimate and shared aspirations. While ensuring the success of the struggles of the nationalists of Africa, Asia, and Latin America against colonialists, neo-colonialists, and imperialists, the new year must be for us and our families a year of freedom, peace, and complete happiness.... While sincerely thanking you for all that your organization has done to help the women of Mali in their heavy but exhilarating task of socialist construction, I ask you, dear friend, to believe in our sincere friendship.[66]
>
> Aoua Kéita

Thus began the new year, and renewed collaboration between the US-RDA and the KDAŽ; Kéita would return to Yugoslavia in October 1966 for an international seminar on social-economic transformations in rural areas. In the speech she gave there, Kéita noted that, in the aftermath of independence, nascent African nations had been forced to confront complex economic problems with very limited resources. Mali, a mostly rural country with no access to the sea, was of little interest to colonial powers, which had merely exploited its natural resources while allowing precolonial structures to deteriorate. Thus, Kéita explained, Mali faced post-independence difficulties stemming from its geography as well as its choice to build a socialist society. And while the US-RDA had been focused primarily on agricultural reform (including the introduction of modern agricultural means and expert supervisory staff) and on educating rural populations, this was not an easy task, due to what she characterized as "the ignorance of our brothers and sisters, who are very attached to ancient methods."[67] As in *Femme d'Afrique*, Kéita here valorizes European scientific progress in this speech, embracing a developmentalist discourse which positioned Africa and Mali as lagging behind Europe.

In fact, she went on to say that the struggle for women's rights in many European countries was in its second or third stage, focused on improving the position of women in the family and in society at large, but that in Mali, this struggle was still in the first stage of trying to improve agricultural production and the lives of agricultural workers. Kéita shared the views of KDAŽ members like Vida Tomšič that the question of female emancipation cannot be disentangled from an overall transformation of the means of production, yet where Tomšič focused on the socialization of reproductive labor through the building of state institutions, Kéita believed that the priority for Mali was comprehensive agricultural reform.

Furthermore, Kéita observed that Malian women were not fully utilizing the rights they had gained, a challenge that Tomšič also highlighted in her writings.[68] Women were represented in all organs of power but were not part of many key decision-making discussions. And in rural areas, women frequently refused to take positions of responsibility. Aware of these challenges, Kéita had worked to amplify the reach of the CSF, most notably by opening almost forty training centers in Bamako and across the country, which offered classes to women that ranged from hygiene to newborn care to civics. The CSF was also working to address illiteracy, which Kéita called a "wound of humanity, of which the peoples of the Third World are the most painful victims."[69] Hence, in every city, functional literacy subcommittees for adult women had been established, to teach them to read, write, and count. This was a relatively difficult mandate to meet, however, as it is never easy to learn an imported language, and local populations spoke what Kéita described as a variety of dialects, lacking any universal living language. The creation of a national language was ongoing, but in the meantime, French remained the official language, and it was French that was taught by the literacy subcommittees. While it is fair to question Kéita's dismissal of local languages as mere dialects, and her prioritization of French, her remarks in this speech and her approach in Mali both point to the challenges of organizing in a multilingual country.[70]

When she returned once again to Yugoslavia in January 1967, Kéita's focus was on developing Malian industry.[71] The country's first factory—for processing fruit and vegetables, and canning fish and meat—had been built with Yugoslav aid, but now needed reserve parts that were produced in Italy and Germany, and Mali did not have the foreign currency to purchase them. Still, she also continued to emphasize the accomplishments of the US-RDA in educating youth and preparing them for employment. At independence only 6 percent of children were going to school, she explained, but that rate was up to 32 percent as of 1967; even if the education of girls remained a significant challenge.[72]

The next month, Vida Tomšič traveled to Mali as part of a trip that included stops in Guinea, Senegal, and Algeria. She had received an official invitation from a women's organization in Guinea to attend the February 9th commemoration of M'Balia Camara's death, which was declared Guinean Women's Day in 1965 to honor the popular anticolonial activist, who had been murdered a decade earlier. Tomšič took the occasion to visit with women's organizations in all four countries, noting later in a report that each operated as specific bureaus or committees within a political party, and were very active. She recounted the work of these women on concrete issues like hygiene, nutrition, and healthcare, but also the innovative ways women were being mobilized and engaged in economic activity, such as through a textile dyeing initiative.[73]

In Mali, Tomšič reported that her visit was very well organized, thanks to the involvement of Kéita.[74] Indeed, Kéita personally saw to it that her Yugoslav friend's stay was enjoyable, inviting Tomšič twice to her home for dinner and assigning her secretary to act as a chaperone. During the visit, Tomšič observed a class at the Foyer de la Femme Malienne in Bamako, where some twenty-five women were learning to sew, read, and write. Women could also attend lectures on marriage legislation and general social issues, as they could at other centers like it across the country.[75] The women Tomšič met in Mali were seeking donations for these educational centers (i.e., notebooks, sewing machines, first aid kits, etc.), and opened her eyes to the extent of Mali's economic troubles. They were willing to take help from any country that would grant it with no strings attached; and on top of Yugoslavia, Kéita had obtained aid for the CSF from the USSR, Poland, and France. She told Tomšič that she had also reached an agreement with the KDAŽ to send a number of Malian girls to Yugoslavia for medical training.[76]

Tomšič later described receiving a very warm welcome across Mali and encountering considerable interest in the Yugoslav antifascist struggle and its system of self-management. She wrote that women were not involved in industrial work but were active in schools and other social activities, and that women activists were mostly midwives and teachers.[77] In fact, many of these activists were the wives of party officials or daughters from wealthy families who had received some formal education in either Mali or France.

Tomšič noted in her report that family and tribal ties continued to play an important role in Mali, and described gender and marriage relations as polygamous, with elements of matriarchy. Interestingly, her reflections on this were mostly neutral, lacking any value judgment regarding polygamy or the organization of Malian social relations. Tomšič thus avoided the "colonial gaze" in her view of the country's social norms. That said, she could not hide her prejudice about Islam or the practice of veiling for women, commenting that "Islam has a less dark outlook for the observer here than in countries where women are under the veil."[78] This position was in line with that of the Yugoslav state, which in 1950 banned the wearing of the veil.[79] Overall, however, her reporting on this visit was remarkably nonjudgmental, demonstrating her true desire to learn and understand. She did not frame conditions in Mali as superior or inferior to those in Yugoslavia, but rather highlighted that both were similarly involved in the fight for women's emancipation; a fight that takes different forms based on local contexts but that has shared goals which open a space for solidarity and friendship.[80]

Back in Yugoslavia, Tomšič wrote to Kéita thanking her for such a warm welcome and her many thought-provoking conversations. She said the KDAŽ would discuss bilateral cooperation with various African countries in the next several days.[81] Kéita responded by inviting a Yugoslav delegation to attend celebrations for the Day of African Women in July 1967, insisting that Mara Rupena of the Yugoslav Red Cross preside over the delegation, and that it should incorporate a member from Slovenia as a thank you for the warm reception she had received there. These celebrations were to include a *kermesse* (festival), a seminar on the role of women in politics and economic development, and a competition for the "prettiest" baby. Pascale Barthélémy and Ophélie Rillon have argued that this prettiest baby contest should be seen as an extension of President Modibo Kéita's gender-conservative politics, which positioned motherhood as the backbone of the nation.[82] Through this lens, Kéita followed the party line by making the competition a part of the Day of African Women. And, in fact, in both Mali and Yugoslavia, in the aftermath of anticolonial and antifascist organizing, women's struggles were to a certain extent domesticated.[83] Yet, when she was interviewed for *Žena*, Kéita insisted that, in this case, the "prettiest" really meant the healthiest (i.e., vaccinated) baby. And while a focus on mother and child may have been in line with party politics, for Kéita—the midwife—women's emancipation was always entangled with reproductive justice, which she saw as an entryway into politics.

Indeed, her autobiography, as well as the archival materials quoted in this chapter, reveal three poles of women's emancipation as Kéita envisioned it: reproductive justice, agricultural reform, and education—all three of which she saw as prerequisites for women's active involvement in politics. But Kéita also understood the importance of transnational solidarity among women who shared this emancipatory objective. So, even beyond her official cooperation with the KDAŽ and friendships with its various members, she developed an important relationship with another Yugoslav woman mentioned in this book, the former Partisan Veda Zagorac.

Aoua Kéita and Veda Zagorac: A Correspondence Across Continents

Kéita met Veda Zagorac in Mali when Zagorac's husband Zdravko Pečar was serving as the Yugoslav ambassador to the country, between 1967 and 1971. Zagorac had previously been the cultural attaché at the Yugoslav Embassy in Tunisia, while her husband, Zdravko Pečar was reporting on the Algerian War, and it was on her initiative that *El Moudjahid*—the newspaper of the Algerian revolution—had been reprinted in Belgrade, an initiative I will discuss in more detail in the following chapter.[84] Zagorac herself had worked as a journalist in Egypt in the early 1950s, reporting on politics, the economy, and women's rights.[85] In Tunisia, she opened a hospital that admitted wounded Algerian revolutionary fighters, and she secured financial aid for the revolution, helped send Algerian students to Yugoslavia, and became a key figure in disseminating the message of the Algerian National Liberation Front.[86] During this time, Zagorac also represented the KDAŽ at many events related to women's rights held across the African continent. For instance, she attended the 1st National Congress of Women from Guinea in 1968, where she offered scholarships to representatives from Portuguese Guinea (now Guinea-Bissau).[87]

Curator Emilia Epštajn explains that, while Zagorac lived in Mali, Kéita ushered her into African society by inviting her to weddings and other special events. Zagorac repaid Kéita in part by inviting her to read excerpts of her still unpublished *Femme d'Afrique* (notably, related to women's education and political work) in the Yugoslav Embassy in Bamako.[88] After Zagorac left Mali in 1971, the two women stayed in touch, exchanging letters over years in correspondence that tells the story of two friends striving to remain in contact and share their lives even after these lives have taken them down different paths. Both trusted nonetheless that they shared similar values and belonged to the same struggle for female emancipation.

In their correspondence, the two women discussed a potential visit of Kéita to the Yugoslav coast. They shared their opinions on political events in their respective countries and reminisced about the days they spent together in Mali. These letters are written by two women who consider each other equals, who were involved in each other's private lives, who planned visits and joint vacations. And they shared their political activities with one another as well. Kéita thus keeps Zagorac updated on the status of *Femme d'Afrique*, and also conveys in her October 1972 letter her gratitude for being invited to speak at the Conference of African Women. Kéita's sense of nostalgia is palpable as she describes her trips to Tanzania, Kenya, and Uganda, which recall a time when her political involvement was at its peak. Yet, her disengagement from politics was clearly never complete, as she writes in 1975 about attending a feminist conference in Dubrovnik. Zagorac, on the other hand, writes about the *griottes* (female storytellers) of Bamako with a note of exoticism and makes a point of sharing news of her mixed-race niece. Still, the letters trace not just one interpersonal connection but a network of political friendships between Malian and Yugoslav women; and it is obvious that Kéita was especially eager to keep up with the lives of her contacts in the Balkans. These experiences and interpersonal connections also led to some concrete projects.

Figure 4. Aoua Kéita and Veda Zagorac in Mali.
The Veda and dr Zdravko Pečar Collection, Belgrade Museum of African Art.

In 1977, the Museum of African Art (Muzej afričke umetnosti, MAU) opened in Belgrade, with Zagorac as one of its founders. The Museum was presented as an "anticolonial" museum built in solidarity with African peoples, where objects were not stolen but either bought or received as gifts, unlike other European museums of its kind. However, Ana Sladojević has questioned the degree to which any museum can truly be anticolonial. Indeed, despite its best intentions, the Museum's permanent exhibit design was ethnological, mirroring other similar museums in Europe after all and leading "to a detachment of the value of what was construed as 'African art' from the agency of African artists, craftswomen, and craftsmen."[89]

To counter a purely ethnological approach, the Museum did exhibit works throughout the years by contemporary African artists including Twins Seven Seven, Yinka Adeyemi, and Jimoh Buraimoh from Nigeria, as well as Kofi Antubam, Nii Amon Kotei, and Albert Osabu Bartimeus from Ghana.[90] Whether this was enough to justify the anticolonial label is debatable, but what is certain is that the Museum's permanent collection contained no references to anticolonial struggles or to Yugoslav-African solidarity. Though anticolonial archives were held in its library, they were only exhibited relatively recently.

In this way, the Museum of African Art is another example of Yugoslav ambivalence vis-à-vis the Global South. Aoua Kéita's political counterparts in Yugoslavia, from Tomšič to Zagorac and Pečar, to other KDAŽ members, actively and earnestly supported anticolonial struggles and newly independent nations, but European discourses and representations had seeped into their understandings of Africa. These relations were therefore marked by a certain "décalage," to borrow from Brent Hayes Edwards: a temporal or spatial gap, "the kernel of precisely that which cannot be transferred or exchanged, the received biases that refuse to pass over when one crosses the water."[91] Yet this never prevented collective action or the formation of deeply valued individual friendships.

In *Scattered Hegemonies*, Inderpal Grewal and Caren Kaplan write that "if feminist political practices do not acknowledge transnational cultural flows, feminist movements will fail to understand the material conditions that structure women's lives in diverse locations."[92] Kéita, Tomšič, and Zagorac believed this, too, and through their collaborations and friendships, sought to "link diverse local practices to formulate a transnational set of solidarities."[93] For Kéita, this began with her work as a midwife and local organizer fighting for independence in Mali, and expanded into collective efforts to build a transnational network of women committed to anti-imperialism and anticapitalism, including members of the KDAž. The political views and practices of these women sometimes overlapped and sometimes diverged, and they knew that women's emancipation would take different forms in different contexts, but they supported each other's organizations, local projects, and personal endeavors because they truly believed they were a part of the same international struggle. Veda Zagorac, and her husband Zdravko Pečar notably played an important role in the Algerian War of Independence.

CHAPTER FIVE

Revolution in Focus: Zdravko Pečar, Dragan Savić, and Veda Zagorac in Algeria

This chapter begins with a photograph taken in 1959 or 1960.[1] Frantz Fanon, Omar Oussedik, and Zdravko Pečar are pictured together in Fanon's apartment in Tunisia during a meeting with Holden Roberto, the exiled Angolan nationalist and anticolonial organizer. I imagine that Fanon, the renowned Martinican psychiatrist and revolutionary who worked in Algeria and participated in its revolution, requires no introduction.[2] As mentioned in the Introduction, Fanon believed that the Algerian revolution could serve as a catalyst to a broader continental uprising, and advocated the formation of an "African legion," which could propel the revolution beyond national borders.[3] It is hardly surprising that he is shown here in conversation with Oussedik—a member of Algeria's National Liberation Front (Front de Libération Nationale, or FLN)[4]—better known by his nom de guerre, Si Tayeb.[5] After all, the Algerian revolution was planned by figures such as Fanon and Oussedik during their exile in Tunisia, and from 1958 to 1960, Oussedik held a post in the Provisional Government of the Algerian Republic (GPRA).[6] What is less obvious is why Zdravko Pečar, a Yugoslav diplomat and journalist, is in their company. The unusual trio captured in Chapter One, of Aimé Césaire, Léopold Sédar Senghor, and Petar Guberina, finds an equally unexpected counterpart here.

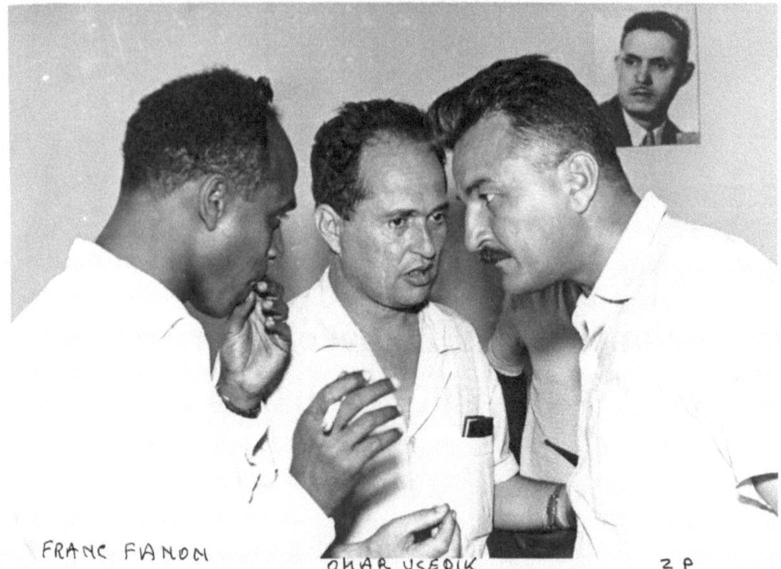

Figure 5. Frantz Fanon, Omar Oussedik and Zdravko Pečar in Fanon's apartment in Tunisia, 1959 or 1960. The Veda and dr Zdravko Pečar Collection, Belgrade Museum of African Art.

I have been aware of this photograph of Fanon, Oussedik, and Pečar for some time, as it has circulated on the internet, been on display at the Non-Aligned exhibit in the Belgrade Museum of African Art, and is stored in the Museum's archive.[7] For years, I have been intrigued by the untold story of revolutionary friendships it tells. Yet, during my research, I found that this photograph was just one of many that told a similar story. In fact, the Belgrade Museum of African Art contains a vast and invaluable written and photographic collection documenting the Algerian War of Independence; an entire archive of friendship and revolution. And it is thanks to Zdravko Pečar, and his wife Veda Zagorac, that this archive exists at all. Both former Partisans and then Yugoslav journalists, the couple founded the Museum, and their personal archives serve as the basis for my exploration here of the involvement of Yugoslavia in the Algerian revolution. Pečar also coordinated a visit to Algeria by the Yugoslav painter and cartoonist Dragan Savić, and I draw equally from his archives.

What these collections reveal is that bonds of friendship and solidarity built between Algerian revolutionaries and their Yugoslav contemporaries played an important role in the Algerian struggle for liberation. Viewing the Algerian revolution through the lens of these Yugoslav archives thus adds another transnational dimension to that struggle. The Algerian War was a fight for independence waged against France, but it also represented an example of anticolonial "worldmaking," an attempt at "reordering the world that sought to create a domination-free and egalitarian international order."[8] As Algerians reached out, seeking to fortify their cause and build connections across the Global South that would help sustain their independence, some friends from faraway places, including Zdravko Pečar, reached back.

The archive Pečar built contains many photographs of the Algerian War that, I argue, represent "utopian demands"—political claims that take "the form not of a narrowly pragmatic reform but of a more substantial transformation of the present configuration of social relations."[9] As we will see, these images prefigure a decolonialized world where friendship plays a crucial role. And this prefiguration should be understood not only in the specific historical context of non-alignment and Yugoslavia's interest in the Algerian anticolonial struggle, but as part of the legacy of Yugoslav Partisan representation.

Yugoslav-Algerian Relations During the Algerian War of Independence

Historian Dragan Bogetić has identified three phases of Yugoslav support to the Algerian independence movement. At the very beginning of the Algerian War, in 1954, this was limited to the sympathetic stance of Yugoslavia within the UN. By 1957, however, the Yugoslav government was sending weapons and humanitarian aid to Algerian revolutionaries via Morocco and Tunisia; and it was in Tunisia that Pečar found himself reporting on the war, during this second phase. Then, in 1961, Yugoslavia officially recognized the GPRA as the legitimate government of Algeria.[10]

Yugoslav-Algerian relations were shaped by several key events over these years. In 1958, after Yugoslavia backed a UN Resolution granting Algerians the right to independence and demanding that France begin negotiations with the GPRA, the French Navy stopped the Yugoslav ship *Slovenia* near Algeria and found it was carrying large quantities of ammunition and military equipment. The incident became a diplomatic scandal, damaging the once-highly valued Yugoslav-French friendship.[11] As President Tito traveled across Asia and Africa from December 1958 through early March 1959, he thus raised the Algerian revolution in conversation with leaders from Indonesia, Burma, Ceylon, Ethiopia, Sudan, and the United Arab Republic, arguing that the non-aligned movement should offer more unified and coordinated support to the Algerian struggle.[12] Yugoslav officials had already held many talks with representatives of the GPRA by this time, including with its President Ferhat Abbas, who visited Yugoslavia in January 1959 and met with Tito to discuss Yugoslavia's official recognition of the provisional Algerian government.

During his visit, Abbas told Yugoslav officials that theirs was the only government which understood the Algerian struggle and had offered help with no ulterior motives. Abdelhafid Boussouf, the GPRA Minister of Communications and Liaison, noted similarly that many of Algeria's allies, even among the Arab states, failed to fully grasp the contours of the country's revolution and were uncomfortable with its popular character; something the Algerians never sensed from Yugoslav leaders. Still, the request of Abbas that Yugoslavia officially recognize the GPRA was initially rejected. As Yugoslav Minister of Foreign Affairs Koča Popović explained to Abbas and his delegation, a de jure recognition in 1959 would have pushed France to sever diplomatic relations entirely with Yugoslavia, hurting both Yugoslavia and Algeria and making it more difficult for the Yugoslavs to send aid. Popović insisted that Yugoslavia was not neutral on this issue, but was simply waiting for more optimal international conditions to emerge before offering official recognition. Reluctantly, Abbas accepted the Yugoslav position, concluding that Algerians needed arms more than they needed de jure recognition, though he asked the Yugoslav delegation to continue advocating for recognition from other countries.[13]

Engagement of this kind was occurring on multiple fronts. For instance, in Tunisia, GPRA Vice President Krim Belkacem and Minister of Information Mhamed Yazid shared their admiration for Yugoslavia in conversations with the Yugoslav ambassador Ilija Topalovski, but also expressed impatience regarding Yugoslavia's choice to delay officially recognizing the provisional government. Yazid contended that Algerians held a special respect for Yugoslavia because they believed the future problems of an independent Algeria would require socialist solutions, and claimed that "the question [of] why Yugoslavia did not recognize their government" was increasingly posed by members of the military. According to

Yazid, this non-recognition served as evidence to Algerians of "the enemy's claim that the Algerian struggle does not enjoy international support and that the majority of global public opinion considers the Algerian war an internal French matter."[14] Vice President Belkacem noted that the GPRA had expected Yugoslavia to be the first country to recognize it, thereby influencing other non-aligned nations.[15]

That said, even if Yugoslav leaders feared France would react to official recognition of the GPRA, they continued sending aid to the Algerians. In February 1959, for example, the *Miami S* departed from Trieste to deliver aid sent by Yugoslav workers' unions to Algerian refugees in Tunisia. Yugoslavia also took in wounded ALN soldiers and granted scholarships to Algerian students. While this aid had been offered clandestinely at the beginning of the war, by 1959, it was done so openly. Hence, while Yugoslavia had not offered de jure recognition of the GPRA, it had done so de facto.[16]

Then, in March 1960, the establishment of an FLN office in Belgrade marked a key development and an important step toward de jure recognition by Yugoslavia of the provisional Algerian government. The office initially lacked official diplomatic status but nonetheless played a crucial role for the FLN, helping reach an agreement on the transfer of more wounded Algerians from Morocco and Tunisia into Yugoslavia, and facilitating Yugoslav advocacy for the FLN in Latin American countries.[17] Yugoslav-Algerian relations grew stronger throughout 1960, and in September, Tito spoke at the UN to mark the sixth anniversary of the Algerian revolution, arguing that the UN should support Algeria's initiative to resolve the crisis through a referendum, because "if a way is not found for a democratic solution as soon as possible, force, and war, are implicitly legalized as means of suppression of the legitimate aspirations of a people."[18]

One year later, in September 1961, Tito offered de jure recognition to the GPRA during the Belgrade Conference of the Non-Aligned Movement, making Yugoslavia the first European country to take this step. His statement was explicit:

> Expressing the deep desire of the people of Yugoslavia, who have, for many years, throughout the entire heroic struggle of the Algerian people, harbored deep sympathy and feelings—I declare on behalf of the Yugoslav government that, since it has already 'de facto' recognized the Algerian government for several years, it has decided to immediately 'de jure' recognize the government of Algeria, whose president is now here among us.[19]

Tito's declaration led France to close its embassy in Belgrade and officially cut diplomatic ties with Yugoslavia in 1962.[20]

At the same time, Yugoslav ties to Algeria were strengthened, and not just through the engagement of GPRA officials. For instance, the Algerian poet, novelist, and playwright Kateb Yacine was also attracted to Yugoslavia, and spent some time there. In a 1961 article published in *Afrique-Action*, Yacine described his friendship with Abdullah, a former Partisan from Sarajevo who sang *malouf*.[21] Yacine offered a very positive vision of Yugoslav self-management, with its schools for workers, extensive maternity leave, and generous salaries and pensions, dismissing any critiques that the system represented a betrayal of socialism. Aid sent by Yugoslavia to African countries was not "a vague sympathy," he said, for it was "truly as brothers that the students of Belgrade demonstrate for Lumumba or raise fifty million dinars for the Algerian refugees."[22] Indeed, Yacine suggested that Yugoslavia shared a certain cultural affinity with Algeria due to the centuries-long Ottoman presence in both places, and was thus a useful example to Algerians.

From the Yugoslav Partisans to the Algerian *Mujahideen*

While Yugoslav-Algerian relations were being shaped and the Algerian War of Independence was advancing, Zdravko Pečar was working as a journalist in Tunisia. At the start of World War II, Pečar had joined the Yugoslav People's Liberation Struggle as a fighter and journalist, writing for the Partisan newspaper *Naprijed*. He was among the few to survive the battle for Ludbreg (in northwest Croatia) and was wounded in Slavonia. Of his experience during the war, Pečar later said: "The hatred of resistance fighters is great, and the eagerness for victory overwhelming."[23]

After the war, Pečar became editor of the daily newspaper *Politika*, and also wrote as a correspondent for other leading dailies and news agencies, such as *Tanjug* and *Borba*, with a primary focus on Africa and the Middle East. When he lived in Tunisia in 1957 and in the summer of 1958, he worked as a war reporter, and sometimes accompanied the ALN battalion led by Major Abderrahmane Bensalem, which often crossed from Tunisia into Algeria to attack French troops. In this way, Pečar participated in the daily lives of ALN fighters, which he documented along with their tactics and strategies. He also engaged with members of the FLN, many of whom were overseeing operations from their exile in Tunisia. In fact, his personal correspondence indicates that his Tunis apartment served as something of an FLN meeting place.

Pečar was getting a front row seat to the political side of revolution, unlike when he fought in Yugoslavia and saw only what was happening on the ground among the guerrillas, and he found that "the leadership of a revolution…is never as pure and beautiful as the soldiers who fight and die for it think it is."[24] He had been in regular contact with GPRA officials and "participated at the very top, in the highest intrigues" of the Algerian struggle, having first met FLN leader Ahmed Ben Bella in 1953 when they were both living in Cairo, where they developed a friendship that continued later in Tunisia.[25] It was from Ben Bella that Pečar claimed to have learned about the beginning of the FLN uprising in 1954, which supposedly made Yugoslavia one of the first countries aware of the upcoming war.[26]

Pečar also knew Houari Boumediene, Chief of Staff of the ALN. The two met in Ghardimaou, a town on the Algerian-Tunisian border where many ALN troops were stationed, and Pečar described Boumediene as crucial to coordinating Yugoslav support for the revolution. In fact, in 1954, Boumediene had commandeered a yacht belonging to the wife of the Jordanian king (with her knowledge), to transport Yugoslav weapons to Algerian revolutionaries. In Ghardimaou, he and Pečar developed a close friendship. The Yugoslav wrote that Boumediene "gave me his bed when I needed to take shelter at night. We toured the border sector together, living and sleeping in dugouts that were under constant fire from French artillery and aviation, day and night."[27] And when Boumediene later founded a school for political commissars in Ghardimaou, Pečar's book *Algeria* was included in the curriculum.[28]

Pečar's 1959 book, which documents his time with the ALN, was well-received by quite a few leaders of the Algerian revolution, and it marked his visible presence in their struggle. After receiving a copy, GPRA President Ferhat Abbas wrote a March 1960 letter to thank Pečar—both officially in the name of the Algerian government, and as a personal friend—for his "incomparable qualities of heart and keen intelligence" informed by his years of experience in "the countries of the East, Black Africa, and North Africa."[29] Pečar believed that his experience as a Yugoslav Partisan also gave him insights into the war in Algeria. And while he acknowledged the difficulties of comparing revolutions, he highlighted certain parallels between the Algerian and Yugoslav fights. Both were led by peasants and workers, and, in the case of Yugoslavia, young intellectuals who "saw in the war…the only way out for their generation."[30] In much the same way, young Algerians (though with fewer intellectuals among them, due to the nature of the colonial system) were left with no other option than outright war against the imperial power.

According to Pečar, it was this similarity—which was frequently emphasized by other Yugoslav proponents of non-alignment as well, including Kardelj and Tito—that facilitated the development of so many Yugoslav-Algerian friendships. In both revolutions, as Pečar saw it, the revolutionary had been misjudged by opponents who underestimated their determination to pursue victory at all costs. In the struggles that ensued, he said, these revolutionaries had "found themselves again," and this experience laid the groundwork for the formation of political alliances.[31]

This argument also appears in correspondence between Pečar and Basil Davidson, a British journalist and historian of Africa, when the two were in contact regarding the publication of Pečar's book, *Alžir do nezavisnosti* (*Algeria to Independence*).[32] Davidson believed Pečar had a unique perspective on the Algerian revolution because the Yugoslav had been a revolutionary himself; and Davidson contended that his own participation in the Yugoslav struggle—when he served for several months as a British liaison to the Partisans in 1943—had helped him understand African history better and write about it differently than other European historians. In Davidson's view, their revolutionary pasts allowed both he and Pečar to see colonized peoples as subjects of history instead of objects of knowledge.[33]

Certainly, there are significant differences between anticolonial struggles and those of the Yugoslav Partisans. Yet, here, I am less interested in the accuracy of this comparison than in the narrative that was built upon it to position Yugoslavs as anticolonial allies. This narrative was adopted by both Yugoslavs and Algerians, and the ALN not only accepted aid from Yugoslavia but permitted Yugoslav journalists, photographers, and filmmakers to spend time with its fighters, capture images of the Algerian revolution, and train Algerians to do the same. They recognized Yugoslavs as fellow revolutionaries with similar ideological values, and understood that, with Yugoslav help, the ALN could counter French war propaganda.

The Algerian War of Independence Through a Yugoslav Lens

Within the Algerian War, there was another war, of images and narratives. As Benjamin Stora has documented, most of the photographs of the war were taken by the French. In fact, the archives of the French Army contain over 100,000 such images; used in the early years of the conflict largely to produce French propaganda focused on normalizing "pacification"—the term France applied to efforts it said were meant to protect and educate a population that was suffering under the violence of the ALN.[34] By 1958, this French campaign had become so reductive that, as Gervereau put it, "Algeria becomes simply 'violence' in the images."[35] Algerians realized they would have to fight a "political-media battle for international visibility," alongside the war for independence.[36]

In this propaganda battle, Algerian revolutionaries found allies in the Yugoslavs, who had experience fighting their own battle of images during World War II. Tito's government dispatched journalists like Pečar to report on the situation in Algeria, and sent professional videographers to document the Algerian revolutionary struggle and train their Algerian counterparts. Mila Turajlić's recent documentary, *Ciné-Guerrillas*, follows the work of cameraman Stevan Labudović, who was selected by Tito to assist the Algerian anticolonial movement by creating films designed to counteract French propaganda.[37] Ultimately, the Algerians wanted to convey a very simple message: that they were winning the war. Meanwhile, France advanced a narrative in the French press that its war of pacification was a success, and that the ALN consisted of small groups of ragtag rebels that the French Army would quickly overcome (a narrative that became more difficult to sustain over time).

The Algerians and Yugoslavs fought propaganda with propaganda. They normalized the idea of the ALN as a national army, taking advantage of the fact that Algerians had developed a national consciousness. This made the outcome of the war practically inevitable; the French just hadn't realized it yet. In *Algeria*, Pečar thus wrote that the French, "not wanting to see the truth about Algeria...are still carried away by illusions that the war is at an end, that the enemy will not last."[38]

The rest of this chapter explores how Pečar worked to dispel these "illusions," both in his reporting and in photography. I combine an analysis of photographs found in his personal collection with a reading of

Algeria. While Pečar also published the more widely known book *Algeria to Independence*, mentioned above, it is lengthy (more than 600 pages) and tells the story of Algerian history from the end of the Roman Empire through independence. In Pečar's more intimate, journalistic account of his experience with the ALN in *Algeria*, I found a better counterpart to his photographic archive.

Reports from Tunisia

While reporting in Tunisia, Pečar covered developments in Algeria extensively, working for both the *Tanjug* news agency and the newspaper *Borba*, among others. He reported the news of Algerian advances and successes in remarkable detail, for example by describing the tactics used to cross the Morice and Challe lines[39]—which served as extra layers of defense at the Algerian-Tunisian border intended to prevent crossings by ALN fighters.[40] Many of Pečar's articles opened by stating, "the leadership of the ALN has announced," making it clear that his reporting echoed ALN communiqués. It was his goal to offer Algerian revolutionaries a means by which they could publicly proclaim their wins, not to highlight numbers of Algerian casualties or the successes of France. As he wrote in *Algeria*, the ALN faced obstacles in publicizing its accomplishments, because it did not have "the technical capabilities to communicate to the world the successes of its units in the fight against the enemy." Pečar explained that "the major global news agencies refuse to transmit these statements through their extensive networks…[so] Algerians are forced to report all these events in *El Moudjahid*, in small letters."[41] He sought to amplify news about the ALN through alternative networks that bypassed mainstream outlets, and by publishing information that wasn't reaching an international audience.[42]

Pečar also reported back to the Yugoslav public when the Algerian and Tunisian press ran stories about Yugoslavia. For instance, he relayed when an article appeared in the *Algerian Worker* about Algerians who traveled to Yugoslavia and received a "warm reception and friendly and fraternal welcome" from Yugoslav workers' unions.[43] Another story chronicled the trip of forty-eight international students (among them five Yugoslavs from five different universities) who participated in building a school in the Tunisian town of Sakiet Sidi Youssef, a project organized by a federation of North African students.[44] And though the French government mobilized in various ways to destroy this project of international student solidarity, the Yugoslavs who participated refused to leave Tunisia until the project was completed.[45]

In the articles Pečar wrote primarily for a Yugoslav audience, he helped build the narrative of Yugoslav-Algerian solidarity; together with Algerian publications that were doing the same for local readers. For instance, in November 1959, *El Moudjahid* published an article conveying good wishes from Algerians to Yugoslavs for the Yugoslav Day of the Republic. According to Pečar, the article described Yugoslavia as "one of the pioneers of active coexistence and positive neutrality," and said, "Its policy of friendship with the Arab and Asian-African world, as well as the undeniable sympathy the country enjoys throughout the world, give it a special place."[46]

Pečar reported the details of specific deliveries of Yugoslav aid to the Algerians as well, such as on 18 March 1960, when Algerian refugees in Tunisia received a package from the Yugoslav Red Cross containing 25 tons of sugar, 10 tons of soap, 4500 pieces of wool clothing, and several hundred tent wings; aid that was officially delivered by Ljiljana Topalovski, wife of the Yugoslav ambassador in Tunisia.[47] Similarly, when the Yugoslav ship *Serbia* had arrived in Morocco a week earlier with Yugoslav aid intended for Algerian refugees, Pečar reported that it was the Yugoslav ambassador's wife, Neda Vilović, who had officially handed it over to the Red Cross.[48] In these and other stories of the revolution, Pečar contributed to constructing a specific narrative: the Algerians were prevailing and had become a nation willing to pay any price for freedom, French "pacification" in Algeria was therefore a lost cause, and Yugoslavia was not just a diplomatic ally to the provisional government but a true friend of the Algerian revolution.

Moreover, stories like the one about Algerian workers in Yugoslavia and about Yugoslav students in Tunisia positioned Yugoslavia as not-quite European. Yugoslavia, which did not share the Western European legacy of racism and colonialism, was a place where Algerian workers felt at home; and it was not strange that Yugoslavs would participate in projects organized by North African students. These articles thus reflected the values of active coexistence and positive neutrality, and when Pečar wrote for Yugoslav readers about the aid given to Algeria, they were meant to feel proud. He was not only reporting on the existing Yugoslav-Algerian friendship, but was trying to activate that friendship and make it even stronger by raising interest among Yugoslavs in the Algerian struggle.

There were few articles in which Pečar offered his own analysis, and it is there where his Yugoslav lens becomes most evident, particularly his belief in worker self-management as liberatory. For example, this comes through in an article entitled, "Tko će zamjeniti kolone?" ("Who will replace the colonizers?"), in which Pečar addressed the nationalization and redistribution of land in Tunisia, arguing that the national bourgeoisie simply wanted to replace the former colonizers as the new owners of the means of production. He highlighted the challenge being mounted to this by more "progressive sectors of society and the administration," which were trying to establish a system of collective land-management.[49]

In many ways, the argument Pečar made in this article echoed Fanon's analysis of the role of the national bourgeoisie.[50] Pečar wrote that some 100,000 hectares of land had been repossessed from European colonizers in the context of reforms meant to prioritize agricultural workers who were still forced to rent this land, and that the Tunisian government was ensuring that large properties containing modern agricultural technology were given to workers' cooperatives and not broken up. Thus, the struggle for national independence was also a class struggle; and in much the same way that Pečar's writing conveyed his confidence in a victory for the ALN, he implied here that any attempt by the bourgeoisie to take power would result in defeat. Tunisia, and hopefully the rest of North Africa, would be joining Yugoslavia in building a world of self-managed socialism.[51] Still, in these rare articles in which Pečar's own ideological positioning was so visible, he mostly separated the struggle of anticolonialism from that of socialism, suggesting that the former was justified and worth supporting regardless of whether the socialist path was taken.

Of course, to support the Algerian revolutionary cause and play his part in the war of images and narratives, Pečar did more than just report for print outlets. He also organized Yugoslav photographers and videographers who crossed from Tunisia into Algeria to document the lives of ALN fighters.[52] Pečar's personal archive contains dozens of photographs from the time he spent with a battalion led by Major Abderrahmane Bensalem, representing a treasure trove for scholars of the Algerian revolution, which remains understudied. These photographs, taken in 1957 and the summer of 1958, capture a pivotal time in the war, as it was in mid-1957 that thousands of people were recruited to build the Morice line, which made border crossings particularly perilous in 1958. This isolated ALN troops even further, made it more difficult to transfer arms, and meant that fewer international journalists were able to enter Algeria.[53] The images shown below were taken in this context, and while various themes appear within them, I would like to underline three: revolutionary friendships, the birth of a nation, and what drives a revolution from within.

Archives of Friendship and Revolution

In her now renowned essay *On Photography*, Susan Sontag observes that "in teaching us a new visual code, photographs alter and enlarge our notions of what is worth looking at and what we have a right to observe. They are a grammar and, even more importantly, an ethics of seeing."[54] This grammar of seeing was precisely what Yugoslav photographers and their Algerian counterparts strove to achieve with the images they captured in Algeria. Algerians were emerging from over a century of colonialism, during which they were treated as subjects of empire not as subject-citizens, and these photographs offered a means of countering the exoticizing impact of the colonial gaze that had positioned them as "other." Indeed, as Sontag puts it, while "photographs give people an imaginary possession of a past that is unreal, they also help people to take possession of space in which they are insecure."[55] And the photographs in Pečar's collection were clearly intended to give ALN fighters, and the civilians supporting them, a sense of confidence in their own revolution and in their right to reclaim their land, even if centuries of colonialism had led them to feel insecure about this. They were also meant to offer future generations an "imaginary possession" of a revolutionary past. Hence, I contend that these photographs are tied to the past, present, and future, simultaneously. Their purpose was to document the revolutionary present at the time and commemorate those who may not survive it, but they served a prefigurative function, too, by portraying the disappearance of a colonial past and the emergence of an independent nation.

While several of the images in Pečar's collection show entire brigades of the ALN, ready for battle, far more of them depict the daily life of soldiers.[56] The focus is not so much on big events and historical battles but rather on the small, everyday moments that helped the ALN survive through multiple years of war. These photographs aimed to demonstrate that the ALN was more than just a group of insurgents; they depicted it as a legitimate national armed force that brought together various segments

Figure 6. Zdravko Pečar with ALN fighters near the Algerian-Tunisian border, 1958. The Veda and dr Zdravko Pečar Collection, Belgrade Museum of African Art.

Figure 7. Zdravko Pečar with two ALN fighters near the Algerian-Tunisian border, 1958. The Veda and dr Zdravko Pečar Collection, Belgrade Museum of African Art.

Figure 8. Zdravko Pečar with an ALN fighter near the Algerian-Tunisian border, 1958. The Veda and dr Zdravko Pečar Collection, Belgrade Museum of African Art.

of the population, including peasants, workers, and intellectuals. In the three photographs above, Pečar is shown among the fighters; erasing the distance between Pečar, the foreigner, and local revolutionaries, and portraying his absolute solidarity. But even more importantly, these images all convey joy, capturing moments in which fighters are smiling and laughing, sharing food, and regarding each other with trust.

Notably, the joy in these images stands in contrast to much of what Pečar wrote about the time he spent with the ALN. In *Algeria*, he described the exhaustion, anxiety, and fear he felt on the frontlines, unsure whether he would make it through the night to see the light of day on some occasions, such as during the battle of Souk Ahras. But the photographs in his collection strive to tell a different story. In fact, the soldiers appear so happy and at ease in these images that they made me think of the recent book by Adrienne Maree Brown on pleasure activism, which may at first seem like an odd association. After all, Brown comes from a tradition of Black, queer feminist writing, and emphasizes pleasure, specifically female bodily pleasure, as a necessary but often forgotten element of liberatory struggles.[57] Arguably, few things are more removed from male soldiers fighting a war in the 1950s, but my focus here is not on sexual pleasure. Instead, it is on the pleasure of the revolution as liberatory, on the joy of this fulfillment.

It is this conception that Brown described in a 2019 interview, noting that pleasure "is about happiness, joy, contentment and satisfaction," and explaining that some people think she is advocating for "pure debauchery… pure escapism," when what she is trying to convey is that pleasure is "about pure aliveness and actually being present for the world around you."[58] Furthermore, as Brown sees it, for people who are burdened by the trauma of historical and systemic harms, pleasure is "about reclaiming what I believe is our birthright. And it's not enough to do it on a personal level."[59]

My aim is not to decontextualize Brown's work on female sexual pleasure, but to harness the larger argument she makes about the revolutionary necessity of reclaiming joy. It is this argument I cannot help but see in Pečar's photographs, which depict a world where colonialism had prevented pure aliveness and presence, had made people subject-objects instead of subject-citizens, had robbed them of their agency, until the ALN soldiers shown in these images were finally able to live and fight for themselves. This is the source of their joy.

But this joy also emerges from revolutionary friendships. One could even suggest that there is a certain degree of homoeroticism among these men. Responsible for each other, struggling together, they have created unprecedented bonds, and this produces unprecedented pleasure. Pečar wrote in *Algeria* of the banter, games, and friendships shared by Algerian fighters: "Jokes bring Algerian soldiers and officers much joy and pleasure. They are always eager and love to tell jokes…and during breaks between major movements and battles, fighters find other ways to have fun and laugh heartily."[60]

This bonding took place against the brutality of colonial relations, which as Aimé Césaire put it, decivilized both the colonizer and the colonized.[61] Revolutionary friendships thus stand in opposition to the dehumanizing dichotomy of colonization. Pečar wanted to make it clear that these friendships would propel the revolution forward; that Algerians were not only winning militarily but that their liberation was inevitable, because any people who find this kind of joy will never accept the misery of subjugation again.

In Pečar's view, this liberation was also inevitable because a nation had emerged out of this network of revolutionaries. In the photograph shown here, of an ALN fighter holding what looks like a radio, both the fighter and the radio are one small part of a larger, and most importantly, modern

Figure 9. ALN soldier holding a radio, 1958. The Veda and dr Zdravko Pečar Collection, Belgrade Museum of African Art.

revolutionary web. As Pečar described in *Algeria*, the ALN had a complex organizational and communication structure that connected "sections, companies, battalions and wilayas," and allowed them to coordinate; bringing the ALN together into a whole.[62] The individual fighter in the image above is also part of a larger network, and that network has come to represent a nation.

In Benedict Anderson's now canonical work on nationalism, he argues that the nation is imagined, because it entails a sense of communion or horizontal comradeship between people who often do not know each other and have never met. According to Anderson, the development of mass vernacular newspapers facilitated the nation, by providing readers the basis to imagine a shared collective experience (in this case, of the news), irrespective of geographical location or social status. The radio depicted in the photograph here serves a similar function to the newspaper. In practical terms, it allows the ALN to share crucial information, but it can also be interpreted as a metaphor for the larger community that exists in the background, the network beyond this soldier that is fighting for the same ideals. Frantz Fanon has discussed the transformative role of the radio in similar terms. Initially, the radio served as a tool of French colonial propaganda, disseminating the colonial narrative and reinforcing the occupiers' control. However, as the Algerian resistance grew, the radio became a powerful means of resistance and solidarity for the Algerian people. It allowed them to receive news, share information, and maintain morale, ultimately contributing to the decolonization process by fostering a collective national consciousness.[63]

It was this larger community that constituted the nation, but it was the ALN that was positioned as its representative. Many photographs thus portray peasants, women, and children, as they interact with ALN soldiers. The photo below, which is also reproduced in *Algeria*, is particularly striking in this sense. Again, it hints at joy, as two soldiers are smiling and laughing with a group of children. But the soldier at the forefront comforts a child who appears to be upset, and the expression of the child who is looking directly into the camera is arresting; joyful but determined.

Here, children are positioned as the future of the Algerian nation, and the ALN as their protectors. The confidence of the child who faces forward in the image reflects the inevitability of Algerian independence. The ALN

Figure 10. Warriors and children (as captioned in *Alžir*, 56). The Veda and dr Zdravko Pečar Collection, Belgrade Museum of African Art.

will win because, behind the revolution are the women, men, and children who make up the Algerian nation. Pečar made a point of this civilian support for the ALN in *Algeria*, recounting that the battalion he was with encountered peasants who "were pleased when they saw that it was their army. They asked about their sons and brothers, about the actions that were in progress, and rejoiced at the report that another helicopter had been shot down."[64]

But it was women who truly drove the revolution from within, supporting the mostly male fighters. The photographs in Pečar's collection capture the determination of women; they are not depicted as victims, shown in tears mourning lost children, or portrayed as they experience violence. Without them, it is clear, the revolution would not have been possible.

Still, despite the active participation of women in the ALN, they are mostly represented as background actors in Pečar's archive. Pečar did publish a 1962 article, "Cinq Djamilah algériennes" ("Five Algerian Djamilahs"), which focused on five female ALN fighters who, after being released from prison, recounted their struggle to be accepted as equals into the ranks of the ALN. It was Pečar's conclusion that women's participation

Figure 11. Algerian women, 1958. The Veda and dr Zdravko Pečar Collection, Belgrade Museum of African Art.

in the independence struggle was leading the old patriarchal way of life to crumble, even as his own writings and photographic archive privileged male fighters and relegated women to the background.[65] In fact, unlike the male gazes, those of women are not turned toward one another.

As we ponder these images, it is a good time to unpack Ariella Azoulay's "civil contract of photography." Azoulay writes that photography's "broad dissemination over the second half of the nineteenth century has created a space of political relations that are not mediated exclusively by the ruling power of the state and are not completely subject to the national logic that still overshadows the familiar political arena."[66] Instead, it is a civil political space that photographers and their subjects conjointly imagine.

In other words, every photograph is an encounter between the photographer, the subject, and the camera. And according to Azoulay, the result is unpredictable. Hence, she sees the photograph not merely as a space of appropriation but also "a space of political relations between those who are governed, a space in which the demand not to be ruled in this way becomes the basis for every civil negotiation."[67] When people are photographed, they are not passive in this process, as they actively participate in the creation of an alternative civic space, in "the rehabilitation of their citizenship in the political sphere."[68]

The colonial world was a world of binaries, where the colonized stood in opposition to the colonizer. The images in Pečar's collection open space for a negotiation of these binaries. They document the emergence of social relations forbidden in the colonial world—like revolutionary friendships—and make room for their becoming. Indeed, through the civil contract of photography, "the governed possess a certain power to suspend the gesture of the sovereign power seeking to totally dominate."[69] The laughter and camaraderie depicted in many of Pečar's photographs from Algeria operate precisely in this way, to suspend existing power relations. The colonized is no longer simply the colonizer's reverse, as he is a fighter, a friend, a parent, and part of a new Algerian nation.

These images also belong to a long legacy of Yugoslav Partisan photography, a legacy that began in the midst of armed struggle—where Pečar's own revolutionary journey began—before the Yugoslavs brought the strategies and techniques they developed in World War II to Algeria. Rastko Močnik has described Partisan cultural production as "a transforming intervention in an aggressive and overly powerful reality...an intervention using representations, but representations that were produced from the perspective of another reality, one that first had to be won in a struggle..."[70] Partisan representations outlined a reality still in the making, fulfilling both a documentary and a prescriptive function by recording a struggle in process and announcing a world yet to be.

Davor Konjikušić explains that at the beginning of World War II, Partisan photographers operated independent from any centralized propaganda system. Instead, "members of the Partisan movement were trained to use cameras, and later their photographs made up the raw materials used to put together newspapers, produce falsified documents, create the Partisan archive and organise exhibitions on the liberated territories."[71] The war needed to be won both on the ground and in representation. The revolution needed to be portrayed as both imminent and unstoppable. As Sonja Horvatinčić writes, "In this sense, the structural function of Partisan photography in Yugoslav memory politics can be compared with that of monuments."[72]

By the time the Algerian War of Independence had begun, the Yugoslavs had institutionalized their propaganda operations and could train others using lessons learned from their own wartime experience:

> Each agitprop brigade, in line with the opportunities and resources available to them (photographers, cameras and materials) should have a photojournalist who films combat, parades, exercises, learning, relaxation, entertainment, the seizing of enemy goods, prisons, enemy losses, our victims, and work from the level of the brigade headquarters to the individual fighters, etc. They should bear in mind that photographs are the most objective images and documents of our struggle and that they are of invaluable historical value.[73]

In the tradition of Yugoslav Partisan photography, images in Pečar's archive represent utopian demands that prefigure "in fragmentary form a different world, a world in which the program or policy that the demand promotes would be considered as a matter of course both practical and reasonable."[74] But these are also more than demands, as their role is to show that the people who are fighting for this world will not lay down their arms until this demand is met. These photographs portray a utopian demand, and one in the midst of being realized.

In *Algeria*, Pečar promises that "without pretensions, often fragmentarily, numerous parts of the mosaic will be lined up in this book, from which the contours and images of that country, its people, their revolutions, hopes and perspectives should emerge."[75] Photographs from his archive accompany the book and serve a similar function, as parts of a fragmentary mosaic of revolution and national consciousness. A fragmentary mosaic puzzled together by Pečar with the help of other Yugoslav artists and journalists.

The Case of Dragan Savić

In 1961, the renowned Yugoslav painter and cartoonist Dragan Savić arrived in Tunisia, having decided to visit his friends Zdravko Pečar and Veda Zagorac on his way back from the United States, where he had just received an award for the "best caricature in the fight for peace." Initially, Savić had no intention to cross into Algeria; but during his stay with Pečar, he met many Algerian revolutionaries, including Frantz Fanon, who convinced him to embed with the ALN to sketch the fighters. This was something Savić had already done for the Yugoslav Partisans when there was no film available during the Yugoslav antifascist struggle. Among the most powerful records of the Partisan fight had thus taken the form of drawings, and it was near the end of the Algerian revolution when it occurred to Pečar that something similar could be done there.

In Pečar's account, Savić was struck by the reality of what he had agreed to do when, before crossing into Algeria, he was told to leave his passport behind; a necessity to avoid being identified as Yugoslav citizens if they were apprehended, so that Yugoslavia's active support for the revolution could remain concealed. This had become standard operating procedure for Pečar, but clarified for Savić the danger of the job at hand.[76] In any case, Savić gathered the courage to cross the border and spent two months with the ALN, drawing fighters and civilians, and painting portraits on the walls next to wounded soldiers.

Savić made hundreds of drawings in these two months, twenty-two of which were published in a 1965 book released by a Yugoslav publishing house in collaboration with the political commissariat of the ALN.[77] The ALN and GPRA were actively involved in selecting the items for publication, and in a June 1962 telegram, Veda Zagorac—then the press attaché in the Yugoslav Embassy in Tunis—informed Savić that Boumediene, Ben Bella, and the GPRA Minister of Information Muhammed Yazid had reviewed nine of

Figure 12. A group of ALN soldiers under the Algerian flag, 1961. Legacy of Dragan Savić, Homeland Museum in Petrovac na Mlavi.

his drawings, and were sending their comments and corrections. They also asked for more drawings that portrayed the action and overall dynamism of the ALN.[78] Given that this telegram was ripped to pieces (and then glued back together by the archivist), it is reasonable to conclude that Savić was not terribly pleased with the corrections he was asked to make; though, we can assume he made some of them, as the book was published. Here, I discuss two of Savić's drawings—both representative of those chosen by the ALN for publication—as well as a photograph from his personal collection, as these three pieces exemplify his contribution to the Algerian propaganda effort. In each case, Savić has positioned the ALN as a victorious national army, and has memorialized the struggle for independence.

The image shown above, in which the Algerian flag appears prominently in the background, portrays the birth of the Algerian nation, represented by four male figures. The determination on their faces, and the collusion evident among them as some read a document we may assume is important, points to their active involvement in the ongoing struggle. The strength and surehandedness of the strokes Savić used to draw their

Figure 13. ALN fighter cutting the Morice line, 1961. Legacy of Dragan Savić, Homeland Museum in Petrovac na Mlavi.

faces and the flag are contrasted by the lighter and less defined strokes he used in their clothing and the background. This evokes a moment of tension and uncertainty in which the flag, and the resolve of those defending it, are the only two inevitabilities.

In this drawing of an ALN soldier cutting the wire fence along the Morice line, the contrast between the firm and steady strokes used to depict the soldier, and the blurrier strokes of the landscape, is even more profound than in the previous drawing.[79] The focus of the viewer is brought to the wire cutters strongly shaded to convey the steadiness and precision with which they are being used. At the same time, the imprecision of the grass in the foreground suggests a tenseness, an unknown danger. And while the context tells us we are looking at the Morice line, there is a certain universality to this image, echoing drawings and figures Savić had sketched to chronicle his own revolution some two decades earlier. In this sense, the drawing depicts an individual Algerian fighter but also an archetype of the revolutionary that reappears in different historical and cultural contexts; an archetype of a Partisan.

Figure 14. Female ALN fighter with older Algerian woman, 11 June 1961. Legacy of Dragan Savić, Homeland Museum in Petrovac na Mlavi.

Beyond his drawings, Savić's personal archive includes a number of photographs of his time with the ALN, many of which show him in conversation with Pečar or ALN members.[80] In fact, Savić's photographs resemble those found in Pečar's archive, reflecting that they were both products of the Partisan tradition. The image shown above caught my eye, however, as it places two women so clearly in the forefront, whereas the photographs in Pečar's collection typically depict women as a group in the background of the revolution.

Savić calls our attention in this photograph to a woman who is not an innocent victim or bystander, but an active revolutionary. She stands next to an older woman, and together these two women represent a generational shift, a divergence marked by the space between the two walls behind them. They stand close together, but are looking in opposite directions; the older woman looking down and to the left (perhaps, toward the past), and the younger woman looking up and to the right (perhaps, toward the future). These women exemplify the opposition between tradition and modernity. But this is Partisan photography, and so the image also offers a prefigurative representation, a glimpse into a new world where modernity is no longer associated with the metropole but with women as revolutionary actors.

Savić later recalled that, in Algeria, he "met wonderful people who had been fighting mercilessly for many years to secure the most sacred right... the right to live in freedom."[81] It was the struggle for this sacred right that he, like Pečar, had tried to capture. But it must be said that neither Pečar nor Savić could have done this without the help of Pečar's wife, Veda Zagorac.

The *El Moudjahid* Arrives in Belgrade

Like Pečar, Zagorac was a former Partisan. At university in the 1930s, she had joined various women's and youth groups, and became a member of the Communist Party of Yugoslavia. During the war, she was editor of the women's journal *Woman in the Struggle* and was a member of the Council of the Women's Antifascist Front. Then, while Pečar was reporting from Tunisia, Zagorac worked at the Yugoslav Embassy in Tunis as a cultural attaché.

There were various ways that Zagorac contributed to the Algerian revolution, but most notable among them was her successful effort to reprint the Algerian revolutionary newspaper *El Moudjahid* in Belgrade.[82] As Pečar explained, he and Zagorac worked together to publish three books of *El Moudjahid*, containing some thirty issues each, because they wanted "to give the Algerian revolution the aura it deserved" and preserve the official newspaper of the ALN "for later generations to use as part of their history."[83] Together with the Yugoslav Embassy in Tunisia and the GPRA's Ministry of Information, Zagorac also initiated the printing of postcards featuring scenes from the Algerian struggle. And, in 1961, she organized the release of the album *Chants d'Algerie*, on the Zagreb-based Jugoton label.

In Pečar's reporting, he sometimes quoted *El Moudjahid* to his Yugoslav readers when the newspaper ran stories about Yugoslav-Algerian relations, such as in his November 1959 article sharing Algerian greetings to Yugoslavs on the Yugoslav Day of the Republic. The *El Moudjahid* article Pečar drew from in that case outlined parallels between the two countries:

> In Algeria as in Yugoslavia, it is the peasants who form the soul and the flesh of the A.L.N. In Algeria as in Yugoslavia, the same savagery of the occupier in its policy of repression and extermination...For us today,

> Yugoslavia is more than an allied country: it is a friendly country—whose support on all fronts has never failed us.[84]

Pečar made similar arguments, comparing the Yugoslav antifascist struggle during World War II and anticolonial struggles in Africa, and positioning Yugoslavia not merely as an ally to Algeria but as a friend to the revolution. Moreover, Pečar recognized that Yugoslavia represented a useful example to the Algerians, and others, as it had been an underdeveloped country before rapidly industrializing due to its system of self-management and direct democracy.

While the reprints of *El Moudjahid* issues held by the Belgrade Museum of African Art are a rich resource on their own, the inside covers of the volumes in which they appear are also fascinating, as they are replete with handwritten messages of friendship. For instance, Colonel Si Nasser wrote:

> To my friends, Mrs. And Mr. Pečar, creators of the bonds of friendship between Algeria and Yugoslavia, and in memory of moments that were both difficult and unforgettable, in the warm action of struggle and friendship, and a joyful outcome that strengthened ties not only between us but between every worthy Yugoslav and every worthy Algerian.

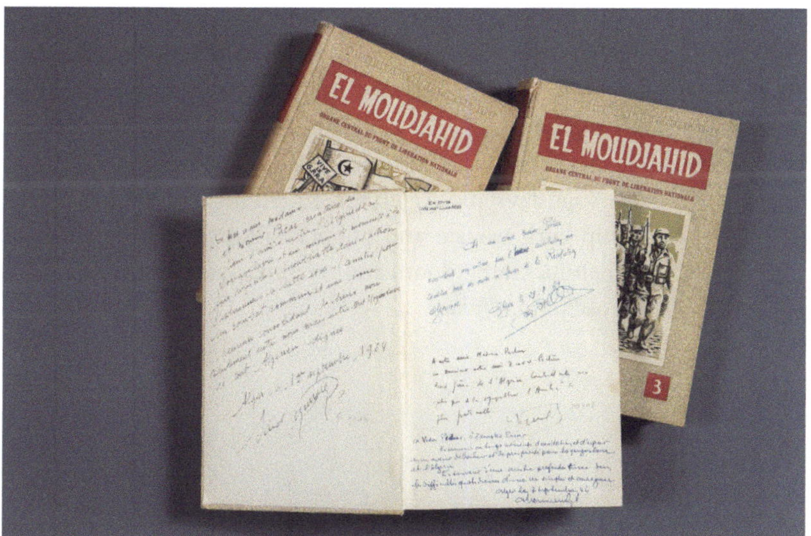

Figure 15. The inside cover of one of the *El Moudjahid* reprints. The Veda and dr Zdravko Pečar Collection, Belgrade Museum of African Art.

The first Algerian president, Ben Bella, wrote an equally personal message, addressed not to the Pečars as a couple, however, but to "my friend Mrs. Pečar"—to whom he sent "all my esteem for the contribution that her entire work represents in favor of the Algerian revolution." It is notable that he thanked her not merely for the publication of the *El Moudjahid* reprints but for the entirety of her work, positioning revolutionary activities as central to her life. Yugoslavs saw themselves as friends of the Algerian revolution, and Algerians knew it to be true.

* * *

Understudied sources that offer new entry points into the history of the Algerian War of Independence may exist in unexpected places, like the Belgrade Museum of African Art. There, Pečar's archive points to transnational connections that were established during the Algerian revolution, with the goal of building a decolonized world. Thus, the photographs it contains do not merely document the reality of the war but represent a new reality in the making; manifested, in part, through revolutionary friendships.

These friendships, some of which are described in this chapter, were the product of a common struggle and of common action. In other words, friendship was both the precondition for, and the result of, this collective fight for freedom. The inside covers of the *El Moudjahid* reprints are graffitied with messages that dance between the personal and the collective, marking individual friendships that paved the way to collective action. In this sense, Zdravko Pečar, Veda Zagorac, and Si Nasser stand in as representatives of all Yugoslavs and Algerians united in a common struggle. This is a friendship both private and public, based equally on intimate moments shared behind closed doors and on public acts of solidarity like the republication of *El Moudjahid.*

Epilogue: The Oasis of Friendship

Alexandra Perisic: If you could have written about Yugoslavia, what would you have said?

René Depestre: To start with, I would have proven that Titoism was not a betrayal of socialism. It was a well-elaborated form of resistance against the dogmatic ideas of Stalinism. It was a unique form of resistance to the totalitarianism of Joseph Stalin. Having lived inside the Stalinist system, I would have been capable of analyzing the Russia-Yugoslav crisis in detail.[1] Then I could have mentioned the origins of Césaire's *Cahier d'un Retour au Pays Natal*. I would have talked about the friendship Césaire had with Guberina. I would have celebrated my encounter with Kostadinka under a tent in the middle of the night, somewhere on the barren outskirts of Zenica. These are unforgettable moments that make you happy to be alive. I'm thrilled that I can mention them today.

While René Depestre never had the chance to write about these topics at length, in *Forgotten Friendships* I have tried to do so. Depestre, Césaire, Senghor, and Kéita were interested in Yugoslavia's peripheral position within Europe as well as its decentralized model of socialism. Friendships with Yugoslav intellectuals as well as visits to Yugoslavia informed their thinking about socialism, internationalism and solidarity. Understanding the Yugoslav origins of Césaire's *Cahier* as well as his lifelong friendship with Petar Guberina allows us to reconsider Négritude as a movement with global aspirations. Similarly, though Senghor has often been accused of cultural essentialism, he believed Slavitude and Négritude could be in dialogue. Even when he broke off with Cuba and settled in Europe, Depestre remained attached to the early communist experiments like the Šamac-Sarajevo railroad. Likewise, though Aoua Kéita is mostly recognized as an anticolonial activist, she belonged to a global web of socialist women fighting for female emancipation. The work of the Yugoslav couple, Zdravko Pečar and Veda Zagorac, is similarly impossible to understand without taking into consideration their deep involvement in the Algerian revolution, which allows us to take the Algerian war beyond the framework of anticolonial nationalism. Though the Francophone writers and activists studied here believed in the specificity of the African diaspora, they remained, throughout their lives, involved in internationalist projects. The historical particularity of their position did not lead them to isolationism. Quite on the contrary. Learning from others was at the heart of their friendships and radical politics. Yet they all also believed that there is an important difference between learning and imitating.

The collaborations and exchanges between these Francophone and Yugoslav intellectuals developed out of friendship. The figure of the friend reappears in archival materials, documentary footage, official documents, and personal correspondence as a crucial category in the building of an alternative globality, among authors who position friendship as central to their understanding of internationalism, justice, and solidarity. In this way, the thinkers featured in this book rescue friendship from the private realm, positioning it as a political category, and offering a theory (and practice) of decolonial friendship. These friendships were personal and intimate, expressed through poetry and writing, yet also extended into the public realm. They had a bearing on public policy and politics, and these friendships were based on a shared vision of a democracy to come, arising from "the network, the interweaving, and the sharing of singularities."[2]

An article in *El Moudjahid* once declared, "Yugoslavia is more than an allied country: it is a friendly country—whose support...has never failed us."[3] The friend is positioned here as more than the ally, they are a solidary figure, an active helper. Friends engage in a common struggle, fighting for a common goal. Friendships are something *done*, they are chosen and built in an acknowledging of difference and a striving for equality. Friendship thus represents "the most enduring and sustaining of the oases, with the resources necessary to withstand the deeply anti-political impulses that inform modernity: the despair of isolation and the anonymity of collectivism."[4] The friendships described in this book moved between personal relations, joint action, and state collaboration, and point precisely to the overlap between the public and the private, the personal and the political. Collaborative political organizing affected how these friends led their private lives, and their personal relations influenced their political opinions and practices. They viewed friendship as a continuous process of learning that leads to personal and social transformation, referring to each other as friends specifically because it underlined the link between personal and social transformation.

The peripheral position of Yugoslavia within Europe and later on its active participation in the Non-Aligned Movement, opened a space for alternative identifications, beyond those which emerged from European imperial centers. The Yugoslav model and the NAM were both products of a desire to push past narratives of division, to build collective systems. We have now come to a time when learning to identify cross-cultural similarities and work across cultural differences is again an incredibly important ethical and political question. The COVID pandemic and the intensifying effects of climate change have made it abundantly clear that we are facing global crises which call for mass social and political movements across borders. As we imagine movements to be, we need to fully understand those that were in order to be able to use them as sources of knowledge, sources of reflection, and sources of inspiration.

As this book has relied on many personal accounts and anecdotes, I end with one of my own, which illustrates for me the importance of centering these friendships for younger generations growing up in what is no longer Yugoslavia.

* * *

In the fall of 2021, I taught a class to university students in Belgrade on European colonialism and anticolonial struggles. The Belgrade Museum of African Art offered an exhibit at the same time entitled the Non-Aligned World, and I visited it with my students. The exhibit focused on the 1961 Belgrade Conference of the NAM, and more generally on the values of anticolonialism, emancipation, equality, peace, cooperation, and solidarity, which were promoted by the movement, and thus by Yugoslavia. After the tour, I asked my students about which piece(s) left the greatest impression, and almost unanimously they responded that the photographs of mass student protests in Belgrade that erupted after the assassination of Congolese Prime Minister Lumumba in 1961 had most surprised and impressed them. They found it remarkable that these students, generations before them, had felt such outrage at something happening so far away; and though they heartily supported this expression of solidarity, most could not imagine their generation responding in the same way.

The few older students in my class were aware of these events, which therefore felt less distant and unfeasible, but younger students had no idea that this kind of solidarity with the Global South had existed in Yugoslavia. Unlike my younger students, I was aware of the chain of events triggered by Lumumba's assassination, and it was another piece in the exhibit that caught my attention. A digital map showed the legacies of the two NAM conferences held in Belgrade, in 1961 and 1989, and included all the monuments, buildings, murals, and paintings made in celebration of non-alignment. Some of them I knew, others I did not. Many, I had passed by numerous times, unaware of their link to the NAM. The curator explained that the plaques identifying this connection are missing in most instances, intentionally removed or never replaced. And so, my own knowledge of Yugoslavia and its involvement with the (rest of the) Global South, contained many gaps. I have written *Forgotten Friendships* to fill some of those gaps, for myself and for my former and future students.

The friendships recounted in this book, nurtured and maintained over decades and shaped by shared experiences of oppression and conflict and peripherality, were tied together by the thread of Yugoslavia. Today, Yugoslavia is no more, and though the wars that broke it into pieces have ended, history itself has become a battleground. As Mila Turajlić explains, due to "Serbia's ambivalent relationship with the legacy of Tito's Yugoslavia," the memory of non-alignment has been "relegated to the domain of personal souvenirs and private memories."[5] In fact, in Serbia, where Partisan contributions to World War II are being erased from school curricula and former Nazi collaborators are being officially exculpated, the narratives of revolutionary interracial friendships from which this book draws exist to challenge the revisionist narratives offered to post-Yugoslav generations.[6] Recentering the Yugoslav history of non-alignment and interracial solidarity defies Serbia's post-Yugoslav embrace of nationalism and white supremacy, and highlights that, despite all its contradictions and limitations, Yugoslavia *chose* to support anticolonial struggles and newly independent nations. This was a choice made once, and a choice that can be made again.

In fact, these stories of interracial friendships carry what Derrida has called "a spectral messianicity."[7] They haunt the contemporary Serbian nationalist narrative, and when pushed into the background, keep returning, continuously reactivated by people seeking to *not* forget.[8] In that sense, these narratives are important to establishing a continuity in Yugoslav memory, where the nationalist wars of the 1990s created a historical rupture. Yet, these are not just Yugoslav narratives; they belong to the Francophone world, to the entirety of the Global South, and as such should be an integral part of Francophone and Global South studies. This book is thus meant for those students and scholars as well.

One of my favorite pastimes in Belgrade is to stroll through the Park of Friendship, the idea for which emerged from youth forest rangers who wanted to honor the 1961 Belgrade Conference of the NAM. They opted to establish a memorial park, where world leaders and famous figures could plant trees as symbols of the international struggle for peace and equality. Fidel Castro, Indira Gandhi, and the Rolling Stones have all planted a tree. But personally, it is Senghor's tree I most love to pass by, as it reminds me that histories are intertwined, that inspiration can be found in unexpected places, and that revolutionary politics require revolutionary friendships.

NOTES

Preface

1. Nika Autor, dir. *Newsreel 242 – Sunny Railways*. Newsreel Front, 2023.

Introduction

1. The curators at the Belgrade Museum of African Art, where this photo and the rest of Pečar's personal archives are held, have not been able to identify who signed this photo. It is my guess, however, that it is Abdelkader Laribi, who is credited as the photographer on many images of Pečar and the ALN that appear in Pečar's 1959 book *Algeria*.

2. When using the term "worldmaking," I rely on the definition offered by Getachew, who argues that "decolonization was a project of reordering the world that sought to create a domination-free and egalitarian international order." See: Adom Getachew, *Worldmaking after Empire: The Rise and Fall of Self-Determination* (Princeton University Press, 2019), 2.

3. For recent reevaluations of the history of the NAM, see: Bojana Videkanić, *Nonaligned Modernism: Socialist Postcolonial Aesthetics in Yugoslavia, 1945–1985* (McGill-Queen's University Press, 2019); Paul Stubbs, ed., *Socialist Yugoslavia and the Non-Aligned Movement: Social, Cultural, Political, and Economic Imaginaries* (McGill-Queen's University Press, 2023); *Southern Constellations: The Poetics of the Non-Aligned*, curated by Bojana Piškur, translated by Tamara Soban (Ljubljana: Moderna galerija, 2019), exhibition catalog.

4. Attempts to decentralize Francophone studies include a 2011 issue of *Contemporary French & Francophone Studies*, which explored the relationship between the Francophone Caribbean and North America, an area that has been underexplored. This work also aimed to shift the focus away from Paris as the primary destination for Francophone immigrants. Similarly, Ignacio Infante's recent book, *After Translation: The Transfer and Circulation of Modern Poetics Across*

the Atlantic, provides a detailed historical account of the role of translation in the transatlantic circulation of modern poetics. The field of Mediterranean studies also offers an important framework for thinking about Francophone literature comparatively. See: Roger Célestin, et al., eds., "The Francophone Caribbean and North America," *Contemporary French & Francophone Studies* 15, no. 1 (2011); and Ignacio Infante, *After Translation: The Transfer and Circulation of Modern Poetics Across the Atlantic* (New York: Fordham University Press, 2013).

5. Adam F. Kola, "The Politics of the Archive in Semi-Peripheries," in *Futures of Comparative Literature*, edited by Ursula Heise (Routledge, 2017).

6. See: Edward Tyerman, *Internationalist Aesthetics: China and Early Soviet Culture* (Columbia University Press, 2022); Anne Garland Mahler, and Paolo Capuzzo, eds., *The Comintern and the Global South: Global Designs/Local Encounters* (Routledge, 2022); Rossen Djagalov, *From Internationalism to Postcolonialism: Literature and Cinema between the Second and the Third Worlds* (McGill-Queen's University Press, 2020).

7. See: Magali Armillas-Tiseyra and Anne Garland Mahler, "Introduction: New Critical Directions in Global South Studies," *Comparative Literature Studies* 58, no. 3 (2021), 466. These methodologies are also associated with the 2007 founding of the journal *The Global South* and the 2016 launch of *The Journal of Global South Studies*.

8. Alfred J. López, "Intentions, Methods, and the Future of Global South Studies," *Comparative Literature Studies* 58, no. 3 (2021): 485–508. Emphasis in original.

9. Armillas-Tiseyra and Mahler, "Introduction: New Critical Directions in Global South Studies," 470.

10. For an analysis of the origin of Global South studies and its relationship to other comparative frameworks, see: Magali Armillas-Tiseyra, "Dislocations," *The Global South* 7, no. 2 (2013): 1–10.

11. Anne Garland Mahler, "Global South," Oxford Bibliographies in Literary and Critical Theory, 25 October 2017, DOI: 10.1093/obo/9780190221911-0055.

12. Anne Garland Mahler, *From the Tricontinental to the Global South: Race, Radicalism, and Transnational Solidarity* (Duke University Press, 2018). The Tricontinental movement formed in 1966 after representatives from the liberation movements of 82 nations in Africa, Asia, and the Americas gathered in Havana.

13. Similarly, in *From Internationalism to Postcolonialism: Literature and Cinema between the Second and the Third Worlds* (McGill-Queen's University Press, 2020), Rossen Djagalov analyzes Cold War-era efforts to build the Third World/Global South project in literature and cinema. However, he focuses specifically on the Afro-Asian Writers Association (1958–1991) and the Tashkent Festival for African, Asian, and Latin American Film (1968–1988).

14. Armillas-Tiseyra and Mahler, "Introduction: New Critical Directions in Global South Studies," 469.

15. Leo Zeilig, *Frantz Fanon: the Militant Philosopher of Third World Revolution* (I.B. Tauris, London, 2016).

16. Ibid.

17. Boaventura de Sousa Santos, "Epistemologies of the South and the Future," *From the European South*, no. 1 (2016): 18–19.

18. Peter Wright has recently questioned the assumed exceptionalism of Cold War Yugoslavia, showing rather that its Global South politics was similar to that of other communist countries. See: Peter Wright, "Challenging Yugoslavia's Internationalist Exceptionalism" in *Re-imagining the Balkans: How to Think and Teach a Region: Festschrift in Honor of Professor Maria N. Todorova*, edited by Theodora Dragostinova and Veneta Ivanova (Amsterdam: De Gruyter, 2023), 269–278. Yet, while Yugoslavia certainly wasn't the only communist country involved in the Global South, its position was in many ways specific due to its involvement in NAM.

19. See: Pascale Barthélémy and Ophélie Rillon, "Aoua Kéita (1912–1980): Anti-Colonial Activist, Nationalist Politician, and Feminist in Mali (West Africa)," in *The Palgrave Handbook of Communist Women Activists around the World*, edited by Francisca de Haan (Springer International Publishing, 2023).

20. Françoise Blum, and Constantin Katsakioris, "Léopold Sédar Senghor et l'Union Soviétique: La Confrontation, 1957–1966." *Cahiers d'Études Africaines* 59, no. 235 (2019): 839–66.

21. K. E. Fleming writes that "the Balkans make up a part of the 'old' model of empire, the late medieval, precolonial empires of the Ottomans and the Habsburgs, both of which followed, more or less explicitly, the imperial model of Rome." See: K. E. Fleming, "Orientalism, the Balkans, and Balkan Historiography," *The American Historical Review* 105, no. 4 (2000): 1218–1233. Similarly, Dušan Bjelić explains that "rather than exploiting natural resources and human labor, the Ottoman Empire...introduced policies of re-population, coupled with policies of religious conversion and polarization, underwritten by perennial military campaigns. Thus Balkan people perceived each other as both colonial rulers *and* as colonial subjects. Serbian nationalism, for example, both celebrates its medieval empire and remembers Ottoman slavery...." See: Dušan Bjelić, "Introduction: Blowing up the 'Bridge'," in *Balkan as Metaphor: Between Globalization and Fragmentation*, edited by Dušan Bjelić and Obrad Savić (Cambridge, MA: MIT Press, 2002), 6.

22. Maria Todorova, *Imagining the Balkans* (New York: Oxford University Press, 2009), 3.

23. Ibid., 15.

24. Ibid., 16.

25. Ibid., 18.

26. Bjelić, "Introduction: Blowing up the 'Bridge'," 3.

27. Fleming, "Orientalism, the Balkans, and Balkan Historiography," 1229.

28. Ibid.

29. Milica Bakić-Hayden, "Nesting Orientalisms: The Case of Former Yugoslavia," *Slavic Review* 54, no. 4 (1995), 918.

30. Catherine Baker, *Race and the Yugoslav Region: Postsocialist, Post-conflict, Postcolonial?* (Manchester University Press, 2018), 108. Here, Baker quotes Linda

Martín Alcoff, who wrote that certain "southern Europeans were sometimes excluded from whiteness and at other times enjoyed a halfway status as almost white, but not quite (unlike those with partial African heritage, no matter how light)." See: Linda Martín Alcoff, "What Should White People Do?" *Hypatia* 13, no. 3 (1998): 6–26.

31. *Martinska-Martinique*, directed by Lawrence Kiiru (Filmoteka 16, 1991).

32. See: Catherine Baker, *Race and the Yugoslav Region: Postsocialist, Post-Conflict, Postcolonial?* (Manchester University Press, 2018); Nemanja Radonjić, "Anti-Colonial Constellations: The Belgrade All-African Students Conference of 1962," in *Eastern Europe, the Soviet Union, and Africa: New Perspectives on the Era of Decolonization, 1950s to 1990s*, edited by Chris Saunders, Helder Adegar Fonseca, and Lena Dallywater (Berlin, Boston: De Gruyter Oldenbourg, 2023), 263–289; Peter Wright, "'Are there Racists in Yugoslavia?' Debating Racism and Anti-blackness in Socialist Yugoslavia." *Slavic Review* 81, no. 2 (2022): 418–441.

33. Wright, "'Are there Racists in Yugoslavia?'," 423.

34. Anikó Imre has thus argued that "the changing situation of Gypsy, or Romani, minorities within Eastern Europe provides a useful lens through which we can examine how whiteness has been called upon to provide legitimacy to the post-socialist nation-state." See: Anikó Imre, "Whiteness in Post-Socialist Eastern Europe: The Time of the Gypsies, the End of Race," in *Postcolonial Whiteness: A Critical Reader on Race and Empire*, edited by Alfred J. Lopez (State University of New York Press, 2005), 80.

35. Baker, *Race and the Yugoslav Region*, 28.

36. Gal Kirn, *Partisan Ruptures: Self-Management, Market Reform and the Spectre of Socialist Yugoslavia*, trans. Borut Praper (London: Pluto Press, 2019), 36.

37. Ibid., 115. This doesn't mean that Yugoslavia ever completely split from the West. In fact, through its non-aligned positioning Yugoslavia developed trade agreements and diplomatic relations with the European Economic Community, became an associate member of the Organisation for Economic Co-operation and Development, and played a key role in the Organization for Security and Co-operation in Europe.

38. Historians have also noted certain divergences between Bandung and Non-Alignment as projects. See: Jeffrey James Byrne, "From Bandung to Havana: Institutionalizing the Contentions of Postcolonial Internationalism," in *The League Against Imperialism: Lives and Afterlives*, edited by Michele Louro, Carolien Stolte, Heather Streets-Salter, and Sana Tannoury-Karam (Leiden University Press, 2020), 371–396; Peter Willetts, "The Foundations of the Non-Aligned Movement: The Trouble with History Is That It Is All in the Past," in *Socialist Yugoslavia and the Non-Aligned Movement: Social, Cultural, Political, and Economic Imaginaries*, edited by Paul Stubbs (McGill-Queen's University Press, 2023), 59–84.

39. Vijay Prashad, *The Darker Nations: A People's History of the Third World* (New York: New Press, 2007), 95.

40. Paul Stubbs has outlined an even longer history of non-alignment, including the Congress Against Colonial Oppression and Imperialism held in Brussels

in February 1927, the formation of the League Against Imperialism and Colonial Oppression, and the Pan-African congresses organized by W.E.B. Dubois from 1919 to 1927. See: Paul Stubbs, "The Emancipatory Afterlives of Non-Aligned Internationalism," Rosa Luxemburg Stiftung, January 2020, https://www.rosalux.de/en/publication/id/41556/. Also see: Jürgen Dinkel, *The Non-Aligned Movement: Genesis, Organization and Politics (1927-1992)*, trans. Alex Skinner (Leiden: Brill, 2019). Literary critic Nataša Mišković has also emphasized the importance of a long history of Afro-Asian solidarity in promoting peaceful coexistence and non-alignment. See: Nataša Mišković, "Introduction," in *The Non-Aligned Movement and the Cold War: Delhi – Bandung – Belgrade*, edited by Nataša Mišković, Harald Fischer-Tiné, and Nada Boskovska (London: Routledge, 2014). Yet, as Dragan Bogetić has noted, regional projects of Asian, African, or Arab unity were also often in contradiction and competition with the global scope of the NAM. See: Dragan Bogetić, "Jugoslavija i borba alžirskog naroda za nacionalno oslobođenje 1954–1962," in *Jugoslavija-Alžir: Zbornik radova sa naučne konferencije*, edited by Miladin Milošević (Beograd: Arhiv Jugoslavije, 2013).

41. See: Prashad, *The Darker Nations*, 98. NB: Yugoslavia sent arms to Egypt when an Anglo-French-Israeli force invaded in retaliation for the nationalization of the Suez Canal.

42. Ibid., 98.

43. See: Mila Turajlić, "Film as the Memory Site of the 1961 Belgrade Conference of Non-Aligned States," in *Socialist Yugoslavia and the Non-Aligned Movement: Social, Cultural, Political, and Economic Imaginaries*, edited by Paul Stubbs (McGill-Queen's University Press, 2023), 203–235.

44. Ibid., 100.

45. Stubbs, "The Emancipatory Afterlives of Non-Aligned Internationalism."

46. Ibid. Also see: Alvin Z. Rubinstein, *Yugoslavia and the Nonaligned World* (Princeton University Press, 1970).

47. *Southern Constellations: The Poetics of the Non-Aligned*, exhibition catalog, 138. In 2019, Slovenian curator Bojana Piškur organized the *Southern Constellations* exhibit, which had a very important role in reassessing the history of the NAM. As Piškur explains, the NAM "envisioned forms of politics that took as their starting point the life of peoples and societies that had been forcibly relegated to the margins of the global economic, political and cultural system" (20). For more information on the exhibit, see: http://www.mg-lj.si/en/exhibitions/2439/southern-constellations-the-poetics-of-the-non-aligned/.

48. Videkanić, *Nonaligned Modernism*, 138.

49. Paul Stubbs, "Socialist Yugoslavia and the Antinomies of the Non-Aligned Movement," *LeftEast*, 17 June 2019, https://lefteast.org/yugoslavia-antinomies-non-aligned-movement/.

50. Radonjić, Nemanja."Anti-Colonial Constellations: The Belgrade All-African Students Conference of 1962," 279.

51. Edvard Kardelj, *The Historical Roots of Non-Alignment* (University Press of America, 1980), 39.

52. Here, Kardelj's argument is quite similar to that of Kwame Nkrumah in his analysis of neocolonialism as the last stage of imperialism; and both were of course influenced by Lenin's view of imperialism as the highest stage of capitalism. See: Kwame Nkrumah, *Neo-Colonialism: The Last Stage of Imperialism* (International Publishers, 1965).

53. Kardelj, *The Historical Roots of Non-Alignment*, 54.

54. Zoran Oklopcic, "Beyond Empty, Conservative, and Ethereal: Pluralist Self-Determination and a Peripheral Political Imaginary," *Leiden Journal of International Law* 26, no. 3 (2013), 517. Also see: Kardelj, *The Historical Roots of Non-Alignment*, 45.

55. For a more in-depth analysis of Yugoslav self-management see: See: Kirn, *Partisan Ruptures*; Vladimir Unkovski-Korica, *The Economic Struggle for Power in Tito's Yugoslavia: From World War II to Non-Alignment* (I.B. Tauris, London [etc.], 2016); and Susan Woodward, *Socialist Unemployment: The Political Economy of Yugoslavia, 1945–1990* (Princeton University Press, 1995).

56. Kirn, *Partisan Ruptures*, 142.

57. It should be noted that "the effective monopoly that the governing party, the League of Communists of Yugoslavia, continued to hold in most sectors of the state, ensured that much of the decentralization remained inconsequential in practice." James Robertson, "Small Socialism: The Scales of Self-Management Culture in Postwar Yugoslavia," *The Slavic Review* 79, no. 3 (2020): 568.

58. Ibid., 566.

59. Rubinstein, *Yugoslavia and the Nonaligned World*, 10.

60. Kardelj, *The Historical Roots of Non-Alignment*, 42.

61. Ibid., 41.

62. This argument was voiced by other African anticolonial activists as well. See: Radonjić, "Anti-colonial Constellations."

63. See: Konstantin Kilibarda, "Non-Aligned Geographies in the Balkans: Space, Race and Image in the Construction of new 'European' Foreign Policies," in *Security Beyond the Discipline: Emerging Dialogues on Global Politics – Selected Proceedings of the Sixteenth Annual Conference of the York Centre for International and Security Studies*, edited by Abhinava Kumar and Derek Maisonville (Toronto: York Centre for International and Security Studies, York University, 2010), 28.

64. Jelena Subotic and Srdjan Vucetic, "Performing Solidarity: Whiteness and Status-seeking in the Non-Aligned World," *Journal of International Relations and Development* 22, no. 3 (2019): 723.

65. Rubinstein, *Yugoslavia and the Nonaligned World*, 134–135.

66. Paul Stubbs, "Introduction: Socialist Yugoslavia and the Non-Aligned Movement: Contradictions and Contestations," in *Socialist Yugoslavia and the Non-Aligned Movement: Social, Cultural, Political, and Economic Imaginaries*, edited by Paul Stubbs (McGill-Queen's University Press: 2023), 4-5.

67. Baker, *Race and the Yugoslav Region*, 119.

68. Jelena Subotic and Srdjan Vucetic have asserted that some of the students to whom Yugoslavia awarded scholarships experienced racism during

their time in Yugoslavia. Similarly, Konstantin Kilibarda has recently shown that many Yugoslav diplomatic texts relating to the NAM also reveal an underlying Eurocentrism. See: Subotic and Vucetic, "Performing Solidarity," 728; and Konstantin Kilibarda, "Non-Aligned Geographies in the Balkans", 28.

69. Nemanja Radonjić, "Studenti iz Afrike u socijalističkoj i nesvrstanoj Jugoslaviji: Prilog istraživanju slike Drugog." *Godišnjak za društvenu istoriju*, no. 3, 2020: 23–53.

70. Wright, "Are there Racists in Yugoslavia?'," 424.

71. Ibid., 419.

72. Paul Stubbs, "Exploring Contradictory Racializations: Socialist Yugoslavia, the Non-Aligned Movement and Decolonial Worldmaking," paper at the international conference *Postcolonial, Decolonial, Postimperial, Deimperial*, Rijeka, May 2024.

73. Aristotle, *Nicomachean Ethics*, trans. Christopher Rowe, edited by Christopher Rowe and Sarah Broadie (Oxford University Press, 2002), 208.

74. For example, see: Graham M. Smith, "Friendship, State, and Nation," in *Friendship and International Relations*, edited by Simon Koschut and Andrea Oelsner (London: Palgrave Macmillan, 2014); Evgeny Roshchin, *Friendship Among Nations: History of a Concept* (Manchester University Press, 2020); Felix Berenskoetter, "Friends, There Are No Friends? An Intimate Reframing of the International," *Millennium* 35, no. 3 (2007): 647–676; and Alexander Wendt, *Social Theory of International Politics* (Cambridge University Press, 1999).

75. Heather Devere and Preston King, *The Challenge to Friendship in Modernity* (Routledge, 2013); Laurence A. Blum, *Friendship, Altruism and Morality* (Routledge, 2009); Janice G. Raymond, *A Passion for Friends: Toward a Philosophy of Female Affection* (Spinifex Press, 2001); and Marilyn Friedman, *What Are Friends For? Feminist Perspectives on Personal Relationships and Moral Theory* (Cornell University Press, 1993).

76. It should be noted that some recent works have tried to address this issue. For instance, Matt Hern and Am Johal have recently proposed a conception of friendship that extends to non-humans. See Matt Hern and Am Johal. *O My Friends, There Is No Friend: The Politics of Friendship at the End of Ecology* (Bielefeld: Transcript Verlag, 2020).

77. Frantz Fanon, *The Wretched of the Earth*, trans. Richard Philcox (New York: Grove Press, 2004).

78. James Mark, Artemy M. Kalinovsky, and Steffi Marung, eds., *Alternative Globalizations: Eastern Europe and the Postcolonial World* (Indiana University Press, 2020), 7.

79. Leela Ghandi, *Affective Communities: Anticolonial Thought, Fin-de-Siècle Radicalism, and the Politics of Friendship* (Duke University Press, 2006), 10.

80. Ibid., 19.

81. Ibid., 20.

82. Paula M. L. Moya, "'Racism is not intellectual': Interracial Friendship, Multicultural Literature, and Decolonizing Epistemologies," in *Decolonizing*

Epistemologies: Latina/o Theology and Philosophy, edited by Ada Maria Isasi-Diaz and Eduardo Mendieta (Fordham University Press, 2012), 174.

83. Ibid., 176.

84. Astrid H. M. Nordin, "Decolonising Friendship," *The Journal of Friendship Studies* 6, no. 1 (2020), 92.

85. Gary Wilder, *Concrete Utopianism: The Politics of Temporality and Solidarity* (Fordham University Press, 2022), 9.

86. Hern and Johal, *O My Friends, There Is No Friend*, 47.

87. Ibid., 22.

88. Rosine Kelz, "Political Friendships to Come? Futurity, Democracy and Citizenship," in *Derrida's Politics of Friendship: Amity and Enmity*, edited by Luke Collison, Cillian Ó Fathaigh, and Georgios Tsagdis (Edinburgh University Press, 2022), 206.

89. Jacques Derrida, *The Politics of Friendship*, trans. George Collins (London: Verso, 1997).

90. According to Derrida, women are often missing from the bonds of fraternal friendship in a way that has been naturalized. Derrida is certainly right to highlight that women are, in this sense, the absent alterity. However, he neglects to mention the racialized other as the counterpoint of European modernity. Rosine Kelz thus notes that "by concentrating on the European canon he is able to analyze its internal exclusionary logic, but misses the opportunity to bring the role of colonialism – and the voices of non-Europeans – more forcefully to the fore." In fact, Derrida mentions Carl Schmitt's concern about the effects of imperialism on the political, but does not fully elaborate on the implications of this on existing theories of friendship. See: Rosine Kelz, "Political Friendships to Come? Futurity, Democracy and Citizenship," 203.

91. Audre Lorde, "The Master's Tools Will Never Dismantle the Master's House," in *Sister Outsider: Essays and Speeches* (Berkeley: Crossing Press, 1984), 111.

92. Édouard Glissant, *Poetics of Relation*, trans. Betsy Wing (University of Michigan Press, 1997), 11.

93. See: Aristotle, *Nicomachean Ethics*, 147–151.

94. Paul Gilroy, *Postcolonial Melancholia* (New York: Columbia University Press, 2005), XV.

95. See: Paul Betts, "A Red Wind of Change: African Press Coverage of Tito's Visits to Decolonizing Africa," in *Tito in Africa: Picturing Solidarity*, edited by Radina Vučetić and Paul Betts (Belgrade: Museum of Yugoslavia, 2017), 69.

96. "…da još jednom doprinesete stvari mira prijateljstva sa narodima Afrike." Telegram from the people of Grljani to Tito, 16 February 1961, AJ (Archives of Yugoslavia, Belgrade) KPR I-2/13.

97. "…želimo ti, druže Tito, lep, sretan i uspešan put u daleke ali prijateljske i uvek bliske zemlje Afrike." Telegram from the Vukovar military post to Tito, 16 February 1961, AJ, KPR, I-2/13.

98. Gayatri Chakravorty Spivak has written that "Teleopoiesis is indeed one of the shocks to the idea of belonging in a collectivity, for it makes a constant and risk-taking effort to affect the distant in a poiesis or imaginative remaking,

without guarantees." See: Gayatri Chakravorty Spivak, "A Note on the New International," *Parallax* 7, no. 3 (2001), 12.

99. Derrida, *The Politics of Friendship*, 29.

100. Roland Arthur Greene, "Review of Death of a Discipline," *SubStance* 35, no. 1 (2006), 155.

101. Gayatri Chakravorty Spivak, *Death of a Discipline* (Columbia University Press, 2003), 34.

102. Homi K. Bhabha, *The Location of Culture* (Routledge, 1994), 4.

103. Arvind Sharma, *Religious Studies and Comparative Methodology: The Case for Reciprocal Illumination* (Albany: State University of New York Press: 2005). Milica Bakić-Hayden uses the term "reciprocal illumination" when talking about the usefulness of Orientalism as a concept for understanding the Balkans. See: Milica Bakić-Hayden, "Ex Orientalism Lux: A Reflection on Differing Legacies of a Concept," in *Re-Imagining the Balkans: How to Think and Teach a Region: Festschrift in Honor of Professor Maria N. Todorova*, edited by Theodora Dragostinova and Veneta Ivanova (De Gruyter Oldenbourg, 2023).

104. Spivak, *Death of a Discipline*, 13.

105. In this respect, my methodology is similar to that outlined by Masha Salazkina in her book *World Socialist Cinema: Alliances, Affinities and Solidarities in the Global Cold War* (University of California Press, 2023).

106. Jane Gallop, *Anecdotal Theory* (Duke University Press, 2002), 2.

107. Joel Fineman, "The History of the Anecdote: Fiction and Fiction," in *The New Historicism*, edited by H. Aram Veeser (New York: Routledge, 1989), 56.

108. Ibid., 61.

109. Patricia J. Saunders, "Fugitive Dreams of Diaspora: Conversations with Saidiya Hartman," *Anthurium* 6, no. 1 (2008), 7.

110. Yohann C. Ripert, "Decolonizing Diplomacy: Senghor, Kennedy, and the Practice of Ideological Resistance," *African Studies Review* 64, no. 2 (2021), 294.

111. *Union Soudanaise–Rassemblement Démocratique Africain* (Sudanese Union–African Democratic Rally).

112. Gary Wilder, *Concrete Utopianism: The Politics of Temporality and Solidarity* (Fordham University Press, 2022), 2.

113. Wilder, *Concrete Utopianism*, 2.

114. Ibid., 3. NB: Wilder does not make a distinction between leftists and liberals, or rather, he includes liberals within the Left. I believe that this distinction is important, and that the position he describes is a liberal position.

115. Ibid., 2.

116. Ibid., 9.

117. Samir Amin, "Towards the Fifth International?" In *Global Political Parties*, edited by Katarina Sehm-Patomaki and Marko Ulvila (London: Zed Press, 2008), 123–143.

118. See the issue of *Globalizations* journal dedicated to Amin's proposal for a Fifth International: *Globalizations* 16, no 7: "An Instrument for the Global Left? Samir Amin's Proposal for a Fifth International," 2019.

Chapter One

1. The title is also sometimes translated into English as *Journal of a Homecoming.*

2. A modified version of this chapter was initially published in *Small Axe*. See: Alexandra Perisic, "Aimé Césaire's Yugoslav Detour," in *Small Axe: A Caribbean Journal of Criticism* 27, no. 2 (71): 1–17. Copyright 2023, Small Axe, Inc. All rights reserved. Republished by permission of the publisher. https://www.dukeupress.edu/

3. Aimé Césaire, *Discourse on Colonialism,* trans. Joan Pinkham (New York: Monthly Review Press, 2001).

4. See: Christopher L. Miller, *The French Atlantic Triangle: Literature and Culture of the Slave Trade* (Duke University Press, 2008); and Gregson Davis, *Aimé Césaire* (Cambridge University Press, 1997).

5. Françoise Vergès has also proposed that Yugoslavia may have represented an important detour for Césaire, but she doesn't develop the idea further. See: Françoise Vergès, "Martinska/Martinique," in *Travelling Communiqué*, edited by Armin Linke, Travelling Communiqué Project Group, Kodwo Eshun, Doreen Mende & Milica Tomić (Spector Books, 2016).

6. Yohann C. Ripert, "Rethinking Négritude: Aimé Césaire & Léopold Sédar Senghor and the Imagination of a Global Postcoloniality" (PhD dissertation, Columbia University, 2017), 2.

7. Jean-Paul Sartre, "Black Orpheus," trans. John MacCombie, *The Massachusetts Review* 6, no. 1 (1964): 13–52.

8. See: Souleymane Bachir Diagne, "La Négritude comme mouvement et comme devenir," *Rue Descartes* 83, no. 4 (2014): 50–61.

9. Anja Jovic Humphrey, "Aimé Césaire and 'Another Face of Europe'." *MLN* 129, no 5 (2014): 1117–1148.

10. Speaking about the journal *Tropiques*, Wilder writes that "rather than critique abstract universality from the standpoint of concrete particularity—or empty form from that of living content, or alienated modernity from that of rooted tradition, or a faceless future from that of a lived past, or a generic humanity from that of a local culture—René Ménil, Suzanne Césaire, and Aimé envisioned an elevated form of concrete universality." See: Gary Wilder, *Freedom Time: Negritude, Decolonization, and the Future of the World* (Duke University Press, 2015), 36.

11. Aimé Césaire, Françoise Vergès, and Matthew B. Smith, *Resolutely Black: Conversations with Françoise Vergès* (Polity, 2020), 1.

12. Ibid., 3.

13. Michael Goebel similarly argues that "transnational and transregional networks and intellectual exchange centered in interwar Paris elucidated the systemic global connections of imperialism and opened new horizons." Michael Goebel, *Anti-Imperial Metropolis: Interwar Paris and the Seeds of Third-World Nationalism* (Cambridge University Press, 2015).

14. Césaire, Vergès, and Smith, *Resolutely Black*.

15. For a more detailed discussion of these publications and Black internationalism in the inter-war period, See: Brent Hayes Edwards, *The Practice of Diaspora: Literature, Translation, and the Rise of Black Internationalism* (Cambridge, MA: Harvard University Press, 2003).

16. *Martinska-Martinique*, directed by Lawrence Kiiru (Filmoteka 16, 1991). All quotations from the documentary used here are drawn from an English transcript published in 2022. See: Sofia Samatar, "Martinska-Martinique," *Caribbean Quarterly* 68, no. 2 (2022): 268–279.

17. Francis Marmande, "Aimé Césaire: 'Ma poésie est née de mon action'," *Le Monde*, 15 March 2006.

18. See: Samatar, "Martinska-Martinique."

19. I explore Senghor's relation to Yugoslavia and to Petar Guberina in Chapter Two.

20. Humphrey, "Aimé Césaire and 'Another Face of Europe'," 1118.

21. Ibid.

22. When Césaire visited Dalmatia in 1935, it was part of the Kingdom of Yugoslavia, an independent but highly underdeveloped and mostly rural country with a literacy rate of around 50 percent.

23. Edward Said, "Third World Intellectuals and Metropolitan Culture," *Raritan* 9, no. 3 (1990): 31.

24. *Martinska-Martinique*, dir. Kiiru.

25. Most of this history is recounted by Césaire in *Martinska-Martinique*. Anja Jovic Humphrey also offers a very detailed account of the friendship Césaire shared with Guberina.

26. Samatar, "Martinska-Martinique," 274.

27. This is the version Césaire reads from in *Martinska-Martinique*. See: Aimé Césaire, *Cahier d'un retour au pays natal* (Paris: Présence Africaine, 1956).

28. Aimé Césaire, "Letter to Maurice Thorez," *Social Text* 28, no. 2 (2010): 146. Emphasis added.

29. Ibid., 150.

30. Ibid., 148.

31. Christopher T. Bonner, "Islands Between Worlds: Caribbean Cold War Literatures," in *The Palgrave Handbook of Cold War Literature*, edited by Andrew Hammond (London: Palgrave Macmillan, 2020), 442.

32. See: Christopher T. Bonner, "The Ferrements of Poetry: The Geopolitical Vision of Aimé Césaire's Cold War Poems," *International Journal of Francophone Studies* 19, no. 3-4 (2016): 298. This designation is of course problematic as it positions a white public figure as the norm, and a Black intellectual as merely its derivative.

33. David Alliot, "Le tapuscrit du Cahier d'un retour au pays natal," Assemblée Nationale, https://www.assemblee-nationale.fr/histoire/aime-cesaire/tapuscrit.asp.

34. *Martinska-Martinique*, dir. Kiiru.

35. Édouard Glissant, *Caribbean Discourse: Selected Essays*, trans. J. Michael Dash (University Press of Virginia, 1989), 20.

36. Celia Britton, *Edouard Glissant and Postcolonial Theory: Strategies of Language and Resistance* (University Press of Virginia, 1999), 25.

37. Glissant credits Michel Benamou with first advancing this theory.

38. Glissant, *Caribbean Discourse*, 21.

39. Ibid., 23.

40. Ibid.

41. Britton, *Edouard Glissant and Postcolonial Theory*, 27.

42. Glissant, cited in ibid.

43. Glissant, *Caribbean Discourse*, 23.

44. Ibid., 22.

45. Mireille Rosello and Robert Postawsko, "'One More Sea to Cross:' Exile and Intertextuality in Aimé Césaire's Cahier d'un retour au pays natal," *Yale French Studies*, no. 83 (1993): 176–195.

46. Vergès, "Martinska/Martinique," 26.

47. The English translation used in this text is that of Eshleman and Smith. See: Aimé Césaire, *Notebook of a Return to the Native Land*, trans. Clayton Eshleman and Annette Smith (Middletown, CT: Wesleyan University Press, 2001), 34. The original French will also be provided in footnotes. Here, the original reads: "Un nègre comique et laid et des femmes derrières moi ricanaient en le regardant. / Il était COMIQUE ET LAID, / COMIQUE ET LAID pour sûr. / J'arborai un grand sourire complice.../ Ma lâcheté retrouvée! / Je salue les trois siècles qui soutiennent mes droits civiques et mon sang minimisé. / Mon héroïsme, quelle farce!"

48. Césaire, *Notebook*, trans. Eshleman and Smith, 34.

49. Rosello and Postawsko, "'One More Sea to Cross'," 181.

50. Césaire, *Notebook*, trans. Eshleman and Smith, 39; the original reads: "j'accepte...j'accepte...entièrement, sans réserve.../ ma race qu'aucune ablution d'hysope et de lys mêlés ne pourrait purifier."

51. Césaire, *Notebook*, trans. Eshleman and Smith, 19; the original reads "... les Antilles qui ont faim, les Antilles grêlées de petite vérole..."

52. Marmande, "Aimé Césaire." The original reads: "A son retour chez lui, il me télégraphie: 'Aimé, qu'est-ce que tu fous à Paris? Tu t'emmerdes, c'est l'été, viens me voir à Zagreb.' Je n'ai pas un sou pour retourner en Martinique, et ce fou m'invite en Croatie. Bref, je prends le train. Au bout, sur le quai, sa famille me réserve un accueil extraordinaire. Les paysages, le découpé de la côte, l'exil, la mer, tout me rappelle la Martinique. Et du troisième étage de la maison, devant un paysage de splendeur qui me rappelait le Carbet, j'aperçois une nuée d'îles: 'Petar, regarde celle-là: c'est ma préférée, comment s'appelle-t-elle?—Martinska!—Mais alors! c'est la Martinique, Pierrot!' Autrement dit, faute d'argent, j'arrive dans un pays qui n'est pas le mien, dont on me dit qu'il se nomme Martinique. 'Passe-moi une feuille de papier!': ainsi commencé-je Cahier d'un retour au pays natal."

53. Édouard Glissant, *Poetics of Relation*, trans. Betsy Wing (University of Michigan Press, 2010), 10.

54. Ibid., 29.

55. *Martinska-Martinique*, dir. Kiiru.

56. Samatar, "Martinska-Martinique," 271.

57. Ibid., 270.

58. Césaire, *Notebook*, trans. Eshleman and Smith, 25; the original reads: "… la jeunesse du bourg se débauche."

59. Césaire, Vergès, and Smith, *Resolutely Black*, 7.

60. Césaire, *Notebook*, trans. Eshleman and Smith, 25; the original reads: "Comme il y a des hommes-hyènes et des hommes-panthères, je serai un homme-juif / un homme-cafre / un homme-hindou-de-Calcutta."

61. Samatar, "Martinska-Martinique," 271.

62. Vergès, "Martinska/Martinique," 29.

63. Césaire, *Notebook*, trans. Eshleman and Smith, 25; the original reads: "J'accepte…j'accepte…/…/ ma race rongée"

64. Samatar, "Martinska-Martinique," 272.

65. Césaire, *Notebook*, trans. Eshleman and Smith, 40; the original reads: "et la détermination de ma biologie, non prisonnière d'un angle facial, d'une forme de cheveux, d'un nez suffisamment aplati, d'un teint suffisamment mélanien, et la négritude, non plus un indice céphalique, ou un plasma, ou un soma, mais mesurée au compas de la souffrance."

66. Césaire, *Notebook*, trans. Eshleman and Smith, 42; the original reads: "Et voici ceux qui ne se consolent point de n'être pas faits à la ressemblance de Dieu mais du diable…"

67. Michael Naas, "The Time of a Detour: Jacques Derrida and the Question of the Gift," *Oxford Literary Review* 18, no. 1/2 (1996): 69.

68. Césaire, *Notebook*, trans. Eshleman and Smith, 36; the original reads: "Ceux qui n'ont inventé ni la poudre ni la boussole"

69. Jean Bernabé, Patrick Chamoiseau, and Raphaël Confiant, *Eloge de la créolité* (Paris: Gallimard, 1989).

70. See: Léopold Sédar Senghor, *Anthologie de la nouvelle poésie nègre et malgache de langue française* (Paris: Presses Universitaires de France, 1948).

71. Sartre, "Black Orpheus," trans. John MacCombie, 16.

72. Ibid., 18.

73. Souleymane Bachir Diagne, "Négritude," *The Stanford Encyclopedia of Philosophy*, edited by Edward Zalta and Uri Nodelman, first published 24 May 2010, revised 24 January 2023, https://plato.stanford.edu/archives/spr2023/entries/negritude/

74. See: Annick Thébia-Melsan and Gérard Lamoureux, eds., *Aimé Césaire: pour regarder le siècle en face* (Maisonneuve & Larose, 2000), 29.

75. Ibid. The original reads: "Le principe de la particularité, précisément par le fait de se développer pour soi jusqu'à la totalité, passe dans l'universel." Césaire made a similar argument on numerous occasions.

76. Miller, *The French Atlantic Triangle*.

77. Diagne, "La Négritude comme mouvement et comme devenir," 51.

78. Ripert, "Rethinking Négritude," 2.

79. Michelle Ann Stephens and Yolanda Martínez-San Miguel, eds., *Contemporary Archipelagic Thinking: Towards New Comparative Methodologies and Disciplinary Formations* (Rowman & Littlefield, 2020), 27.

80. Ibid., 41.

81. Marmande, "Aimé Césaire."

82. Antonio Benítez Rojo, *The Repeating Island: The Caribbean and the Postmodern Perspective*, trans. James E. Maraniss (Duke University Press, 1996), 2.

83. Césaire, *Notebook*, trans. Eshleman and Smith, 28; the original reads: "Et mon île non-clôture..."

84. James Clifford has thus spoken about Césaire's "poetics of neologism." See: James Clifford, "A Poetics of Neologism: Aimé Césaire," in *The Predicament of Culture: Twentieth-Century Ethnography, Literature, and Art* (Harvard University Press, 1988). And Gregson Davis has analyzed the "syntactical ambiguity" of Césaire, resulting from uncommon sentence constructions and infrequent punctuation, in his introduction to the English translation of Césaire's *Non-Vicious Circle*. See: Aimé Césaire, *Non-Vicious Circle*, trans. Gregson Davis (Stanford University Press, 1984).

85. "Au bout du petit matin..."

86. "Au bout du petit matin bourgeonnant d'anses frêles les Antilles.../.../ Au bout du petit matin, sur cette plus fragile épaisseur de terre que dépasse de façon humiliante son grandiose avenir—les volcans éclateront.../.../ Au bout du petit matin, cette ville inerte et ses au-delà de lèpres.../.../ Au bout du petit matin, le morne au sabot inquiet et docile..."

87. Brent Hayes Edwards has in fact proposed a reading of *Cahier* through a theory of anaphora, focusing specifically on Césaire's negative definition of Négritude in the poem: "Ma négritude n'est pas une pierre, sa surdité ruée / Contre la clameur du jour / ma négritude n'est pas une taie d'eau morte sur l'œil mort de la terre / ma négritude n'est ni une tour ni une cathédrale." Edwards argues that anaphoras in *Cahier* "may not have to do with 'regularity,' nor with what other critics have diagnosed either as 'invariance'...or as rhythmic primitivism (an evocation of 'tribal frenzy' and 'delirium' that would somehow be 'properly African and concrete'." Rather, "it may be precisely the element of repetition that adds a qualification, an element of uncertainty, to a proposition that could otherwise be taken as a singular declaration." See: Brent Hayes Edwards, "Aimé Césaire and the Syntax of Influence," *Research in African Literatures* 36, no. 2 (2005): 8. I would like to build on Edwards' analysis, and thus to think about Césaire's anaphoras as forming an archipelago.

88. Wilder, *Freedom Time*, 23.

89. Césaire, *Notebook*, trans. Eshleman and Smith, 26–27; the original reads: "Partir. Mon cœur bruissait de générosités emphatiques. Partir...j'arriverais lisse et jeune dans ce pays mien et je dirais à ce pays dont le limon entre dans la composition de ma chair: 'J'ai longtemps erré et je reviens vers la hideur désertée de

vos plaies.' /.../ Et je lui dirais encore: 'Ma bouche sera la bouche des malheurs qui n'ont point de bouche, ma voix, la liberté de celles qui s'affaissent au cachot du désespoir.' /.../ Et voici que je suis venu!"

90. "Dans cette destruction se manifesteront à titre égal les qualités de toutes les races et un monde nouveau se bâtira avec le concours de toutes les races." Césaire, *Cahier d'un retour au pays natal*, 14.

91. I agree with Gary Wilder that Césaire is interested less in "criticizing modern universality from the standpoint of black particularity than to project a model of humanity onto the world stage from an Antillean perspective." See: Wilder, *Freedom Time*, 24.

92. Nick Nesbitt, "Antinomies of Double Consciousness in Aimé Césaire's 'Cahier d'un retour au pays natal'," *Mosaic: An Interdisciplinary Critical Journal* 33, no. 3 (2000): 125.

93. Aimé Césaire, *Discours sur le colonialisme suivi de Discours sur la Négritude* (Paris: Présence Africaine, 2004). "l'histoire d'une communauté dont l'expérience apparaît, à vrai dire, singulière avec ses déportations de populations, ses transferts d'hommes d'un continent à l'autre, les souvenirs de croyances lointaines, ses débris de cultures assassinées."

94. Nesbitt, "Antinomies of Double Consciousness," 111.

95. Samatar, "Martinska-Martinique," 274.

96. Noëlle Diamant-Berger, "René Depestre pleure Aimé Césaire: 'Je suis redevenu orphelin'," *Negritude* (blog), 23 April 2008, https://aime-cesaire.blogspot.com/2008/04/ren-depestre-pleure-aim-csaire-je-suis.html. The original reads: "Et savez-vous ce que Césaire m'a dit? Tu sais, tu auras été le meilleur d'entre nous, car tu as gardé l'innocence de la fraternité. Toi, tu n'as jamais connu la haine."

97. Wilder, *Freedom Time*, 3.

98. Petar Guberina, *Zvuk i Pokret u Jeziku* (Zagreb: Matica Hrvatska, 1952).

99. Ibid., 24. The original reads: "artikulirana riječ, koja je težila oslobađanju od prirodne nužde, i prirodni zvuk i pokret (vrednote govornog jezika), koji je bio vezan za prirodnu stvarnost."

100. Ibid., 26. The original reads: "oponašanje...kretanja i promjena stvari u prirodi."

101. Ibid., 92–93. The original reads: "Čujemo kako veliki crnački književnik Aimé Césaire iznosi svoj revolt zbog situacije u kolonijama...Sve riječi, koje je upotrebio Aimé Césaire pokreti su, prijetnje rukom, srdžba izražena pokretima i zvukovima, kao da slušamo ritam sinkopirane muzike."

102. "L'émotion est nègre, comme la raison est hellène." This is one of Senghor's most contentious statements about Négritude. Léopold Sédar Senghor, *Liberté I, Négritude et humanisme* (Paris: Seuil, 1964): 288.

103. Petar Guberina, *Povezanost Jezičkih Elemenata* (Zagreb: Matica Hrvatska, 1952).

104. Ibid., 75. The original reads: "Gledanje na jezične elemente sa stanovišta forme, bez obzira na povezanost s drugim izražajnim elementima, dovodi dalje

do toga, da se počešće iz 'karaktera,' koji se daje pojedinim izoliranim rečima, oblicima, izvlači 'karakter' i tip mišljenja ovog naroda, koji tim i takvim jezikom govori."

105. Ibid., 87. In the original, Guberina discusses these French thinkers in French; it reads: "Le sauvage...donne par exemple aux considérations spatiales une attention plus grande peut être que n'en accordent nos languages aux considérations temporelles...Or, le temps est d'un degré d'abstraction plus élevé que l'espace."

106. See: Diagne, "Négritude."

107. Guberina, *Povezanost Jezičkih Elemenata*, 89. The original (again in French) reads: "Le Bantou considère tout ce qui existe, soit comme une force influente, soit au contraire comme une force influencée, étrangère à sa vie ou liée à sa vie...En Europe on conçoit les choses séparément, sans rapport intérieur, indépendantes les unes des autres..."

108. *Martinska-Martinique*, dir. Kiiru.

Chapter Two

1. "Afrika je dio moga života i s kulturnog i s emocionalnog stanovišta. Kad sam 1961. stupio prvi put na afričko tlo, kad me Senghor pozvao na proslavu nezavisnosti Senegala, to je bio najveći doživljaj u mome životu." Guberina made this statement in an interview he gave to *Danas* in December 1989, which has since been re-published in several places. See: Petar Guberina, "Politika Je Progutala Jezik," in *Drugo čitanje*, edited by Mirko Galić (Zagreb: Matica Hrvatska, 2007).

2. "J'ai eu, moi aussi, comme c'était la mode au Quartier Latin, dans les années 30, ma crise de slavophilie, favorisée, il est vrai, par la fréquentation d'un camarade yougoslave, Petar Guberina, devenu depuis, un des plus grands linguistes de notre temps." Léopold Sédar Senghor, Response to the Toast Made by President Josip Broz Tito, 2 September 1975, AJ, KPR, I-3-a/103-10.

3. Gary Wilder, *Freedom Time: Negritude, Decolonization, and the Future of the World* (Duke University Press, 2015), 136.

4. Frantz Fanon, *The Wretched of the Earth*, trans. Richard Philcox (New York: Grove Press, 2004), 11.

5. Wilder, *Freedom Time*, 136.

6. Ibid., 135.

7. He described this experience in his 1948 poetry collection *Hosties noires* (*Black Sacrifices*).

8. Benyamin Neuberger, "The African Concept of Balkanisation," *The Journal of Modern African Studies* 14, no. 3 (1976): 523.

9. Ibid.

10. This federation of eight French colonial territories, the capital of which was located in Senegal, was first restructured and renamed in 1958, and then collapsed in 1960.

11. On 28 September 1958, a constitutional referendum was held throughout the French Union (i.e., French colonial territories) on whether to adopt the new French Constitution, which would grant four months to each territory to decide whether to remain an overseas territory, become a state of the French Community, or become an overseas department. By voting "no", Guinea opted for outright independence.

12. Neuberger, "The African Concept of Balkanisation," 524.

13. "Tout ce que l'on peut admettre, c'est que l'on crée éventuellement, par traité si les circonstances sont favorables, une assemblée consultative du type de celle de l'Assemblée consultative de Strasbourg, de celle du Conseil nordique ou de l'Union balkanique." Léopold Sédar Senghor, "Pour une République Fédérale," *Politique étrangère* 21, no. 2 (1956): 165–174.

14. Léopold Sédar Senghor, "Balkanisation ou Fédération," *Afrique Nouvelle* (December 1956).

15. Wilder, *Freedom Time*, 155.

16. See: Léopold Sédar Senghor, "Je vous dis que la France est un arbre vivant," address to the French National Assembly, 29 January 1957.

17. "on veut à tout prix empêcher toute solidarité politique et administrative entre des territoires que tout lie, non seulement les structures économiques, mais encore la race, la culture, l'organisation administrative et les aspirations politiques." Ibid.

18. "par les pouvoirs du haut-commissaire, mais exercés par l'État, c'est-à-dire en fait par la métropole. Comme si l'on pouvait faire le bonheur des peuples sans leur participation active!" Ibid.

19. "toutes ces solidarités naturelles dont on veut nous priver." Ibid.

20. "Mais nous sommes aujourd'hui en 1957, au XXe siècle, à l'heure où les États et les empires les plus forts sont de structure fédérale: USA, URSS, Inde, Canada, Brésil, Allemagne occidentale, Yougoslavie et, plus près de nous, l'Angleterre qui va donner l'indépendance à la Gold Coast au sein du Commonwealth, lequel a cessé d'être britannique. Fédérer effraye certains membres de l'Assemblée. Mais, mes chers collègues, fédérer n'est pas séparer. Fédérer, au sens étymologique du mot, c'est lier, mais sans étouffer, on l'oublie trop souvent." Ibid.

21. Léopold Sédar Senghor, "Rapport sur la doctrine el le programme du parti," in *Nation et voie africaine du socialisme* (Paris: Présence Africaine, 1961), 7.

22. "si la balkanisation de l'Afrique noire de langue française devait se maintenir, ils n'auraient plus qu'à fermer les portes de leurs usines." Ibid., 21.

23. "Un peuple n'est pas réellement indépendant quand, acquise l'indépendance nominale, ses dirigeants importent, telles quelles, des institutions—politiques, économiques, sociales, culturelles—qui sont, ailleurs, les fruits naturels de la géographie, de l'histoire, de la race." Ibid., 8.

24. For further discussion and also existing critiques of The First World Festival of Negro Arts, See: David Murphy, *The First World Festival of Negro Arts, Dakar 1966: Contexts and Legacies* (Liverpool: Liverpool University Press, 2016); Nijah Cunningham, "Quiet Dawn: Time, Aesthetics, and the Afterlives of Black Radicalism," PhD diss. (Columbia University, 2015).

25. Wilder, *Freedom Time*, 214.

26. Senghor, *Liberté 1* (Paris: Seuil, 1964), 9.

27. Wilder, *Freedom Time*, 206.

28. "La structure fédérale—la décentralisation et la déconcentration—sera étendue, dans le cadre même de l'Etat fédéré, aux collectivités régionales et communales jusque dans les domaines économique et social. Les structures yougoslaves, adaptées à nos réalités, nous serviront, en l'occurrence, de modèle. Ainsi nous comblerons le vide qui existe actuellement entre l'Etat fédéré et le village." Senghor, "Rapport sur la doctrine el le programme du parti," 72.

29. Maria Todorova, *Imagining the Balkans* (New York: Oxford University Press, 2009), 35.

30. Telegram from Assistant Secretary of State for Foreign Affairs to the Cabinet of the President of the Republic, 9 June 1961, AJ, KPR, I-3-a/103-10.

31. "Report on Senegal Compiled by the State Secretariat for Foreign Affairs," 15 July 1961, AJ, KPR, I-3-a/103-10.

32. Wilder, *Freedom Time*, 208.

33. Mamadou Diouf, "Senegalese Development: From Mass Mobilization to Technocratic Elitism," in *International Development and the Social Sciences: Essays on the History and Politics of Knowledge*, edited by Frederick Cooper and Randall Packard (University of California Press, 1997), 304.

34. Mamadou Diouf explains that "the political entrepreneurs were able to successfully resist the Diaist enterprise. The marabouts developed a certain capacity to turn the new structures to their advantage, they gained a direct foothold, for the first time, in the modern sectors (the cooperatives and the CERS). The traders who controlled the most important economic network, the groundnut network, were the principal victims of this policy." See: Diouf, "Senegalese Development," 305.

35. See: Valérie Nivelon, "La voix Mamadou Dia (3/3) en exclusivité sur RFI," *La Marche du Monde*, RFI, 17 April 2020; and Valérie Nivelon, "Mamadou Dia parle, histoire d'une archive inédite," RFI, 25 January 2019, https://www.rfi.fr/fr/afrique/20190125-mamadou-dia-parle-histoire-archive-inedite-senegal-senghor.

36. It should be noted that Senegal wasn't the only African country where leaders believed that postcolonial socialist projects could draw on traditional rural organizations. In Tanzania, for instance, Julius Nyerere built the national development program around the concept of *ujamaa* (familyhood), which he believed reflected communitarian values of the precolonial past. See: Priya Lal, *African Socialism in Postcolonial Tanzania: Between the Village and the World* (Cambridge University Press, 2015).

37. Nivelon, "La voix Mamadou Dia (3/3) en exclusivité sur RFI."

38. Ljubica Spaskovska, "Comrades, Poets, Politicians: Aco Šopov, Léopold Sédar Senghor and the Cultural Politics of Non-Alignment" (presented at the Towards a Conjuctural Political Economy of Non-Alignment and Cultural Politics Research Workshop, Rijeka, 27–29 September 2021).

39. Aco Šopov, *Pesna na crnata žena* (Skopje: Misla, 1976).

40. The Award of the Anti-Fascist Council of the People's Liberation of Yugoslavia (AVNOJ Award for short) was the highest state award in the Socialist Federal Republic of Yugoslavia (SFRJ) from 1966 to 1990. It was granted to those creators in the field of art and science whose works had a special significance for the development of SFRJ.

41. "Песник је истраживач. Али истраживач нарочите врсте. Он трага за нечим чега нема и што не постоји у природном реду ствари, откривајући њихов дубљи и трајни смисао. Песма постоји јер не постоји у том реду. У противном, она постаје голи податак који нема никакве уметничке вредности." Miodrag Drugovac, "Razgovor sa Acom Šopovim," *Književne novine*, 15 August 1970, 12.

42. Léopold Sédar Senghor, "La voie africaine du socialisme: nouvel essai de définition," in *Liberté II: Nation et Voie Africaine du Socialisme* (Paris: Seuil, 1971), 287.

43. "Песма није само свест о егзистенцији, она је и свест о себи, и због тога се и потврђује и остварује у непрекидном судару и са стварношћу и са самом собом. Другим речима, она је свест о непрекидно мењаној људској стварности и сопственог бића." Šopov, "Песма је свест о непрекидно мењаној стварности."

44. Африка је на мене — на пример — огромно утицала: она је пре свега била невероватно откриће за мене. Отишао сам тамо с потпуно погрешним представама, иако сам се припремао да тај сусрет буде што безболнији. За то своје „откриће" црне Африке највише дугујем богатој поезији Леополда Сенгора. Он ми је више казао о Африци него брда књига које сам прочитао! Он је од веровања, легенди, прича, успео да направи поезију која је један прави песнички универзум. Цео свет је сагледао кроз једно мало, непознато сенегалско место — своје родно место.

Сенгор је за мене један од највећих песника савременог света и сјајан пример шта поезија значи: колико може да каже човеку, без обзира колико је он, на први поглед, странац и туђин. Из тога сам за себе извукао драгоцен наук: ако човек хоће да боље упозна себе, своју земљу, свој народ, онда он мора да добро зна и друге. И друго: кад себе и своју средину сагледаш из друге перспективе, рецимо из афричке, многе ствари које те код куће тиште постану много разумљивије, неке сасвим друкчије. А поезија у оба случаја игра неслућено велику улогу! Aco Šopov, "Poezija Otkriva Svet," *Politika*, 15 February 1976.

45. "Telo tvoje crna maslina, / Najtamnija bronza, najdublji zvuk, / Zvuk tam-tama tvojih predaka, iz njihove / Starinske kore." Šopov, *Pesna na crnata žena*.

46. "Еден духовен свет, лоциран на мал географски простор како што е крајот на Серерите во Сенегал, израснува пред наши очи во свет со универзални димензии и универзално значење. Со магичноста на поетскиот збор Сенгор го преобразува овој свет во исклучив поетски универзум, секому близок и достапен." Leopold Sedar Sengor, *Poezija: Izbor*, trans. Aco Šopov (Skopje: Nova Makedonija, 1975).

47. "можат да се нурнат во неизмерните длабини на душата и духовниот свет на својот роден крај и од него да излезат со пораки за човештвото." Sengor, *Poezija: Izbor.*

48. "Штип и Жоал / Еден под Исарот / друг на Океанот / А исти љубови / исти бранувања / и исти поетски маки и сонувања." See: "Во Штип и во Жоал" in *Pesna na crnata žena.*

49. In 2006, on the occasion of the Senghor Year in Macedonia, Aco Šopov's daughter published a bilingual French-Macedonian selection of fifty poems by the Senegalese and Macedonian poets, underlining their similarities. See: Jasmina Šopova, *Sengor – Šopov: Paraleli* (Skopje: Sigmapres, 2006).

50. Telegram from the Yugoslav Embassy in Dakar to the Ministry of Foreign Affairs, 25 April 1975, AJ, KPR, I-3-a/103-10.

51. "se Marksove i Lenjinove misli rasvetljavaju i primenjuju u Jugoslovenskim uslovima." Telegram from the Yugoslav Embassy in Dakar to the Ministry of Foreign Affairs, 25 April 1975, AJ, KPR, I-3-a/103-10.

52. Note from Ministry of Foreign Affairs to President Tito, 7 February 1974, AJ, KPR, I-3-a/103-10.

53. The exhibit was funded entirely by the Senegalese government.

54. Yugoslav Ministry of Foreign Affairs, "Information About the Struga Poetry Evening of 1975," 28 August 1975, AJ, KPR, I-3-a/103-10.

55. Janet G. Vaillant, *Black, French, and African: A Life of Léopold Sédar Senghor* (Harvard University Press, 2013), 325.

56. Ibid., 319.

57. Ibid., 325.

58. Ibid.

59. Ibid., 330.

60. Wilder, *Freedom Time.*

61. Vaillant, *Black, French, and African*, 330.

62. Minutes from the Conversation between Josip Broz Tito and Léopold Sédar Senghor, 2 September 1975, AJ, KPR, I-3-a/103-10.

63. The OERS was founded in 1968 in yet another attempt by Senghor to encourage regional federalism and de-balkanize Africa. Senghor described its founding as "the first time that [African] states are creating a confederation." However, when political tensions between Senegal and Guinea escalated, Guinea withdrew from the organization, significantly weakening it. See: Senghor cited in Robert A. Mortimer, "From Federalism to Francophonia: Senghor's African Policy," *African Studies Review* 15, no. 2 (1972): 291.

64. Ibid.

65. "parmi les pays d'Europe qui sont, pour nous du Tiers-Monde, non précisément un modèle, mais un exemple significatif." Senghor, Response to the Toast Made by President Josip Broz Tito.

66. Souleymane Bachir Diagne, "A Note on African Socialism," *African Arts* 54, no. 3 (2021) : 1.

67. "les choses, comme les vivants, sont en perpétuel devenir. Elles renferment, en elles, leur propre négation—sans parler de l'action réciproque des unes sur les autres—des contradictions intérieures, qui, développant leur mouvement naturel, amèneront la destruction de ces choses, plus exactement, leurs transformations en de nouvelles synthèses ou symbioses, en de nouvelles réalités." Senghor, "Rapport sur la doctrine el le programme du parti," 62.

68. Souleymane Bachir Diagne, *Postcolonial Bergson*, trans. Lindsay Turner (Fordham University Press, 2019), 54.

69. " C'est grâce à l'autogestion que le travailleur yougoslave a pu échapper aux contraintes qui entravaient l'épanouissement de sa personne, et cela dans le respect des principes de liberté individuelle et de développement communautaire." Senghor, Response to the Toast Made by President Josip Broz Tito.

70. Ibid.

71. "Partis des textes mêmes de Marx et d'Engels, vous en avez fait une relecture lucide à la lumière de vos réalités nationales et de celles de notre XXe siècle. Synthèse donc, plus exactement symbiose, c'est à dire œuvre vivante, entre le Plan et le Marché, la contrainte de la discipline, imposée par les réalités, et la liberté de la pensée créatrice, qui est la conquête de l'homme." Senghor, Response to the Toast Made by President Josip Broz Tito.

72. Léopold Sédar Senghor, "De la Négritude," in *Liberté V: Le dialogue des cultures* (Paris: Seuil, 1993), 18.

73. Ibid., 19.

74. Pierre Teilhard de Chardin was a French Jesuit priest, scientist, paleontologist, theologian, philosopher, and teacher. He was the author of several influential theological and philosophical texts.

75. Léopold Sédar Senghor, *Pierre Teilhard De Chardin Et La Politique Africaine* (Paris: Seuil, 1962).

76. Léopold Sédar Senghor, *On African Socialism* (New York: Praeger, 1964), 135.

77. Léopold Sédar Senghor, "Hommage à Pierre Teilhard De Chardin," in *Liberté V: Le dialogue des cultures* (Paris: Seuil, 1993).

78. Senghor, *On African Socialism*, 140.

79. Ibid., 146.

80. Diagne, "A Note on African Socialism," 1.

81. The New International Economic Order (NIEO) consists of a series of proposals put forward by developing countries to dismantle economic colonialism and reduce dependency, aiming to create a new, interdependent global economy. Though the United Nations General Assembly adopted the Declaration for the Establishment of a New International Economic Order in 1974, developed countries blocked its implementation. For a more detailed discussion of NIEO, See: Adom Getachew, *Worldmaking after Empire: The Rise and Fall of Self-Determination* (Princeton University Press, 2019).

82. See: Senghor, Response to the Toast Made by President Josip Broz Tito.

83. See: Léopold Sédar Senghor, "Preface," in *The New International Economic Order: Philosophical and Socio-Cultural Implications*, edited by Hans Köchler (International Progress Organization, 1980).

84. "Pour nous Sénégalais, ni l'Islam ni le Christianisme, et moins encore le Colonisateur, n'ont réussi à altérer fondamentalement nos valeurs culturelles, celles de la Négritude, qu'exprime, avec tant de force, chacune des six ethnies qui forment notre nation. Ces valeurs de l'Islam et du Christianisme, comme les valeurs européennes au demeurant, nous les avant tout simplement intégrées dans notre héritage culturel.

Il me plait de constater que, pour vous aussi, malgré des siècles de domination, qu'il s'agisse de l'Empire ottoman ou de celui de Habsbourg, l'âme populaire yougoslave est restée fidèle à ses traits culturels: aux valeurs éternelles de la Slavitude…

C'est dans cet esprit, que vous avez, depuis 1948, élaboré—et pratiqué—un fédéralisme des républiques et des régions, dans le but ultime est de favoriser les valeurs originales, populaires, de chaque ethnie, toutes valeurs dont la symbiose permettra au peuple yougoslave d'atteindre, dans le domaine culturel, un développement maximum. C'est encore Marx qui parlait du 'charme éternel' de l'art grec parce que fils de 'l'imagination populaire'…

La coopération yougoslave-sénégalaise s'est nouée au lendemain de notre indépendance nationale. Je forme l'espoir qu'a l'occasion de ce voyage et de nos entretiens, nous adoptions un certain nombre de mesures qui renforceront cette coopération, non seulement de la construction socialiste, mais encore de l'édification de la Civilisation de l'Universel." Senghor, Response to the Toast Made by President Josip Broz Tito.

85. Léopold Sédar Senghor, press conference, Struga Poetry Evenings, broadcast on Radio Belgrade, 1975, Radio Belgrade Archive.

86. Ibid.

87. Ibid.

88. I borrow this term from Yohann Ripert, See: Yohann C. Ripert, "Rethinking Négritude: Aimé Césaire & Léopold Sédar Senghor and the Imagination of a Global Postcoloniality" (PhD diss., Columbia University, 2017).

89. Patrick Williams and Laura Chrisman, eds., *Colonial Discourse and Post-Colonial Theory: A Reader* (Columbia University Press, 1994), 31.

90. *Leopold Sedar Senghor*, directed by Kiril Cenevski (1975).

91. Williams and Chrisman, *Colonial Discourse and Post-Colonial Theory*, 34.

92. "Jezik, pojedini vokali i konsonanti izlaze is crnačkog umjetnika kao arhitektonski ili plastični materijal koji gradi jezičnu cjelinu u kojoj ječi zajedničnim glasom i ton i glas i riječ i rečenica. I to ne zbog toga sto bi afrički jezici bili primitivni ili siromašni, ili što bi bili na stadiju slijepe imitacije prirodnih glasova… nego zato što je ritmički element muzike u svakom momentu prisutan i sklapa glasove riječi u harmoničnu cjelinu." Petar Guberina, "Postface," *Genij Afrike* (Zagreb: Stvarnost, 1969), 306.

93. Petar Guberina, "Guberina's Report to the Federal Institute for Technological, Cultural and Scientific Cooperation About His Trip to Senegal," Scientific and technological cooperation SFRJ-Senegal, Vol. 465, ф1718, Archives of Yugoslavia. These documents were destroyed in a flood and are no longer available in the Archives; thus, I am extremely thankful to Nemanja Radonjić for sharing copies with me.

94. "Leopold Sedar Sengor je odjednom zastao. Stajao je kraj starih zidina srednjovekovne crkve sv. Pantelejmona, na uzvišici, tačno u podne, zadivljen posmatrao zelenkastu liniju jezera koja se spajala s horizontom. Ranije su nam rekli da predsednik Republike Senegal, političar i najveći živi pesnik Afrike, laureat 'Zlatnog venca Struških večeri poezije za 1975. godinu' i naš dragi gost, ovako uobičava da nad vodama, bilo da je u Sengalu na Atlantiku ili na obali Sene, ili kao sada u Ohridu, ispituje svoje prave doživljaje, i kao čovek i kao poeta." Léopold Sédar Senghor, "Još se nisam odužio ženi," interview by Dušan Grbić, *Ilustrovana Politika*, n.879, 9 September 1975.

Chapter Three

1. Charles Forsdick, "Local, National, Regional, Global: Glissant and the Postcolonial Manifesto," in *Caribbean Globalizations, 1492 to the Present Day*, edited by Eva Sansavior and Richard Scholar (Liverpool University Press, 2015), 230.

2. Chris Bongie, *Friends and Enemies: The Scribal Politics of Post/Colonial Literature* (Liverpool University Press, 2008), 329. Similarly, Jean-Marie Salien writes that, in 1988, when he published *Hadriana in All My Dreams*, "Depestre was in the midst of a transition from writer of public interest (decolonization, Marxism, anti-imperialism) to a writer of private interest (eroticism, aestheticism)." See: Jean-Marie Salien, "Croyances populaires haïtiennes dans *Hadriana dans tous mes rêves* de René Depestre," *The French Review* 74, no. 1 (2000): 82–93. And, according to Philip Kaisary, once he achieved literary fame, Depestre renounced any explicit political engagement. See: Philip Kaisary, *The Haitian Revolution in the Literary Imagination: Radical Horizons, Conservative Constraints* (University of Virginia Press, 2014).

3. Katell Colin-Thebaudeau described Depestre's later work as "nothing more than an unbridled praisesong to pleasure and the body," for instance. See: K. Colin-Thebaudeau, "Rene Depestre: The Ground Made Flesh," *Etudes françaises* 41, no. 2 (2005), 50.

4. See: Alexandra Perisic and René Depestre, "A Secret Love Affair: An Interview with René Depestre," *Transition* 128 (2019): 108–118.

5. John Rodden, *Performing the Literary Interview: How Writers Craft Their Public Selves* (University of Nebraska Press, 2001), 10.

6. In fact, most scholars have described the literary interview as a hybrid genre, somewhere between the personal and the objective. See: Anneleen Masschelein, Christophe Meurée, David Martens, and Stéphanie Vanasten. "The Literary Interview: Towards a Poetics of a Hybrid Genre." *Poetics Today* 35.1–2 (2014): 1–49; Stephen Arkin, "Composing the Self: The Literary Interview as Form." *International Journal of Oral History* 4, no.1 (1983): 12–18.

7. By 1932, Aragon had announced his break with Breton and surrealism, due to his commitment to communist politics and socialist-realist aesthetics.

8. "Je suis en train de résoudre, grâce à Aragon, le conflit où se débattait mon individualisme formel." René Depestre, "Lettre À Charles Dobzynski," *Les lettres françaises* 573 (1955), 5.

9. Ibid.

10. "Un débat autour des conditions d'une poésie nationale chez les peuples noirs."

11. "Un débat autour des conditions d'une poésie nationale chez les peuples noirs," *Présence Africaine* 4 (1955): 36–38.

12. "est-il vrai que tu doutes de la forêt natale / de nos voix rauques de nos cœurs qui nous remontent amers / de nos yeux de rhum rouge de nos fruits incendiés / se peut-il / que les pluies de l'exil / aient détendu la peau de tambour de ta voix." Aimé Césaire and Nicolas Guillén, "Réponse à Depestre poète haïtien (Eléments d'un art poétique)," *Présence Africaine* 1/2 (1955): 113–15.

13. "ce n'est pas la communauté de langue ni de race qui détermine le caractère national d'une culture, mais en dernière analyse, les conditions de vie, les conditions de développement historique propres à chaque pays." René Depestre, "Réponse à Aimé Césaire (Introduction à un art poétique haïtien)," *Présence Africaine* 4 (1955): 45.

14. Kaiama L. Glover, "'The Francophone World Was Set Ablaze': Pan-African Intellectuals, European Interlocutors and the Global Cold War," *Postcolonial Studies* 24, no. 4 (2021): 464–483.

15. René Depestre, *Bonjour et adieu à la négritude: Suivi de Travaux d'identité* (Paris: R. Laffont, 1980).

16. The positions of Césaire and Depestre have been considered different enough that Martin Munro based his doctoral dissertation on this comparison, for instance. See: Martin Munro, *Shaping and Reshaping the Caribbean: The Work of Aimé Césaire and René Depestre* (Leeds, UK: Maney Publishing for the Modern Humanities Research Association, 2000).

17. Christopher T. Bonner, "Islands Between Worlds: Caribbean Cold War Literatures," in *The Palgrave Handbook of Cold War Literature*, edited by Andrew Hammond (London: Palgrave Macmillan, 2020), 439.

18. "…eut l'effet d'une bombe tant elle s'était placée dans le droit fil de l'esprit contestataire qui avait été celui du surréalisme, à ses débuts, dans le Paris des années 20." René Depestre, *Le métier à métisser* (Paris: Stock, 1998), 101.

19. "Le pays tout entier se trouvait à nos côtés. On peut imaginer l'allégresse d'André Breton devant la sorte de 'Mai 68' avant la lettre que les jeunes d'Haïti lui offraient, en hommage aux valeurs libertaires du surréalisme." Ibid., 102.

20. Ibid.

21. Paul B. Miller, "¿Un cubano más?: An Interview with René Depestre about his Cuban Experience," *Afro-Hispanic Review* 34, no. 2 (2015): 172.

22. Ibid., 170.

23. Forsdick, "Local, National, Regional, Global"; and Joan Dayan, "'Hallelujah for a Garden-Woman': The Caribbean Adam and His Pretext," *The French Review* 59, no. 4 (1986): 581–595.

24. It should be noted that in various writings, including the 1992 poem "Adieu à la révolution" ("Farewell to the Revolution") and the 1998 essay collection *Ainsi parle le fleuve noir* (*So Speaks the Black River*), Depestre publicly renounced radical politics.

25. Dayan, "'Hallelujah for a Garden-Woman'," 581.

26. René Depestre, *Alléluia pour une femme-jardin: récits d'amour solaire* (Montréal: Leméac, 1973), 91.

27. Joan Dayan, "France Reads Haiti: René Depestre's Hadriana Dans Tous Mes Rêves," *Yale French Studies* 83 (1993): 154–175. For an extensive overview of the reception of *Hadriana*, See: Kaiama Glover, *A Regarded Self: Caribbean Womanhood and the Ethics of Disorderly Being* (Duke University Press, 2021).

28. Glover, *A Regarded Self*, 74.

29. Hal Wylie, Review of *Éros dans un train chinois: Neuf histoires d'amour et un conte de sorcier* by René Depestre, *World Literature Today* 66, no. 1 (1992) : 189.

30. Robert J. Hartwig, "Review of *Éros dans un train chinois* by René Depestre," *The French Review* 65, no. 6 (1992): 1077–1078.

31. Miller, "¿Un cubano más?" 166.

32. Ibid., 175.

33. *Pruga Šamac-Sarajevo: Dar Omladine Titu i Narodu* (Zagreb: Novo pokoljenje, 1947).

34. Sweden's Olof Palme, Canada's Pierre Trudeau, and Belgium's Pierre Alechinsky all joined international brigades. See: Andrea Matošević and Tanja Petrović, *Duh Pruge: Zbornik Radova o Knjizi E.P. Thompsona* (Belgrade: Fabrika Knjiga, 2020).

35. Once a member of the Communist Party of Great Britain (which he left after the 1956 Soviet invasion of Hungary), Thompson was a prominent voice in both the British New Left of the 1950s and the Nuclear Disarmament Campaign of the 1980s. He remains most widely known as the author of *The Making of the English Working Class* (1963), in which he traced the emergence of a working-class identity in early nineteenth-century Britain.

36. Edward P. Thompson, ed. *The Railway: An Adventure in Construction* (Helsinki: Rab-Rab Press, 2020), 13.

37. Ibid., 74.

38. Nika Autor, dir. *Newsreel 242—Sunny Railways*. Newsreel Front, 2023.

39. "borba sa silama prirode, borba sa greškama prošlosti, borba sa predrasudima i rđavim nasleđima u nama, otpočeće građenje prve veće pruge normalnog koloseka u Bosni i Hercegovini." See: Matošević and Petrović, *Duh Pruge: Zbornik Radova o Knjizi E.P. Thompsona*, 112.

40. " Deux cent neuf mille garçons et filles se proposaient en 199 journées de labeur de construire une ligne ferroviaire. Ils avaient à poser 300 kilomètres de rails, 429 000 traverses, 289 appareils d'aiguillage. On aurait aussi à percer 9 tunnels et à édifier 803 ouvrages en béton, y compris 9 ponts d'une longueur totale de 2 469 mètres." René Depestre, "La jupe," in *Éros dans un train chinois* (Paris: Gallimard, 1993), 61.

41. Thompson, *The Railway*, 64.

42. See: Matošević and Petrović, *Duh Pruge: Zbornik Radova o Knjizi E.P. Thompsona.*

43. Ibid.

44. See: Nicole Lindstrom, "Yugonostalgia: Restorative and Reflective Nostalgia in Former Yugoslavia," *East Central Europe* 32, no. 1–2 (2005): 227–237.

45. See: Matošević and Petrović, *Duh Pruge: Zbornik Radova o Knjizi E.P. Thompsona*, 160.

46. "Dans le train en gare du Nord, à notre arrivée dans le compartiment, deux garçons tenaient compagnie à deux demoiselles. Durant les deux cents premiers kilomètres, il n'y eut pas plus de dix-neuf mots d'échanges entre nous six. Chantal et moi, on était assis dans le sens de la marche, côté couloir. On était tout à notre fringale de vivre. En face de nous les deux beautés, visiblement parisiennes du seizième arrondissement, ne décampaient pas de leur quant-à-soi des beaux quartiers. Côté fenêtre, les jeunes gens, gais lurons à fleurs de mots et de peau du Midi, se moquaient d'elles, sans retenue, dans un occitan flamboyant. Ils étaient de Lézignan-Corbières." Depestre, "La jupe," 55.

47. "Écoutez, dis-je, parlant à la cantonade, le monde se remet à peine d'un conflit meurtrier. C'est le premier été qui rouvre à la jeunesse les frontières de l'Europe. Pour sûr les jeunes Yougoslaves qui nous ont invités seraient dépités de voir débarquer chez eux une tribu de rabat-joie aux têtes d'enterrement." Depestre, "La jupe," 56.

48. "Le côté païen et solaire de mon tempérament d'homme de la caraïbe situe d'emblée ma vision de l'amour à l'inverse de l'expérience douloureuse qui a marqué l'aventure historique de l'Eros occidental." Depestre, *Le métier à métisser* (Paris: Stock, 1998), 105.

49. Depestre, *Bonjour et adieu à la négritude.*

50. Depestre, *Le métier à métisser*, 107.

51. "Aux caraïbes, à l'heure du coq et du jardin enchanté, homme et femme se débarrassent allègrement du sentiment du péché. Ils se laissent dehors mourir de faim et de soif, tandis qu'ils font l'amour, en êtres libres et souverains qui reinventent les quatres saisons, la foire aux étoiles, la roue magique de la beauté, dans un état de poésie et d'émerveillement follement réciproque". Ibid.

52. See: Mimi Sheller, *Citizenship from Below: Erotic Agency and Caribbean Freedom* (Duke University Press, 2012); M. Jacqui Alexander, *Pedagogies of Crossing: Meditations on Feminism, Sexual Politics, Memory, and the Sacred* (Duke University Press, 2005); and Kamala Kempadoo, *Sexing the Caribbean: Gender, Race, and Sexual Labor* (New York: Routledge, 2004).

53. "Puis-je vous demander encore une faveur? / Laquelle? dit-elle. / Comment vous appelez-vous? / Kostadinka Crnojévitch. Et vous? / Marc Zénon." Depestre, "La jupe," 49.

54. Glover, *A Regarded Self*, 77.

55. "J'ignorais que son prénom était également fameux: en 1943, au temps des offensives de la guérilla yougoslave, c'était elle le légendaire commandant Dinka des communiqués de la B.B.C." Depestre, "La jupe," 49.

56. Titograd is the former name of the current Montenegrin capital, Podgorica.

57. The past conditional is sometimes called the past unreal because it is used to describe events that either never happened or did happen but are being described as if they didn't. In English, past conditionals often begin with "if…", as in "if this had happened, this would have (or could have) happened." Thus, English speakers often refer to the past conditional in French as the "could have, should have, would have" construction.

58. "Le fait est là: je ne remettrai jamais le pied au pays de ma superbe Slave du Sud. L'âge d'homme- si lourd à porter dans mon pays natal- a coincé mes jours et mes humbles travaux à des milliers de kilomètres de Kostadinka. Le feu de sa cheminée ne m'accueillera pas en vieux copain, un tendre soir d'hiver." Depestre, "La jupe," 51.

59. "Il était une fois une jeune fille yougoslave et un étudiant haïtien. J'avais alors vingt-deux ans. Pour moi, c'était, effectivement, 'le plus bel âge de la vie.'" Depestre, "La jupe," 52.

60. "Elle était alors tout, tout nue dans mes bras." Ibid, 49.

61. "Pourrions-nous converser un instant? demandai-je / C'est l'heure de rentrer, dit-elle. Peut-être un autre jour, si vous y tenez, camarade? / Demain? / Elle prit un moment de réflexion. / Oui demain, pourquoi pas? / Puis-je obtenir une autre faveur? / Laquelle? / Comment vous appelez-vous? / Kostadinka Crnojévitch. Et vous? / Marc Zénon." Ibid, 65.

62. "Ecoutez, camarade Xiluan, faites-moi un plaisir, voulez-vous? / Lequel, illustre hôte? / Ne m'appelez pas ainsi." Ibid., 13.

63. Jodi Dean, *Comrade: An Essay on Political Belonging* (Verso Books, 2019), 9.

64. Ibid., 29.

65. Ibid.

66. "Ce scandale venait confirmait ce qui se répétait en messe basse depuis les quatre semaines que nous étions là: on réprimait sévèrement toute relation amoureuse entre les jeunes filles yougoslaves et les volontaires étrangers. Chaque nuit les patrouilles de miliciens qui rôdaient autour des campements, soi-disant pour nous protéger d'éventuelles incursions des « oustachis », veillaient en réalité sur le pucelage des vierges du cru." Depestre, "La jupe," 68.

67. "Ce matin-là, à la brigade, on lui trouva 'plus de charmes que jamais les fées.' C'était si vrai, a-t-on dit, que les deux militaires venus pour l'arrêter la laissèrent toutefois terminer son ballet du lumineux matin d'août." Ibid., 74.

68. See: Matošević and Petrović, *Duh Pruge: Zbornik Radova o Knjizi E.P. Thompsona*, 41.

69. "Puis je lis d'autres nouvelles de lui, du recueil intitulé Eros dans un train chinois et je m'arrête sur quelques histoires qui se passent dans les pays communistes qui, à ce révolutionnaire chassé de sa patrie, ont ouvert alors leurs bras. Avec étonnement et tendresse, j'imagine aujourd'hui ce poète haïtien, la tête bourrée de folles fantaisies érotiques, traversant le désert stalinien dans ses pires années où régnait un puritanisme invraisemblable et où la moindre liberté érotique était chèrement payée." Milan Kundera, *Une rencontre* (Paris: Gallimard, 2009), 106–107.

70. Nataša Kovačević, *Narrating Post/Communism: Colonial Discourse and Europe's Borderline Civilization* (Routledge, 2008), 2.

71. "Calmez-vous, les potes, intervint Chantal, après tout c'est leur affaire. Nos 'spirales' à la française ont un demi-siècle d'avance sur les mœurs de l'époque!" Depestre, "La jupe," 68.

Chapter Four

1. "Chère amie, / Votre lettre que Vous m'avez envoyés par la camarade Veda Zagorac m'a fait un grand plaisir.... Si bien tellement loin l'un de l'autre, nous travaillons à des questions semblables, notamment comment développer la société pour que puisse la femme, elle aussi, devenir le sujet ayant les mêmes droits. Bien sûr, ça ne dépend seullement des organisations féminines tant que du développement, du progrès général." Vida Tomšič, Letter to Aoua Keita, 7 October 1971, AJ 142, Socijalistički savez radnog naroda Jugoslavije (SSRNJ), A-631. NB: All translations are by the author. While the Archives of Yugoslavia have Tomšič's letter in its French original, Kéita's response is only available in its Serbian translation. As Tomšič's French wasn't flawless, the letter contains some errors, which have been maintained in the English translation to remain as faithful to the original as possible.

2. Pascale Barthélémy and Ophélie Rillon argue that Kéita was sidelined by her cousin's socialist government for being too moderate. See: Pascale Barthélémy and Ophélie Rillon, "Aoua Kéita (1912–1980): Anti-Colonial Activist, Nationalist Politician, and Feminist in Mali (West Africa)." In *The Palgrave Handbook of Communist Women Activists around the World*, edited by Francisca de Haan (Springer International Publishing, 2023).

3. "Draga prijateljice, / Potvrđujem prijem Vašeg pisma od 7 oktobra, koje me je jako obradovalo. Pošto nisam imala Vašu adresu, zadnje pismo sam uputila preko naše prijateljice Vede Zagorac, znajući da će Vam ga ona predati. Znate, moja draga Vido, da sam u Brazavilu uzgredno (sa nekim, tj, mužem, prim.prev.) a ne kao funkcioner na dužnosti. Od januara 1967. nemam više nikakvu funkciju. Prilikom raspuštanja Politbiroa i Nacionalne skupštine, što se desilo avgusta 1967. i januara 1968, mene su samovoljno udaljili od svih odgovornih funkcija nacionalnih i međunarodnih. Moje nacionalne funkcije dodeljene su Mariam

Travélé supruzi bivšeg Predsednika Republike Mali, moga rođaka Modibo Keite. Veda koja je živela izvesno vreme tamo, mora da Vam je o tome pričala. Ali, ja ni malo nisam dekuražirana, jer za mene borba traje i nastaviće se do konačnog oslobođenja Kontinenta i ekonomskog i podjednako društvenog razvoja svih afričkih slojeva." Aoua Kéita, Letter to Vida Tomšič, 3 November 1971, AJ 142 (SSRNJ), A-631.

4. Tomšič also held many important posts in both the Yugoslav federal government and Slovene republican bodies, including Minister of Social Policy in the Slovene government, President of the Assembly of Slovenia, President of the House of Nations of the Assembly of Yugoslavia, and Member of the Presidency of SR Slovenia. She also served as president of the Women's Antifascist Front (*Antifašistička fronta žena*, AFŽ) between 1948 and 1952. See: Chiara Bonfiglioli, "On Vida Tomšič, Marxist Feminism, and Agency," *Aspasia* 10, no. 1 (2016): 145–151.

5. The Women's Antifascist Front (AFŽ) was founded in 1942, in Bosanski Petrovac, and played an important role in the communist resistance to Nazi occupation. It was dissolved in 1953, after which various organizations addressing women's issues came together in the Union of Women's Societies of Yugoslavia, and from that, the Conference for the Social Activity of Women of Yugoslavia emerged in 1961 as a social organization operating within the Socialist Alliance of the Working People of Yugoslavia (SSRNJ).

6. Kéita, Letter to Vida Tomšič, 3 November 1971.

7. See more in Barthélémy and Rillon, "Aoua Keita (1912–1980)."

8. See: Ljiljana Burcar, "Brisanje Dosega Jugoslavenskog Socijalističkog Feminizma," in *Ljevica Nakon Opovrgnute Revolucije*, edited by Srećko Pulig (Zagreb: Jesenski i Turk, 2020).

9. Barthélémy and Rillon, "Aoua Keita (1912–1980)," 489.

10. Aoua Kéita, *Femme d'Afrique: la vie d'Aoua Kéita racontée par elle-même* (Présence Africaine, 1975).

11. See: Barthélémy and Rillon, "Aoua Keita (1912–1980)"; and Jane Turrittin, "Aoua Kéita and the Nascent Women's Movement in the French Soudan," *African Studies Review* 36, no. 1 (1993): 59–89.

12. Bonfiglioli, "On Vida Tomšič, Marxist Feminism, and Agency," 147. Also see: Barthélémy and Rillon, "Aoua Keita (1912–1980)." Barthélémy and Rillon discuss Kéita's "socialist internationalism," notably her links with the USSR, China, North Korea, and the Democratic Republic of Viet Nam, but they do not discuss connections between Malian and Yugoslav women activists.

13. Breny Mendoza, "Transnational Feminisms in Question," *Feminist Theory* 3, no. 3 (2002): 300.

14. Ibid., 302.

15. Ibid., 296.

16. Chandra Talpade Mohanty, *Feminism without Borders: Decolonizing Theory, Practicing Solidarity* (Duke University Press, 2003), 2–3.

17. Ibid., 7.

18. Inderpal Grewal and Caren Kaplan, *Scattered Hegemonies: Postmodernity and Transnational Feminist Practices* (University of Minnesota Press, 1994), 3.

19. Mendoza, "Transnational Feminisms in Question," 304.

20. Chiara Bonfiglioli and Kristen Ghodsee, "Vanishing Act: Global Socialist Feminism as the 'Missing Other' of Transnational Feminism—A Response to Tlostanova, Thapar-Björkert and Koobak (2019)," *Feminist Review* 126, no. 1 (2020): 168. Bonfiglioli and Ghodsee were responding to another article, in which Madina Tlostanova, Suruchi Thapar-Björkert, and Redi Koobak criticized a lack of "theoretical, temporal and spatial intersections of postcolonial and postsocialist feminisms, investigating the echoing and untranslatable experiences, concepts and ideas between the two critical discourses." See: Madina Tlostanova, Suruchi Thapar-Björkert, and Redi Koobak, "The Postsocialist 'Missing Other' of Transnational Feminism?" *Feminist Review* 121, no. 1 (2019): 81–87.

21. Bonfiglioli and Ghodsee, "Vanishing Act," 168.

22. Kristen Ghodsee, *Second World, Second Sex: Socialist Women's Activism and Global Solidarity During the Cold War* (Duke University Press, 2018).

23. Bonfiglioli and Ghodsee, "Vanishing Act," 168. Ghodsee has offered an illuminating account of strategic alliances between Bulgarian and Zambian women as well; but where Ghodsee delineates women's partnerships in the context of the UN Conferences on Women, I focus on collaborations between two women's organizations, the CSF and KDAŽ, as well as individual friendships that emerged from them. See: Ghodsee, *Second World, Second Sex*.

24. Mendoza, "Transnational Feminisms in Question," 297.

25. Kéita, *Femme d'Afrique*.

26. "Sage-femme en retraite / Ancien député / Ancien membre du bureau politique national / de l'U.S.R.D.A." Ibid.

27. Turrittin, "Aoua Kéita and the Nascent Women's Movement in the French Soudan."

28. Annette K. Joseph-Gabriel, *Reimagining Liberation: How Black Women Transformed Citizenship in the French Empire* (University of Illinois Press, 2019), 151.

29. "Notre position est unique et connue...pourquoi aurions-nous peur? Nous ne sommes pas fonctionnaires. On ne peut, ni nous muter, ni nous rétrograder, ni nous licencier. Nous sommes notre commandant, nous sommes notre gouverneur." Kéita, *Femme d'Afrique*, 148.

30. See: Vida Tomšić, *Žena U Razvoju Socijalističke Samoupravne Jugoslavije* (Jugoslovenska stvarnost, 1980).

31. "Il n'y avait ni maternité ni matériel d'obstétrique. Le médecin-chef, malgré toute sa bonne volonté, n'avait pu mettre à ma disposition que deux pinces, une paire de ciseaux, un flacon de teinture, un peu d'alcool à bruler, du coton, des compresses, des bandes." Kéita, *Femme d'Afrique*, 31.

32. "...un des premiers bâtiments en dur de Gao." Kéita, *Femme d'Afrique*, 45.

33. Tomšić discusses her views on reproductive justice in *Žena U Razvoju Socijalističke Samoupravne Jugoslavije*. For further analysis of her activism

surrounding these issues, see: Bonfiglioli, "On Vida Tomšič, Marxist Feminism, and Agency."

34. "Tu observes, tu t'occupes des camarades...tu nous représentes au bureau et tu votes. Ce sera déjà une grande contribution. Evite surtout de parler de politique." Kéita, *Femme d'Afrique*, 65.

35. "...conseil d'ainé: retirez-vous de la politique, elle n'est pas bonne pour les hommes et elle peut être fatale pour une femme." Kéita, *Femme d'Afrique*, 176.

36. "Je ferai de la politique jusqu'au bout." Ibid.

37. "...les activités politiques et syndicales...de l'Afrique entière." Kéita, *Femme d'Afrique*, 161.

38. "...une atmosphère irrespirable pour la pauvre sage-femme de brousse." Kéita, *Femme d'Afrique*, 355.

39. The Senegalese Tirailleurs were a colonial infantry in the French Army made up of recruits from French West Africa, formed in 1857 and finally disbanded in 1964.

40. "...la nécessité de consolider les résultats obtenus à la suite de la première conférence mondiale des femmes travailleuses et sur la décision du bureau exécutif...relative à l'organisation d'un séminaire international à l'intention des militantes syndicales." Kéita, *Femme d'Afrique*, 358.

41. "...cette participation a servi dans une grande mesure à la prise de conscience des femmes travailleuses du Soudan. Elle a eu aussi un élément déterminant dans la création de l 'intersyndicat des femmes travailleuses du Soudan." Ibid.

42. "Dans la deuxième capitale de la République démocratique allemande, étaient réunis les représentants des centaines de millions de travailleurs de tous les pays de tous les continents. Ils étaient venus dans cette partie de l'Europe pour étudier leurs problèmes et trouver des solutions satisfaisantes pour tous, sans distinction de race, de couleur, d'idéologie ou de religion. Cette rencontre des colonisés et des colonisateurs...fut pour moi très révélatrice." Kéita, *Femme d'Afrique*, 359.

43. "...il y avait tout un monde entre ce que j'avais appris et ce que je vivais." Ibid.

44. "...libérée à la fois du joug colonial et de tout autre préjugé rétrograde." Kéita, *Femme d'Afrique*, 361.

45. "L'indépendance politique fut le grand couronnement de nos efforts et des sacrifices de nos martyrs. Mais la lutte n'était pas terminée pour autant. Elle continue et continuera encore longtemps pour la liberté, la démocratie et la paix universelle." Kéita, *Femme d'Afrique*, 395.

46. "Lors de ma prise de conscience, vers l'âge de six–sept ans, Bamako était une petite ville de huit mille habitants à peine." Kéita, *Femme d'Afrique*, 15.

47. Letter from Latinka Perović to the Executive Committee of the Women of Mali, June 1962, AJ 142 (SSRNJ), A-631.

This effort to establish connections with women's organizations in Mali was part of a general KDAŽ effort to build bilateral agreements with groups across the Global South. In fact, as Chiara Bonfiglioli explains, after the Soviet-Yugoslav split, the Yugoslav Antifascist Women's Front (which was later transformed into

KDAŽ) was expelled from the Women's International Democratic Federation (WIDF) in 1949. To counteract this international isolation, Yugoslav representatives endeavored to establish their own bilateral connections with women's organizations worldwide. The decision to expel Yugoslavia was overthrown in 1956, yet Yugoslavia refused to rejoin the WIDF at that point, opting instead to pursue bilateral agreements. See Chiara Bonfiglioli, "Representing Women's Non-Aligned Encounters: A View from Yugoslavia," in *Socialist Yugoslavia and the Non-Aligned Movement: Social, Cultural, Political, and Economic Imaginaries*, edited by Paul Stubbs (McGill-Queen's University Press, 2023), 37–59.

48. Letter from the Executive Committee of the Women of Mali to the Conference for the Social Activity of Women, July 1962, AJ 142 (SSRNJ), A-631.

49. KDAŽ, Zabeleška O Poseti Ambasadora Malija Konferenciji Za Društvenu Aktivnost Žena (Note on the Visit of the Ambassador of Mali to the Conference for the Social Activity of Women), March 1963, AJ 142 (SSRNJ), A-631.

50. "qui ont constamment et fermement soutenu le people du Mali dans sa lutte de libération et de construction nationale." Letter from the Ambassador of the Republic of Mali to the President of the Conference for the Social Activity of Yugoslav Women, 1963, Fond 142 (SSRNJ), Archives of Yugoslavia.

51. KDAŽ, Razgovor Sa Ambasadorom Malija, Gosp. Ture (Conversation with the Ambassador of Mali, Mr. Touré), May 1965, AJ 142 (SSRNJ), A-631.

52. For Kéita's collaboration with Soviet activists, See: Barthélémy and Rillon, "Aoua Keita (1912–1980); Tatiana Smirnova and Ophélie Rillon, "When Malian Women Looked to the USSR (1961–1991): The Challenges of Female Educational Cooperation," *International Journal of African Historical Studies* 54, no. 3 (2021): 457–478.

53. KDAŽ, Zabeleška O Poseti Gdje. Ave Keite Jugoslaviji 26. maj- 15. jun 1965 god (Note on the Visit of Ms. Aoua Keita to Yugoslavia May 26th–June 15th, 1965), AJ 142 (SSRNJ), A-631.

54. KDAŽ, Pomoć Jugoslovenskog Crvenog Krsta i Konferencije Za Društvenu Aktivnost Žena Jugoslavije Maliju 1965. i 1966. godine (Aid from the Yugoslav Red Cross and the Conference for the Social Activity of Women of Yugoslavia to Mali in 1965 and 1966), AJ 142 (SSRNJ), A-631.

55. Aoua Kéita, Letter to the President of the Conference for the Social Activity of Women of Yugoslavia, 1965, AJ 142 (SSRNJ), A-631.

56. "Ce voyage à travers la République Fédérative de Yougoslavie m'a permis d'une part de mieux connaitre le peuple Yougoslave et de l'apprécier hautement. D'autre part, il m'a permis de profiter de vos expériences qui me seront d'une très grande utilité pour la formation sociale des femmes de mon pays." Ibid.

57. *Žena* was published by the Croatian branch of the Yugoslav state socialist women's organization, known as the Union of Women's Societies (SŽD) from 1953 to 1961, and the Conference for the Social Activity of Women (KDAŽ) after 1961. For a history of the magazine and its representation of Global South female activists, see: Bonfiglioli, "Representing Women's Non-Aligned Encounters: A View from Yugoslavia."

58. "vrvjelo je mnogim primjerima hrabrosti, herojstva i entuzijazma žena Malija, koje su uvijek u najtežim časovima potezale čak i oružje, makar i najprimitivnije poput otrovnih strijela, ili se služile lukavstima da bi zadavale kolonizatoru odlučne udarce." "Ava Keita: Mjesto Malijke U Slobodi," *Žena*, July 1965.

59. See Bonfiglioli, "Representing Women's Non-Aligned Encounters: A View from Yugoslavia."

60. "prva ćelija u razvoju čovječanstva." Ibid.

61. Ibid.

62. "les soins qu'on apporte non seulement à l'émancipation des femmes, mais aussi au développement économique et à l'élévation du niveau culturel et éducatif du peuple, ce qui présente certainement une des conditions principales de chaque progrès réel et de la pleine émancipation des femmes." Jelica Marić, Letter to Aoua Keita, 1965, AJ 142 (SSRNJ), A-631.

63. Savica Hočevar, Letter to Aoua Keita, 1965, AJ 142 (SSRNJ), A-631.

64. "qui s'inscrit dans le cadre de la solidarité internationale si chère à toutes les femmes de bonne volonté dont vous faites partie." Aoua Kéita, Letter to Savica Hočevar, January 1966, AJ 142 (SSRNJ), A-631.

65. Aoua Kéita, Postcard to Jelica Marić, AJ 142 (SSRNJ), A-631.

66. "Bien chère amie, /…Les femmes du Mali fondent beaucoup d'espoir sur l'année 1966 et souhaitent ardemment qu'elle voit la satisfaction de nos légitimes et communes aspirations. Tout en couronnant de succès les luttes des nationalistes d'Afrique, d'Asie et d'Amérique Latine contre les colonialistes, les néo-colonialistes et les impérialistes, l'année nouvelle doit être pour nous et nos foyers une année de liberté dans la quiétude et le bonheur les plus complets.… Tout en vous remerciant très sincèrement de tout ce que votre organisation a fait pour aider les femmes du Mali dans leur lourde mais exaltante tache qu'est la construction socialiste, je vous prie, chère amie, de croire à notre sincère amitié." Aoua Kéita, Letter to the President of the Conference of Yugoslav Women, 8 January 1966, AJ 142 (SSRNJ), A-631.

67. "l'ignorance de nos frères et sœurs qui tiennent beaucoup aux méthodes millénaires." Aoua Kéita's Speech at the 5th International Seminar Organized by Kdaž, 1966, AJ 142 (SSRNJ), A-631, 4.

68. See: Vida Tomšič, *Žena U Razvoju Socijalističke Samoupravne Jugoslavije.*

69. "cette plaie de l'humanité dont les peuples du Tiers-Monde sont les plus douloureuses victimes." Aoua Kéita's Speech at the 5th International Seminar Organized by Kdaž, 1966, AJ 142 (SSRNJ), A-631, 6.

70. Ibid.

71. Kéita's visit was aimed in part at collecting donations for a Women's Day lottery she was organizing, for which she received 10 large transistors, 2 small transistors, and 40 scarfs from the KDAŽ.

72. KDAŽ, Zabeleška O Razgovoru Sa Auom Keitom (A Note on a Conversation with Aoua Kéita), 24 January 1967, AJ 142 (SSRNJ), A-631.

73. Vida Tomšič, *Izveštaj O Poseti Ženskim Organizacijama U Maliju, Gvineji I Senegalu, 7–19. Februara 1967. godine* (*Report on the Visit to Women's Organizations in Mali, Guinea, and Senegal, 7–19 February 1967*), AJ 142 (SSRNJ), A-631.

74. Tomšič spent five nights in Mali.

75. Tomšič, *Izveštaj O Poseti Ženskim Organizacijama U Maliju, Gvineji I Senegalu.*

76. Ibid.

77. Ibid.

78. "...muslimanstvo ima ovde za posmatrača manje mračan vid nego u zemljama gde je žena pod zarom." Ibid.

79. For a more in-depth discussion on Yugoslav politics toward the veil See: Gordana Stojaković, "Poruke o zaru i feredži u AFŽ štampi na srpskom jeziku (1947–1951): slučaj Kosmet," *Ženski Muzej*, 27. decembra 2021. https://zenskimuzejns.org.rs/2021/12/27/poruke-o-zaru-i-feredzi-u-afz-stampi-na-srpskom-jeziku-1947-1951-slucaj-kosmet/

80. Ibid.

81. Vida Tomšič, Letter to Aoua Kéita, 1967, AJ 142 (SSRNJ), A-631.

82. Barthélémy and Rillon, "Aoua Keita (1912–1980)," 486.

83. For a discussion of the situation in Yugoslavia, see Bonfiglioli, "Representing Women's Non-Aligned Encounters: A View from Yugoslavia."

84. Prior to her involvement in the Algerian war, Zagorac had experience as a Partisan. A student of philosophy and economics, she joined the League of Communist Youth of Yugoslavia and quickly rose through the ranks of the Yugoslav Communist Party. Before and after World War II, she wrote for various newspapers on women's issues, and during the war, she joined the antifascist fight. Significantly less has been written about the important contributions of Zagorac than about those of her husband, though Emilia Epštajn has recently offered a much-needed analysis of her life and work. See: Emilia Epštajn, "Tragom Vede Zagorac U Muzeju Afričke Umetnosti," in *Feministička Teorija Je Za Sve*, edited by Adriana Zaharijević and Katarina Lončarević (Belgrade: Institut za Filozofiju i Društvenu Teoriju, 2018).

85. Nemanja Radonjić, "Drums of Revolution: Veda Zagorac and Zdravko Pečar," in *Nyimpa Kor Ndzidzi*, edited by Ana Sladojević and Emilija Epštajn (Belgrade: Museum of African Art, 2017).

86. *Jugoslovenska Svedočanstva O Alžirskoj Revoluciji—Arhivski Omnibus* (*Yugoslav Testimonies of the Algerian Revolution—Archival Omnibus*), curated by Mila Turajlić, et al., Belgrade Museum of African Art, 18 March–11 June 2023.

87. Veda Zagorac, Letter to Kdaž after the Congress of Guinean Women, 1968, AJ 142 (SSRNJ), A-631.

88. Epštajn, "Tragom Vede Zagorac U Muzeju Afričke Umetnosti."

89. Ana Sladojević, "An Anticolonial Museum," *Europe Now*, no. 50, Council for European Studies (2023), https://www.europenowjournal.org/2023/02/21/an-anticolonial-museum/.

90. Ibid.

91. Brent Hayes Edwards, *The Practice of Diaspora: Literature, Translation, and the Rise of Black Internationalism* (Harvard University Press, 2003), 14.

92. Grewal and Kaplan, *Scattered Hegemonies*, 17.

93. Ibid., 19.

Chapter Five

1. All the photographs included in this chapter are held at the Belgrade Museum of African Art as part of the Veda and dr Zdravko Pečar Collection.

2. Fanon provides an account of the Algerian revolution in his 1959 book, *L'An V de la révolution algérienne* (published in English as *A Dying Colonialism*). See: Frantz Fanon, *L'An V de la révolution algérienne* (Paris: François Maspero, 1959).

3. Leo Zeilig, *Frantz Fanon: The Militant Philosopher of Third World Revolution* (London: I.B. Tauris, 2016), 116.

4. The FLN was created in 1954 by the Revolutionary Committee of Unity and Action (Comité Révolutionnaire d'Unité et d'Action), a group of Algerian militants seeking to unite factions of the country's nationalist movement. By mid-1956, almost every Algerian nationalist organization had joined the FLN, which was then reorganized so that it resembled a provisional government. For example, it featured a five-member executive body, as well as a legislative body consisting of all the district heads. The National Liberation Army (Armée de Libération Nationale, or ALN), under the command of Col. Houari Boumediene, acted as the military arm of the FLN.

5. Oussedik joined the Parti du peuple algérien (PPA) headed by Messali Hadj when he was only 22. He also participated in the formation of an armed clandestine network, the Organisation spéciale (OS). In 1948 he was arrested by France and imprisoned in the Blida military prison, where he was tortured. After his release in 1951, he settled in France, where he was active in the Algerian labor movement. He returned to Algeria to join the FLN in 1955. After holding a post in the Provisional Government of the Algerian Republic (GPRA) from 1958 to 1960, he worked as the FLN representative in Guinea, and then, following independence in 1962, served as the ambassador of Algeria in the Soviet Union, Bulgaria, India, and Italy.

6. In May 1958, the French Fourth Republic fell, and general Charles de Gaulle was brought back to power. Several months later, on 19 September 1958, the Provisional Government of the Algerian Republic was established in Cairo, with Ferhat Abbas as its first president. Abbas sent a message to President Tito that day, explaining that the formation of the GPRA had already been discussed at the Tangier Conference, a gathering of representatives from newly independent Morocco and Tunisia and the FLN. The decision came in response to the announcement of a constitutional referendum scheduled for September 1958 in which voters (including those in Algeria) would be asked to approve the constitution of the French Fifth Republic, written by de Gaulle himself. According to Abbas, the fact that Algerians were expected to weigh in on the internal matters of France in the midst of a war for independence constituted a provocation. See: Letter from President of the GPRA Ferhat Abbas to Zdravo Pečar, 30 March 1960, Veda and dr Zdravko Pečar Collection, Belgrade Museum of African Art.

7. In March 2023 an exhibit entitled "Yugoslav Testimonies of the Algerian Revolution—Archival Omnibus" opened at the Belgrade Museum of African Art. Curators Mila Turajlić, Maja Medić, Ana Knežević, and Emilia Epštajn exhibited

material and oral testimonies by Yugoslavs who actively participated in the Algerian revolution, including this photograph of Fanon, Oussedik, and Pečar.

8. Adom Getachew, *Worldmaking after Empire: The Rise and Fall of Self-Determination* (Princeton University Press, 2019), 2.

9. Kathi Weeks, *The Problem with Work: Feminism, Marxism, Antiwork Politics, and Postwork Imaginaries* (Duke University Press, 2011), 176.

10. Dragan Bogetić, "Jugoslavija i borba alžirskog naroda za nacionalno oslobođenje 1954–1962," in *Jugoslavija-Alžir: Zbornik radova sa naučne konferencije*, edited by Miladin Milošević (Beograd: Arhiv Jugoslavije, 2013).

11. Ibid. Also see: Ljubodrag Dimić, "Jugoslavija i Alžir 1961–1965," in *Jugoslavija-Alžir: Zbornik radova sa naučne konferencije*, edited by Miladin Milošević (Beograd: Arhiv Jugoslavije, 2013).

12. Bogetić, "Jugoslavija i borba alžirskog naroda…1954–1962." Also see: Jože Smole and Rudi Štajduhar, eds., *Predsednik Tito u zemljama Azije i Afrike* (Beograd: Kultura, 1959).

13. Minutes of Yugoslav-Algerian Talks, 8 June 1959, KPR, I-3-a/2-1, Archive of Yugoslavia. Notably, the Algerian delegation also left Yugoslavia with three projectors and twenty documentary and fiction films about the Yugoslav national-liberation struggle in World War II, gifted to them by the Information Secretariat, as the Algerians had expressed an interest in studying Yugoslav guerrilla tactics. See: Mila Turajlić, "Filmske Novosti: Filmed Diplomacy," *Nationalities Papers* 49, no. 3 (2021): 483–503.

14. "Nepriznavanje pomaže tvrdnju neprijatelja, da borba Alžira ne uživa međunarodnu podršku i da pretežni deo svetske javnosti smatra Alžirski rat unutrašnjim problemom Francuske." Yazid and Belkacem quoted in: Dragan Bogetić, "The Yugoslav Support to the Algerian People Struggle for Independence in the Final Phase of the Algerian War 1958–1962," *Istorija 20. veka*, no. 3 (2012).

15. Ibid.

16. Bogetić, "Jugoslavija i borba alžirskog Naroda…1954–1962"; Dragomir Bondžić, "Studenti iz Alžira u Jugoslaviji 1958–1965," in *Jugoslavija-Alžir: Zbornik radova sa naučne konferencije* (Beograd: Arhiv Jugoslavije, 2013); and Leo Mates, *Međunarodni odnosi socijalističke Jugoslavije* (Beograd: Nolit, 1976).

17. Bogetić, "The Yugoslav Support to the Algerian People…1958–1962."

18. "Problem rata u Alžiru nalazi se pred nama već punih šest godina, a da do danas u tom pogledu nije zabilježen nikakav napredak ka jednom zadovoljavajućem rješenju. Narod Alžira koji i dalje podnosi teške žrtve za zadobijanje svoje slobode—čime zadužuje sve narode, koji se bore za mir, nezavisnost i ravnopravnost—traži prirodna i zakonita prava na samoopredjeljenje. Ta prava mu je prošle godine i Francuska u načelu pri-znala, ali su pregovori koji su uslijedili pokazali, na žalost, da francuska strana nije izvukla one praktične zaključke koji proizilaze iz prava na samoopredjeljenje, zbog čega su i uslovi pregovaranja bili neprihvatljivi za predstavnike Alžira. U takvoj situaciji vlada Alžira traži izlaz iz situacije putem referenduma pod kontrolom ove naše Organizacije, što mi sa svoje strane možemo samo pozdraviti i podržati…Ako se ne nađe put za što skorije

demokratsko rješenje, implicitno se u stvari legalizuje sila kao sredstvo za gušenje legitimnih aspiracija jednog naroda, pa time praktično i rat." Tito quoted in: Bogetić, "The Yugoslav Support to the Algerian People Struggle for Independence in the Final Phase of the Algerian War 1958–1962," 164–165.

19. "Izražavajući duboku želju naroda Jugoslavije, koji prema alžirskom narodu već niz godina, tokom čitave njegove herojske borbe, gaji duboke simpatije i osjećanja—izjavljujem u ime jugoslovenske vlade da je ona, s obzirom da već više godina 'de fakto' priznaje alžirsku vladu, riješila da neodložno 'de jure' prizna vladu Alžira, čiji se predsjednik nalazi danas ovdje među nama." Tito quoted in: Bogetić, "The Yugoslav Support to the Algerian People Struggle for Independence in the Final Phase of the Algerian War 1958–1962," 165–166.

20. Dragan Petrović, *Francusko-jugoslovenski odnosi u vreme Alžirskog rata 1952–1964* (Beograd: Institut za međunarodnu politiku i privredu, 2009).

21. Malouf is a musical genre from Algeria, Libya, and Tunisia of Iberian origin, introduced to populations in the Maghreb by Andalusian refugees.

22. "une vague sympathie...c'est réellement en frères que les étudiants de Belgrade manifestent pour Lumumba ou recueillent cinquante millions de dinars pour les réfugiés algériens." See: Kateb Yacine, *Minuit passé de douze heures: écrits journalistiques, 1947–1989* (Paris: Editions du Seuil, 1999), 127. In fact, large student protests erupted in Belgrade after Lumumba's assassination.

23. Pečar cited in: Nemanja Radonjić, "Drums of Revolution: Veda Zagorac and Zdravko Pečar," in *Nyimpa Kor Ndzidzi*, edited by Sladojević Ana and Emilija Epštajn (Belgrade: The Museum of African Art, 2017), 162. For more on Pečar's life and his involvement with Algeria, also see: Olivier Hadouchi, *Images of Non-Aligned and Tricontinental Struggles*, trans. Mark Brogan (Museum of Contemporary Art Belgrade, 2016).

24. "...vrhuška jedne revolucije...nikada nije ni izdaleka onako čista i lepa onako kao što misle vojnici koji za nju vojuju i umiru." Zdravko Pečar, "Slučaj Dragana Savića," Veda and dr Zdravko Pečar Collection, Belgrade Museum of African Art.

25. "...sudelovao sam na samom vrhu, na najvišim intrigama" (ibid.). Ben Bella was one of the principal leaders of the revolution and later became the first prime minister (1962–63) and first elected president (1963–65) of independent Algeria.

26. "Dolazio je u moj stan da bi diskutovao o unutarnjim odnosima FLN-ALN, kao i problemima tadašnjih odnosa FLN sa Francuskom. Meni lično se zahvalio na opširnom i poštenom pisanju u jugoslovenskoj štampi o alžirskoj borbi i pokretu, a posebno zbog napisane knjige o Alžiru." ("He used to come to my apartment to discuss internal FLN-ALN relations, as well as the problems of FLN's relations with France at the time. He personally thanked me for the extensive and honest writing in the Yugoslav press about the Algerian struggle and movement, and especially for the book written about Algeria"). Zdravko Pečar, "Beleška O Ben Beli," Veda and dr Zdravko Pečar Collection, Belgrade Museum of African Art.

27. "Ustupio mi je i ležaj kad je trebalo noću da se sklonim. Zajedno smo obilazili granični sector, živelo se i spavalo pod zemunicama koje su bile pod

neprestanom paljbom francuske artiljerije i avijacije i to dano-noćno." Zdravko Pečar, "Houari Boumedienne," Veda and dr Zdravko Pečar Collection, Belgrade Museum of African Art.

28. Zdravko Pečar, *Alžir* (Beograd: Kultura, 1959). The book was translated into French in 1987 under the title *Algérie, témoignage d'un reporter yougoslave sur la guerre d'Algérie* (*Algeria, Testimony of a Yugoslav Reporter on the Algerian War*). NB: After serving as Chief of Staff of the ALN, Boumediene served as defense minister under Ben Bella. In 1965, he staged a military coup, installed himself as President of Algeria, and imprisoned Ben Bella before placing him under house arrest (from which he was finally released in 1980). From Pečar's writing, is it is clear the Yugoslav condemned the coup and remained loyal to Ben Bella.

29. "des qualités de cœurs incomparables et une vive intelligence…pays d'Orient, d'Afrique Noire et d'Afrique du Nord." Letter from President of the GPRA Ferhat Abbas to Zdravo Pečar, 1960, Veda and dr Zdravko Pečar Collection, Belgrade Museum of African Art.

30. "u ratu…videli jedini izlaz svojih generacija." Zdravko Pečar, "Le Caractère Populaire De La Révolution Algerienne," Veda and dr Zdravko Pečar Collection, Belgrade Museum of African Art.

31. "našao ponovo sam sebe." Ibid.

32. Zdravko Pečar, *Alžir do nezavisnosti* (Beograd: Prosveta, 1967). Davidson was chief of Britain's clandestine Special Operations Executive Yugoslav Section in Cairo from 1942 to mid-1943, before he spent several months in Bosnia serving as a liaison with the Partisans, an experience he described in his 1946 book, *Partisan Picture*. See: Basil Davidson, *Partisan Picture* (Bedford Books, 1946). Davidson also helped Pečar get his book reviewed by the journal *Jeune Afrique*.

33. Letters from Basil Davidson to Zdravko Pečar, Veda and dr Zdravko Pečar Collection, Belgrade Museum of African Art.

34. See: Laurent Gervereau and Benjamin Stora, eds., *Photographier la guerre d'Algérie* (Marval, 2004).

35. "L'Algérie devient 'violence' tout court dans les images." Laurent Gervereau, "Les hésitations des photographes professionnels," in *Photographier la guerre d'Algérie*, edited by Laurent Gervereau and Benjamin Stora (Marval, 2004), 38.

36. "bataille politico-médiatique de la visibilité internationale." Abdelmadjid Merdaci, "Une guerre Algérienne au fond des yeux," in *Photographier la guerre d'Algérie*, edited by Laurent Gervereau and Benjamin Stora (Marval, 2004), 166.

37. *Ciné-Guerrillas: Scenes from the Labudovic Reels*, directed by Mila Turajlić (2022).

38. "krijući sve više danak u krvi alžirskom ratu i ne želeći da sagledaju istinu o Alžiru, Francuzi se i dalje zanose iluzijama da je rat pri kraju, da neprijatelj neće izdržati." Pečar, *Alžir*, 8.

39. The Challe line (named for General Maurice Challe) was built in 1959 to reinforce the existing Morice line (named for then French Minister of Defense André Morice), built in 1957, consisting of an electric fence and minefield built parallel to the border.

40. See: Zdravko Pečar, "Alžirski Ustanici Mestimično Probili Šalov Pojas," Veda and dr Zdravko Pečar Collection, Belgrade Museum of African Art.

41. "Vrhovna komanda NOV Alžira nema tehničkih mogućnosti da svetu saopštava uspehe svojih jedinica u borbi s neprijateljem...Velike svetske novinske agencije odbijaju da putem svoje razgranate mreže prenesu ta saopštenja izvanredno bogata i potpuno sveža...Alžirci su primorani da u *El Mužahidu* sitnim slovima beleže sve te akcije." Pečar, *Alžir*, 62.

42. Similarly, Ahmed Bedjaoui said that the primary objective of films made during the Algerian War of Independence was to "provide journalists around the world with images showing a people mobilized in the fight for their freedom." See: Ahmed Bedjaoui, *Cinéma et guerre de libération: Algérie, des batailles d'images* (éditions Chihab, 2014), 89.

43. "topao prijem i prijateljski i bratski doček..." Zdravko Pečar, "Jugoslavija je veliki i iskren prijatelj Alžira," Veda and dr Zdravko Pečar Collection, Belgrade Museum of African Art.

44. Zdravko Pečar, "Naši studenti u Tunisu," Veda and dr Zdravko Pečar Collection, Belgrade Museum of African Art.

45. Zdravko Pečar, "Studenti najavili da neće napustiti Tunis," Veda and dr Zdravko Pečar Collection, Belgrade Museum of African Art.

46. "jedan od prvoboraca aktivne koegzistencije i pozitivnog neutralizma"; "Njena politika prijateljstva sa arapskim i azijsko-afričkim svetom, kao i neosporne simpatije koje ta zemlja uživa u celom svetu, daju joj posebno mestu." Zdravko Pečar, "Pisanje Alžirskog 'Al Mudžahida' Povodom Dana Republike," Veda and dr Zdravko Pečar Collection, Belgrade Museum of African Art.

47. Zdravko Pečar, "Pomoć Jugoslovenskog Crvenog Križa Alžirskim Izbeglicama," Veda and dr Zdravko Pečar Collection, Belgrade Museum of African Art. These reports also underline the crucial role that Tunisia played in the Algerian war. Yet as Jeffrey Byrne has argued, the Tunisian government wasn't always enthusiastic to play this role as they were afraid of straining too much their relation with France. See: James Jeffrey Byrne, *Mecca of Revolution: Algeria Decolonization and the Third World Order* (New York, NY: Oxford University Press, 2019).

48. Zdravko Pečar, "Deo Jugoslovenske Pomoći Za Alžirske Izbeglice Dopremljen U Kazablanku," Veda and dr Zdravko Pečar Collection, Belgrade Museum of African Art.

49. Zdravko Pečar, "Tko Će Zamjeniti Kolone?" Veda and dr Zdravko Pečar Collection, Belgrade Museum of African Art.

50. See: Frantz Fanon, *The Wretched of the Earth*, trans. Richard Philcox (New York: Grove Press, 2004).

51. Pečar, "Tko Će Zamjeniti Kolone?"

52. In fact, Pečar was commissioned by Yugoslav Newsreels to write a script for a documentary about the Algerian War.

53. Gervereau and Stora, *Photographier la guerre d'Algérie*.

54. Susan Sontag, *On Photography* (Rosetta Books, 2005), 3.

55. Ibid., 9.

56. Much of the footage captured by Yugoslav photographers and filmmakers was shared with the Algerians, for example to make the documentary film *Dzazaïrouna* (*Our Algeria*), in the summer of 1960. As Mila Turajlić writes, "Dzazaïrouna is generally considered the first documentary signed by the newly-created Service Cinéma of the Ministry of Information of the GPRA, and a group of Algerian and French filmmakers came to Belgrade to participate in the editing and voice-over recording of the film, making it a truly collectivist work and an example of Third Cinema." See: Turajlić, "Filmske Novosti: Filmed Diplomacy," 492. The movie was also screened at the UN during a 1960 discussion of the Algerian War.

57. Adrienne Maree Brown, *Pleasure Activism: The Politics of Feeling Good* (AK Press, 2019).

58. Catherine Lizette Gonzalez, "In 'Pleasure Activism,' Adrienne Maree Brown Dares Us to Get In Touch With Our Needs," *Colorlines*, 26 February 2019, https://www.colorlines.com/articles/pleasure-activism-adrienne-maree-brown-dares-us-get-touch-our-needs.

59. Ibid.

60. "Alžirskim vojnicima i oficirima mnogo radosti i zadovoljstva pričinjavaju šale. Uvek su spremni i vole da prepričavaju viceve…za vreme odmora između velikih pokreta i borbi borci nalaze i druge načine da se zabave i od srca nasmeju." Pečar, *Alžir*, 59–60.

61. Aimé Césaire, *Discours sur le colonialisme suivi de Discours sur la Négritude* (Paris: Présence Africaine, 2004).

62. "Sekcije, čete, bataljoni i vilaje povezani su na određenim sektorima odličnom radiomrežom." Pečar, *Alžir*, 42.

63. Fanon, *L'An V de la révolution algérienne*.

64. "su bili zadovoljni kada su videli da je to njihova vojska. Raspitivali su se o svojim sinovima i braći, o akcijama koje su bile u toku i radovali se izveštaju da je opet jedan helikopter srušen. Prijatelj iz strane zemlje bio je centar pažnje, a on je sa čuđenjem slušao kako ti ljudi tačno izgovaraju ime njegovog Tita, koji je ovde zaista bio i njihov, jer im je on više nego njegova zemlja bio poznat i blizak." Pečar, *Alžir*, 56.

65. For a more detailed account of women's involvement in the ALN, see: Djamila Amrane, *Des femmes dans la guerre d'Algérie: entretiens* (Paris: Editions Khartala, 1994); Diane Sambrone, *Femmes musulmanes: guerre d'Algérie, 1954–1962* (Paris: Editions Autrement, 2007).

66. Ariella Azoulay, *The Civil Contract of Photography* (Princeton University Press, 2008), 12.

67. Ibid., 16.

68. Ibid., 17.

69. Ibid., 21

70. Močnik quoted in: Davor Konjikušić, *Red Glow: Yugoslav Partisan Photography and Social Movement, 1941–1945* (Berlin: De Gruyter, 2021), 19.

71. Ibid., 26.

72. Ibid., 18.

73. Ibid., 109.

74. Weeks, *The Problem with Work*, 176.

75. "bez pretenzija, često fragmentarno, nizaće se u ovoj knjizi brojni delovi mozaika iz kojih bi trebalo da se pojave konture i slike te zemlje, njenih ljudi, njihove revolucije, nadanja i perspektiva" Pečar, *Alžir*, 9.

76. Zdravko Pečar, "Slučaj Dragana Savića," Veda and dr Zdravko Pečar Collection, Belgrade Museum of African Art.

77. Dragan Savić, *Alžir* (Beograd, 1965).

78. Telegram from Veda Zagorac to Dragan Savić, 21 June 1962, Legat Dragana Savića (Bequest of Dragan Savić), *Zavičajni muzej Petrovac na Mlavi* (Homeland Museum Petrovac na Mlavi).

79. The two drawings are included in Savić's *Alžir*. Copies can also be found in the personal collection of Savić, in the Homeland Museum Petrovac na Mlavi.

80. Savić's personal collection held by the Homeland Museum Petrovac na Mlavi includes cartoons related to Algeria as well as photographs he took during the time he spent with the ALN.

81. "upoznao sam divne ljude koji su se već niz godina bespoštedno borili kako bi se izborili za najsvetije pravo, a to je život u slobodi." Dragan Savić, "Svedočanstvo o epopeji", *Borba*, 11 July 1982.

82. These reprints are available at the Belgrade Museum of African Art, in three volumes.

83. "Želeći toj alžirskoj revoluciji da damo onaj oreol koji joj je trebalo dati… da ga kasnija pokolenja koriste kao deo svoje istorije." Zdravko Pečar, "Slučaj Dragana Savića."

84. "En Algérie comme en Yougoslavie ce sont les paysans qui forment l'âme et la chair de l'A.L.N. En Algérie comme en Yougoslavie, même sauvagerie de l'occupant dans sa politique de répression et d'extermination…Pour nous actuellement, la Yougoslavie est plus qu'un pays allié: c'est un pays ami—dont l'aide sur tous les plans ne nous a jamais fait défaut." "29 Novembre: Fête de la République Yougoslave," *El Moudjahid*, no. 56, 27 November 1959, Veda and dr Zdravko Pečar Collection, Belgrade Museum of African Art.

Epilogue

1. Though in our interview, Depestre emphasized his support for Titoism, in 1949, he had expressed his anger over the Yugoslav-Soviet split. In the communist journal *L'Humanité*, he openly accused Tito of betraying the socialist youth he had collaborated with on the Šamac-Sarajevo worksite. At the time, the West had embraced the Yugoslav-Soviet split and initiated economic aid to Yugoslavia. Depestre feared that Yugoslavia might fully align with the West, thus turning the

Šamac-Sarajevo railroad—built by international socialist youth—into a tool for socialism's enemies. His frustration was rooted in a strong attachment to the "sunlit memory" of horizontal democracy he experienced in Bosnia. Although critical of Yugoslav leadership, Depestre asserts in the article that he still believes in the country's socialist youth. Depestre did not mention this article in our interview, which I only discovered afterward. While I can't say for certain why, I suspect it's because, as Yugoslavia ended all military and security agreements with the United States, refused to join NATO, and turned its focus toward the Global South and the Non-Aligned Movement, Depestre regained faith in the Yugoslav project. In our 2017 conversation, he emphasized his lasting solidarity with the youth of Šamac-Sarajevo, omitting (or perhaps forgetting) the challenges that arose along the way. See Parti communiste français, "Tito a trahi la jeunesse yougoslave," *L'Humanité: journal socialiste quotidien*, 28 October, 1949. I am extremely grateful to Kaiama Glover for bringing this article to my attention.

2. Leela Ghandi, *Affective Communities: Anticolonial Thought, Fin-de-Siècle Radicalism, and the Politics of Friendship* (Duke University Press, 2006), 19.

3. The article shared the greetings of Algerians to Yugoslavs on the Yugoslav Day of the Republic in 1959. "29 Novembre: Fête de la République Yougoslave," *El Moudjahid*, no. 56, 27 November 1959, Veda and dr Zdravko Pečar Collection, Belgrade Museum of African Art.

4. Ibid.

5. Mila Turjalić, "Film as the Memory Site of the 1961 Belgrade Conference of Non-Aligned States," in *Socialist Yugoslavia and the Non-Aligned Movement: Social, Cultural, Political, and Economic Imaginaries*, ed. Paul Stubbs (McGill-Queen's University Press, 2023), 204.

6. For an analysis of historical revisionism in contemporary Serbia see: Jelena Đureinović, *The Politics of Memory of the Second World War in Contemporary Serbia: Collaboration, Resistance and Retribution* (London: Routledge, 2020); Dubravka Stojanović, *Prošlost dolazi: Promene u tumačenju prošlosti u srpskim udžbenicima istorije 1913–2021* (Beograd: Biblioteka XX vek, 2023).

7. Jacques Derrida and Eric Prenowitz, "Archive Fever: A Freudian Impression," *Diacritics* 25, no. 2 (1995), 29.

8. Here I include all the scholars cited throughout this book who are working on the Non-Aligned Movement.

BIBLIOGRAPHY

Abdelmadjid, Merdaci. "Une guerre Algérienne au fond des yeux." In *Photographier la guerre d'Algérie*, edited by Laurent Gervereau and Benjamin Stora. Marval, 2004.

Alexander, M. Jacqui. *Pedagogies of Crossing: Meditations on Feminism, Sexual Politics, Memory, and the Sacred*. Duke University Press, 2005.

Alliot, David. "Le tapuscrit du Cahier d'un retour au pays natal." Assemblée Nationale. Accessed 23 June 2023. https://www.assemblee-nationale.fr/histoire/aime-cesaire/tapuscrit.asp.

Amin, Samir. "Towards the fifth international?" In *Global Political Parties*, edited by Katarina Sehm-Patomaki and Marko Ulvila, London: Zed Press, 2008, 123–143.

Amrane, Djamila. *Des femmes dans la guerre d'Algérie: entretiens*. Paris: Editions Khartala, 1994.

Aristotle. *Nicomachean Ethics*. Translated by Christopher Rowe. Edited by Christopher Rowe and Sarah Broadie. Oxford University Press, 2002.

Arkin, Stephen. "Composing the Self: The Literary Interview as Form." *International Journal of Oral History* 4, no.1 (1983): 12–18.

Armillas-Tiseyra, Magalí. "Dislocations." *The Global South* 7, no. 2 (2013): 1–10.

Armillas-Tiseyra, Magalí and Anne Garland Mahler. "Introduction: New Critical Directions in Global South Studies." *Comparative Literature Studies* 58, no. 3 (2021): 465–84.

Autor, Nika. dir. *Newsreel 242 – Sunny Railways*. Newsreel Front, 2023.

"Ava Kéita: Mjesto Malijke U Slobodi." *Žena*, July 1965.

Azoulay, Ariella. *The Civil Contract of Photography*. Princeton University Press, 2008.

Baker, Catherine. *Race and the Yugoslav Region: Postsocialist, Post-conflict, Postcolonial?* Manchester University Press, 2018.

Bakić-Hayden, Milica. "Nesting Orientalisms: The Case of Former Yugoslavia." *Slavic Review* 54, no. 4 (1995): 917–931.

Barthélémy, Pascale, and Ophélie Rillon. "Aoua Kéita (1912–1980): Anti-Colonial Activist, Nationalist Politician, and Feminist in Mali (West Africa)." In *The Palgrave Handbook of Communist Women Activists around the World*, edited by Francisca de Haan. Springer International Publishing, 2023.

Basil, Davidson. *Partisan Picture.* Bedford Books, 1946.

Bastian, Jeannette. *Owning Memory: How a Caribbean Community Lost Its Archives and Found Its History.* Westport, CT: Bloomsbury, 2003.

Bedjaoui, Ahmed. *Cinéma et guerre de libération: Algérie, des batailles d'images.* éditions Chihab, 2014.

Benítez Rojo, Antonio. *The Repeating Island: The Caribbean and the Postmodern Perspective.* Translated by James E. Maraniss. Duke University Press, 1996.

Berenskoetter, Felix. "Friends, There Are No Friends? An Intimate Reframing of the International." *Millennium* 35, no. 3 (2007): 647–676.

Bernabé, Jean, Patrick Chamoiseau, and Raphaël Confiant. *Eloge de la créolité.* Paris: Gallimard, 1989.

Betts, Paul. "A Red Wind of Change: African Press Coverage of Tito's Visits to Decolonizing Africa." In *Tito in Africa: Picturing Solidarity*, edited by Radina Vučetić and Paul Betts. Belgrade: Museum of Yugoslavia, 2017.

Bhabha, Homi K. *The Location of Culture.* Routledge, 1994.

Bjelić, Dušan. "Introduction: Blowing up the 'Bridge'." In *Balkan as Metaphor: Between Globalization and Fragmentation*, edited by Dušan Bjelić and Obrad Savić. Cambridge, MA: MIT Press, 2002.

Blum, Françoise, and Constantin Katsakioris. "Léopold Sédar Senghor et l'Union Soviétique: La Confrontation, 1957–1966." *Cahiers d'Études Africaines* 59, no. 235 (2019): 839–66.

Blum, Laurence A. *Friendship, Altruism and Morality.* Routledge, 2009.

Bogetić, Dragan. "Jugoslavija i borba alžirskog naroda za nacionalno oslobođenje 1954–1962." In *Jugoslavija-Alžir: Zbornik radova sa naučne konferencije*, edited by Miladin Milošević. Beograd: Arhiv Jugoslavije, 2013.

Bogetić, Dragan. "The Yugoslav Support to the Algerian People Struggle for Independence in the Final Phase of the Algerian War 1958–1962." *Istorija 20. veka*, no. 3 (2012): 155–169.

Bonfiglioli, Chiara. "On Vida Tomšič, Marxist Feminism, and Agency." *Aspasia* 10, no. 1 (2016): 145–151.

Bonfiglioli, Chiara, and Kristen Ghodsee. "Vanishing Act: Global Socialist Feminism as the 'Missing Other' of Transnational Feminism – A Response to Tlostanova, Thapar-Björkert and Koobak (2019)." *Feminist Review* 126, no. 1 (2020): 168–172.

Bongie, Chris. *Friends and Enemies: The Scribal Politics of Post/Colonial Literature.* Liverpool University Press, 2008.

Bonner, Christopher T. "Islands Between Worlds: Caribbean Cold War Literatures." In *The Palgrave Handbook of Cold War Literature*, edited by Andrew Hammond, 315–332. London: Palgrave Macmillan, 2020.

Bonner, Christopher T. "The Ferrements of Poetry: The Geopolitical Vision of Aimé Césaire's Cold War Poems." *International Journal of Francophone Studies* 19, no. 3–4 (2016): 275–300.

Britton, Celia. *Edouard Glissant and Postcolonial Theory: Strategies of Language and Resistance.* University Press of Virginia, 1999.

Brown, Adrienne Maree. *Pleasure Activism: The Politics of Feeling Good.* AK Press, 2019.

Burcar, Ljiljana. "Brisanje Dosega Jugoslavenskog Socijalističkog Feminizma." In *Ljevica Nakon Opovrgnute Revolucije*, edited by Srećko Pulig. Zagreb: Jesenski i Turk, 2020.

Byrne, Jeffrey James. "Beyond Continents, Colours, and the Cold War: Yugoslavia, Algeria, and the Struggle for Non-Alignment." *The International History Review* 37, no. 5 (2015): 912–932.

Byrne, Jeffrey James. "From Bandung to Havana: Institutionalizing the Contentions of Postcolonial Internationalism." In *The League Against Imperialism: Lives and Afterlives,* edited by Michele Louro, Carolien Stolte, Heather Streets-Salter, and Sana Tannoury-Karam. Leiden University Press, 2020: 371–396.

Byrne, Jeffrey James. *Mecca of Revolution: Algeria, Decolonization, and the Third World Order.* New York, NY: Oxford University Press, 2019.

Célestin, Roger, Eliane Dalmolin, Alec G. Hargreaves & Martin Munro, eds. "The Francophone Caribbean and North America." *Contemporary French & Francophone Studies* 15, no. 1 (2011).

Cenevski, Kiril, dir. *Leopold Sedar Senghor.* 1975.

Césaire, Aimé. *Non-Vicious Circle.* Translated by Gregson Davis. Stanford University Press, 1984.

Césaire, Aimé. *Discours sur le colonialisme suivi de Discours sur la Négritude.* Paris: Présence Africaine, 2004.

Césaire, Aimé. *Cahier d'un retour au pays natal.* Paris: Présence Africaine, 1956.

Césaire, Aimé. *Notebook of a Return to the Native Land.* Translated by Clayton Eshleman and Annette Smith. Middletown, CT: Wesleyan University Press, 2001.

Césaire, Aimé. "Letter to Maurice Thorez." *Social Text* 28, no. 2 (2010): 145–152.

Césaire, Aimé. *Discourse on Colonialism.* Translated by Joan Pinkham. New York: Monthly Review Press, 2000.

Césaire, Aimé, Françoise Vergès, and Matthew B. Smith. *Resolutely Black: Conversations with Françoise Vergès.* Polity, 2020.

Césaire, Aimé and Nicolas Guillén. "Réponse à Depestre poète haïtien (Eléments d'un art poètique)." *Présence Africaine* 1/2 (1955): 113–15.

Chakravorty Spivak, Gayatri. "A Note on the New International." *Parallax* 7, no. 3 (2001): 12–16.

Clifford, James. *The Predicament of Culture: Twentieth-Century Ethnography, Literature, and Art.* Harvard University Press, 1988.

Colin-Thébaudeau, Katell. "René Depestre: la terre faite chair." *Études françaises* 41, no. 2 (2005): 43–56.

Collison, Luke, Cillian Ó Fathaigh, and Georgios Tsagdis. *Derrida's Politics of Friendship: Amity and Enmity.* Edinburgh University Press, 2022.

Cunningham, Nijah. "Quiet Dawn: Time, Aesthetics, and the Afterlives of Black Radicalism." PhD diss., Columbia University, 2015.

Davis, Gregson. *Aimé Césaire.* Cambridge University Press, 1997.

Dayan, Joan. "France Reads Haiti: René Depestre's Hadriana Dans Tous Mes Rêves." *Yale French Studies* 83 (1993): 154–175.

Dayan, Joan. "'Hallelujah for a Garden-Woman': The Caribbean Adam and His Pretext." *The French Review* 59, no. 4 (1986): 581–595.

de Sousa Santos, Boaventura. "Epistemologies of the South and the Future." *From the European South*, no. 1 (2016): 17–29.

Dean, Jodi. "From Allies to Comrades," *Liberation School*, 9 September 2019. https://www.liberationschool.org/from-allies-to-comrades/.

Dean, Jodi. *Comrade: An Essay on Political Belonging.* Verso Books, 2019.

Depestre, René. "Lettre À Charles Dobzynski." *Les lettres françaises* 573 (1955).

Depestre, René. "Réponse à Aimé Césaire (Introduction à un art poétique haïtien)," *Présence Africaine* 4 (1955): 42–62.

Depestre, René. *Alléluia pour une femme-jardin: récits d'amour solaire.* Montréal: Leméac, 1973.

Depestre, René. *Le mât de cocagne.* Paris: Gallimard, 1979.

Depestre, René. *Le métier à métisser.* Paris: Stock, 1998.

Depestre, René. *Hadriana dans tous mes rêves.* Paris: Gallimard, 1988.

Depestre, René. *Bonjour et adieu à la négritude: suivi de Travaux d'identité.* Paris: R. Laffont, 1980.

Derrida, Jacques. *Archive Fever: A Freudian Impression.* Translated by Eric Prenowitz. University of Chicago Press, 1996.

Derrida, Jacques. *The Politics of Friendship.* Translated by George Collins. London: Verso, 1997.

Devere, Heather, and Preston King. *The Challenge to Friendship in Modernity.* Routledge, 2013.

Diagne, Souleymane Bachir. "A Note on African Socialism." *African Arts* 54, no. 3 (2021): 1–4.

Diagne, Souleymane Bachir. "La Négritude comme mouvement et comme devenir." *Rue Descartes* 83, no. 4 (2014): 50–61.

Diagne, Souleymane Bachir. "Négritude." *The Stanford Encyclopedia of Philosophy*, edited by Edward Zalta and Uri Nodelman. First published 24 May 2010, revised 24 January 2023. https://plato.stanford.edu/archives/spr2023/entries/negritude/.

Diagne, Souleymane Bachir. *Postcolonial Bergson.* Translated by Lindsay Turner. Fordham University Press, 2019.

Diamant-Berger, Noëlle. "René Depestre pleure Aimé Césaire: 'Je suis redevenu orphelin'." *Negritude* (blog), 23 April 2008. https://aime-cesaire.blogspot.com/2008/04/ren-depestre-pleure-aim-csaire-je-suis.html.

Digeser, P. E. *Friendship Reconsidered: What It Means and How It Matters to Politics*. Columbia University Press, 2016.

Dimić, Ljubodrag. "Jugoslavija i Alžir 1961–1965." In *Jugoslavija-Alžir: Zbornik radova sa naučne konferencije*, edited by Miladin Milošević. Beograd: Arhiv Jugoslavije, 2013.

Diouf, Mamadou. "Senegalese Development: From Mass Mobilization to Technocratic Elitism." In *International Development and the Social Sciences: Essays on the History and Politics of Knowledge*, edited by Frederick Cooper and Randall Packard. University of California Press, 1997.

Djagalov, Rossen. *From Internationalism to Postcolonialism: Literature and Cinema between the Second and the Third Worlds*. McGill-Queen's University Press, 2020.

Dragomir, Bondžić. "Studenti Iz Alžira U Jugoslaviji 1958–1965." In *Jugoslavija-Alžir: Zbornik Radova Sa Naučne Konferencije Alžir, 27 Januar 2013*. Beograd, 2013.

Dragostinova, Theodora and Veneta Ivanova, eds. *Re-Imagining the Balkans: How to Think and Teach a Region. Festschrift in Honor of Professor Maria N. Todorova*. Oldenbourg: De Gruyter Oldenbourg, 2023.

Drugovac, Miodrag. "Razgovor sa Acom Šopovim." *Književne novine*, 15 August 1970.

Đureinović, Jelena. *The Politics of Memory of the Second World War in Contemporary Serbia: Collaboration, Resistance and Retribution*. London: Routledge, 2020.

Edwards, Brent Hayes. *The Practice of Diaspora: Literature, Translation, and the Rise of Black Internationalism*. Harvard University Press, 2003.

Edwards, Brent Hayes. "Aimé Césaire and the Syntax of Influence." *Research in African Literatures* 36, no. 2 (2005): 1–18.

Epštajn, Emilia. "Tragom Vede Zagorac U Muzeju Afričke Umetnosti." In *Feministička Teorija Je Za Sve*, edited by Adriana Zaharijević and Katarina Lončarević. Belgrade: Institut za Filozofiju i Društvenu Teoriju, 2018.

Fanon, Frantz. *L'An V de la révolution algérienne*. Paris: François Maspero, 1959.

Fanon, Frantz. *The Wretched of the Earth*. Translated by Richard Philcox. New York: Grove Press, 2004.

Fineman, Joel "The History of the Anecdote: Fiction and Fiction." In *The New Historicism*, edited by H. Aram Veeser. New York: Routledge, 1989.

Fleming, K. E. "Orientalism, the Balkans, and Balkan Historiography." *The American Historical Review* 105, no. 4 (2000): 1218–1233.

Forsdick, Charles. "Local, National, Regional, Global: Glissant and the Postcolonial Manifesto." In *Caribbean Globalizations, 1492 to the Present Day*, edited by Eva Sansavior and Richard Scholar. Liverpool University Press, 2015.

Friedman, Marilyn. *What Are Friends For? Feminist Perspectives on Personal Relationships and Moral Theory*. Cornell University Press, 1993.

Gallop, Jane, *Anecdotal Theory*. Duke University Press, 2002.

Gervereau, Laurent. "Les hésitations des photographes professionnels." In *Photographier la guerre d'Algérie*, edited by Laurent Gervereau and Benjamin Stora. Marval, 2004.

Gervereau, Laurent, and Benjamin Stora, eds. *Photographier la guerre d'Algérie*. Marval, 2004.

Getachew, Adom. *Worldmaking after Empire: The Rise and Fall of Self-Determination*. Princeton University Press, 2019.

Ghandi, Leela. *Affective Communities: Anticolonial Thought, Fin-de-Siècle Radicalism, and the Politics of Friendship*. Duke University Press, 2006.

Ghodsee, Kristen. *Second World, Second Sex: Socialist Women's Activism and Global Solidarity During the Cold War*. Duke University Press, 2018.

Gilroy, Paul. *Postcolonial Melancholia*. New York: Columbia University Press, 2005.

Glissant, Édouard. *Poetics of Relation*. Translated by Betsy Wing. University of Michigan Press, 2010.

Glissant, Édouard. *Caribbean Discourse: Selected Essays*. Translated by J. Michael Dash. University Press of Virginia, 1989.

Glover, Kaiama L. "'The Francophone World Was Set Ablaze': Pan-African Intellectuals, European Interlocutors and the Global Cold War." *Postcolonial Studies* 24, no. 4 (2021): 464–483.

Glover, Kaiama L. *A Regarded Self: Caribbean Womanhood and the Ethics of Disorderly Being*. Duke University Press, 2021.

Gonzalez, Catherine Lizette. "In 'Pleasure Activism,' Adrienne Maree Brown Dares Us to Get in Touch with Our Needs," *Colorlines*, 26 February 2019. https://www.colorlines.com/articles/pleasure-activism-adrienne-maree-brown-dares-us-get-touch-our-needs.

Greene, Roland Arthur, "Review of Death of a Discipline," *SubStance* 35, no. 1 (2006): 154–159.

Grewal, Inderpal, and Caren Kaplan. *Scattered Hegemonies: Postmodernity and Transnational Feminist Practices*. University of Minnesota Press, 1994.

Guberina, Petar. "Izvještaj o putu u Senegal", "Guberina's Report to the Federal Institute for Technological, Cultural and Scientific Cooperation About His Trip to Senegal." Scientific and technological cooperation SFRJ-Senegal, AJ 465, ф1718, 8 February 1976.

Guberina, Petar. "Politika Je Progutala Jezik." In *Drugo čitanje*, edited by Mirko Galić. Zagreb: Matica Hrvatska, 2007.

Guberina, Petar. "Postface." In *Genij Afrike*. Zagreb: Stvarnost, 1969.

Guberina, Petar. *Povezanost Jezičkih Elemenata*. Zagreb: Matica Hrvatska, 1952.

Guberina, Petar. *Zvuk i Pokret u Jeziku*. Zagreb: Matica Hrvatska, 1952.

Hadouchi, Olivier. *Images of Non-Aligned and Tricontinental Struggles*. Translated by Mark Brogan. Museum of Contemporary Art Belgrade, 2016.

Hartwig, Robert J. "Review of *Éros dans un train chinois*, by René Depestre." *The French Review* 65, no. 6 (1992): 1077–1078.

Hern, Matt, and Am Johal. *O My Friends, There Is No Friend: The Politics of Friendship at the End of Ecology*. Bielefeld: Transcript Verlag, 2020.

Hočevar, Savica. Letter to Aoua Kéita, 1965. AJ 142 (SSRNJ), A-631.

Hsu, Hua. "What Jacques Derrida Understood About Friendship," *New Yorker*, 3 December 2019. https://www.newyorker.com/books/second-read/what-jacques-derrida-understood-about-friendship.

Imre, Aniko. "Whiteness in Post-Socialist Eastern Europe: The Time of the Gypsies, the End of Race." In *Postcolonial Whiteness: A Critical Reader on Race and Empire*, edited by Alfred J. Lopez. State University of New York Press, 2005.

Infante, Ignacio. *After Translation: The Transfer and Circulation of Modern Poetics Across the Atlantic*. New York: Fordham University Press, 2013.

Joseph-Gabriel, Annette K. *Reimagining Liberation: How Black Women Transformed Citizenship in the French Empire*. University of Illinois Press, 2019.

Jovic-Humphrey, Anja. "Aimé Césaire and 'Another Face of Europe'." *MLN* 129, no. 5 (2014): 1117–1148.

Jugoslovenska Svedočanstva O Alžirskoj Revoluciji – Arhivski Omnibus (*Yugoslav Testimonies of the Algerian Revolution – Archival Testimonies*), curated by Mila Turajlić, Maja Medić, Ana Knežević & Emilia Epštajn, Belgrade Museum of African Art, 18 March–11 June 2023.

Kaisary, Philip. *The Haitian Revolution in the Literary Imagination: Radical Horizons, Conservative Constraints*. University of Virginia Press, 2014.

Kardelj, Edvard. *The Historical Roots of Non-Alignment*. University Press of America, 1980.

Kéita, Aoua. *Aoua Kéita's Speech at the 5th International Seminar Organized by KDAŽ*. AJ 142 (SSRNJ), A-631, Konferencija za Društvenu Aktivnost Žena (KDAŽ).

Kéita, Aoua. *Femme d'Afrique: la vie d'Aoua Kéita racontée par elle-même*. Présence Africaine, 1975.

Kéita, Aoua. Letter to Savica Hočevar, January 1966. AJ 142 (SSRNJ), A-631.

Kéita, Aoua. Letter to the President of the Conference for the Social Activity of Women of Yugoslavia, 1965. AJ 142 (SSRNJ), A-631.

Kéita, Aoua. Letter to the President of the Conference for the Social Activity of Women of Yugoslavia, 8 January 1966. AJ 142 (SSRNJ), A-631.

Kéita, Aoua. Letter to Vida Tomšič, 3 November 1971. AJ 142 (SSRNJ), A-631.

Kéita, Aoua. Postcard to Jelica Marić [no date]. AJ 142 (SSRNJ), A-631.

Kelz, Rosine. "Political Friendships to Come? Futurity, Democracy and Citizenship." In *Derrida's Politics of Friendship: Amity and Enmity*, edited by Luke Collison, Cillian Ó Fathaigh, and Georgios Tsagdis. Edinburgh University Press, 2022.

Kempadoo, Kamala. *Sexing the Caribbean: Gender, Race, and Sexual Labor*. New York: Routledge, 2004.

Kiiru, Lawrence, dir. *Martinska-Martinique*. Filmoteka 16, 1991.

Kilibarda, Konstantin. "Non-Aligned Geographies in the Balkans: Space, Race and Image in the Construction of New 'European' Foreign Policies." In *Security Beyond the Discipline: Emerging Dialogues on Global Politics – Selected*

Proceedings of the Sixteenth Annual Conference of the York Centre for International and Security Studies, edited by Abhinava Kumar and Derek Maisonville. Toronto: York Centre for International and Security Studies, York University, 2010.

Kirn, Gal. *Partisan Ruptures: Self-Management, Market Reform and the Spectre of Socialist Yugoslavia*. Translated by Borut Praper. London: Pluto Press, 2019.

Kola, Adam F. "The Politics of the Archive in Semi-Peripheries." In *Futures of Comparative Literature*, edited by Ursula Heise. Routledge, 2017.

KDAŽ. *Pomoć Jugoslovenskog Crvenog Krsta i Konferencije Za Društvenu Aktivnost Žena Jugoslavije Maliju 1965. i 1966. godine* (*Aid from the Yugoslav Red Cross and the Conference for the Social Activity of Women of Yugoslavia to Mali in 1965 and 1966*), AJ 142 (SSRNJ), A-631.

KDAŽ. Razgovor Sa Ambasadorom Malija, Gosp. Ture (Conversation with the Ambassador of Mali, Mr. Touré), May 1965. AJ 142 (SSRNJ), A-631.

KDAŽ. Zabeleška O Poseti Ambasadora Malija Konferenciji Za Društvenu Aktivnost Žena (Note on the Visit of the Ambassador of Mali to the Conference for the Social Activity of Women), March 1963. AJ 142 (SSRNJ), A-631.

KDAŽ. Zabeleška O Razgovoru Sa Auom Keitom (A Note on a Conversation with Aoua Kéita), 24 January 1967. AJ 142 (SSRNJ), A-631.

Konjikušić, Davor. *Red Glow: Yugoslav Partisan Photography and Social Movement, 1941–1945*. Berlin: De Gruyter, 2021.

Kovačević, Nataša. *Narrating Post/Communism: Colonial Discourse and Europe's Borderline Civilization*. Routledge, 2008.

Kundera, Milan. *Une rencontre*. Paris: Gallimard, 2009.

Lal, Priya. *African Socialism in Postcolonial Tanzania: Between the Village and the World*. Cambridge University Press; 2015.

League of Communists of Yugoslavia. *The Programme of the League of Yugoslav Communists: Adopted by the VII. Congress of the League of Yugoslav Communists Held from 22 to 26 April, 1958 in Ljubljana*. 1958.

Letter from the Ambassador of the Republic of Mali to the President of the Conference for the Social Activity of Yugoslav Women, 1963. AJ 142 (SSRNJ), A-631.

Letters from Basil Davidson to Zdravko Pečar. The Veda and dr Zdravko Pečar Collection, Belgrade Museum of African Art.

Letter from the Executive Committee of the Women of Mali to the Conference for the Social Activity of Women, July 1962. AJ 142 (SSRNJ), A-631.

Letter from President of the GPRA Ferhat Abbas to Zdravko Pečar, 30 March 1960. The Veda and dr Zdravko Pečar Collection, Belgrade Museum of African Art.

Lindstrom, Nicole. "Yugonostalgia: Restorative and Reflective Nostalgia in Former Yugoslavia." *East Central Europe* 32, no. 1–2 (2005): 227–237.

López, Alfred J. "Intentions, Methods, and the Future of Global South Studies." *Comparative Literature Studies* 58, no. 3 (2021): 485–508.

Lorde, Audre. *Sister Outsider: Essays and Speeches*. Berkeley: Crossing Press, 1984.

Mahler, Anne Garland. "Global South." Oxford Bibliographies in Literary and Critical Theory, 25 October 2017. DOI: 10.1093/obo/9780190221911-0055.

Mahler, Anne Garland. *From the Tricontinental to the Global South: Race, Radicalism, and Transnational Solidarity.* Duke University Press, 2018.

Mahler, Anne Garland, and Paolo Capuzzo, eds. *The Comintern and the Global South: Global Designs/Local Encounters.* Routledge, 2022.

Marić, Jelica. Letter to Aoua Kéita, 1965. AJ 142 (SSRNJ), A-631.

Mark, James, Artemy M. Kalinovsky, and Steffi Marung, eds. *Alternative Globalizations: Eastern Europe and the Postcolonial World.* Indiana University Press, 2020.

Marmande, Francis. "Aimé Césaire: 'Ma poésie est née de mon action'." *Le Monde*, 15 March 2006.

Masschelein, Anneleen, Christophe Meurée, David Martens, and Stéphanie Vanastan. "The Literary Interview: Towards a Poetics of a Hybrid Genre." *Poetics Today* 35, no. 1–2 (2014): 1–49.

Mates, Leo. *Međunarodni odnosi socijalističke Jugoslavije.* Beograd: Nolit, 1976.

Matošević, Tanja and Andrea Petrović. *Duh Pruge: Zbornik Radova O Knjizi E.P. Thompsona.* Belgrade: Fabrika Knjiga, 2020.

Melaku, Tsedale M., Angie Beeman, David G. Smith & W. Brad Johnson. "Be a Better Ally," *Harvard Business Review* (November–December 2020).

Mendoza, Breny. "Transnational Feminisms in Question." *Feminist Theory* 3, no. 3 (2002): 295–314.

Mignolo, Walter. "Foreword. On Pluriversality and Multipolarity." In *Constructing the Pluriverse: The Geopolitics of Knowledge*, edited by Bernd Reiter. Duke University Press, 2018.

Miller, Christopher L. *The French Atlantic Triangle: Literature and Culture of the Slave Trade.* Duke University Press, 2008.

Minutes from the Conversation between Josip Broz Tito and Léopold Sédar Senghor, 2 September 1975. AJ, KPR, I-3-a/103-10.

Minutes of Yugoslav-Algerian Talks, 8 June 1959, AJ, KPR, I-3-a/2-1.

Mišković, Nataša. "Introduction." In *The Non-Aligned Movement and the Cold War: Delhi—Bandung—Belgrade*, edited by Nataša Mišković, Harald Fischer-Tiné, and Nada Boskovska. London: Routledge, 2014.

Mohanty, Chandra Talpade. *Feminism without Borders: Decolonizing Theory, Practicing Solidarity.* Duke University Press, 2003.

Mortimer, Robert A. "From Federalism to Francophonia: Senghor's African Policy." *African Studies Review* 15, no. 2 (1972): 283–306.

Moya, Paula M. L. "'Racism is not intellectual': Interracial Friendship, Multicultural Literature, and Decolonizing Epistemologies." In *Decolonizing Epistemologies: Latina/o Theology and Philosophy*, edited by Ada Maria Isasi-Diaz and Eduardo Mendieta. Fordham University Press, 2012.

Munro, Martin. *Shaping and Reshaping the Caribbean: The Work of Aimé Césaire and René Depestre.* Leeds, UK: Maney Publishing for the Modern Humanities Research Association, 2000.

Murphy, David. *The First World Festival of Negro Arts, Dakar 1966: Contexts and Legacies*. Liverpool: Liverpool University Press, 2016.

Naas, Michael. "The Time of a Detour: Jacques Derrida and the Question of the Gift." *Oxford Literary Review* 18, no. 1/2 (1996): 67–86.

Nesbitt, Nick. "Antinomies of Double Consciousness in Aimé Césaire's 'Cahier d'un retour au pays natal'." *Mosaic: An Interdisciplinary Critical Journal* 33, no. 3 (2000): 107–128.

Neuberger, Benyamin. "The African Concept of Balkanisation." *The Journal of Modern African Studies* 14, no. 3 (1976): 523–529.

Nivelon, Valérie. "La voix Mamadou Dia (3/3) en exclusivité sur RFI." *La Marche du Monde*, RFI, 17 April 2020.

Nivelon, Valérie. "Mamadou Dia parle, histoire d'une archive inédite." RFI, 25 January 2019, https://www.rfi.fr/fr/afrique/20190125-mamadou-dia-parle-histoire-archive-inedite-senegal-senghor.

Nkrumah, Kwame. *Neo-Colonialism: The Last Stage of Imperialism*. International Publishers, 1965.

Nordin, Astrid HM. "Decolonising Friendship." *The Journal of Friendship Studies* 6, no. 1 (2020): 88–114.

Note from Ministry of Foreign Affairs to President Tito, 7 February 1974. AJ, KPR, I-3-a/103-10.

Oklopcic, Zoran. "Beyond Empty, Conservative, and Ethereal: Pluralist Self-Determination and a Peripheral Political Imaginary." *Leiden Journal of International Law* 26, no. 3 (2013): 509–529.

Parti communiste français. "Tito a trahi la jeunesse yougoslave." *L'Humanité: journal socialiste quotidien*, 28 October, 1949.

Pečar, Zdravko. *Alžir.* Beograd: Kultura, 1959.

Pečar, Zdravko. "Cinq Djamilah algériennes," 1962. The Veda and dr Zdravko Pečar Collection, Belgrade Museum of African Art.

Pečar, Zdravko. *Alžir do nezavisnosti*. Beograd: Prosveta, 1967.

Pečar, Zdravko. "Alžirski Ustanici Mestimično Probili Šalov Pojas." The Veda and dr Zdravko Pečar Collection, Belgrade Museum of African Art.

Pečar, Zdravko. "Beleška O Ben Beli." The Veda and dr Zdravko Pečar Collection, Belgrade Museum of African Art.

Pečar, Zdravko. "Deo Jugoslovenske Pomoći Za Alžirske Izbeglice Dopremljen U Kazablanku." The Veda and dr Zdravko Pečar Collection, Belgrade Museum of African Art.

Pečar, Zdravko. "Houari Boumedienne." The Veda and dr Zdravko Pečar Collection, Belgrade Museum of African Art.

Pečar, Zdravko. "Jugoslavija Je Veliki i Iskren Prijatelj Alžira." The Veda and dr Zdravko Pečar Collection, Belgrade Museum of African Art.

Pečar, Zdravko. "Le Caractère Populaire De La Révolution Algérienne." The Veda and dr Zdravko Pečar Collection, Belgrade Museum of African Art.

Pečar, Zdravko. "Naši studenti u Tunisu." The Veda and dr Zdravko Pečar Collection, Belgrade Museum of African Art.

Pečar, Zdravko. "Pisanje Alžirskog 'Al Mudžahida' Povodom Dana Republike." The Veda and dr Zdravko Pečar Collection, Belgrade Museum of African Art.

Pečar, Zdravko. "Pomoć Jugoslovenskog Crvenog Križa Alžirskim Izbeglicama." The Veda and dr Zdravko Pečar Collection, Belgrade Museum of African Art.

Pečar, Zdravko. "Slučaj Dragana Savića." The Veda and dr Zdravko Pečar Collection, Belgrade Museum of African Art.

Pečar, Zdravko. "Studenti Najavili Da Neće Napustiti Tunis." The Veda and dr Zdravko Pečar Collection, Belgrade Museum of African Art.

Pečar, Zdravko. "Tko Će Zamjeniti Kolone?" The Veda and dr Zdravko Pečar Collection, Belgrade Museum of African Art.

Perisic, Alexandra. "Aimé Césaire's Yugoslav Detour." *Small Axe: A Caribbean Journal of Criticism* 27, no. 2 (71): 1–17.

Perisic, Alexandra, and René Depestre. "A Secret Love Affair: An Interview with René Depestre." *Transition* 128 (2019): 108–118.

Perović, Latinka. Letter to the Executive Committee of the Women of Mali, June 1962. AJ 142 (SSRNJ), A-631.

Petrović, Dragan. *Francusko-jugoslovenski odnosi u vreme Alžirskog rata 1952–1964.* Beograd: Institut za međunarodnu politiku i privredu, 2009.

Prashad, Vijay. *The Darker Nations: A People's History of the Third World.* New York: New Press, 2007.

Pruga Šamac-Sarajevo: Dar Omladine Titu i Narodu. Zagreb: Novo pokoljenje, 1947. https://hip.eindigo.net/?pr=i&id=154695

Radonjić, Nemanja. "*Anti-Colonial Constellations*: The Belgrade All-African Students Conference of 1962." In *Eastern Europe, the Soviet Union, and Africa: New Perspectives on the Era of Decolonization, 1950s to 1990s*, edited by Chris Saunders, Helder Adegar Fonseca, and Lena Dallywater. Berlin, Boston: De Gruyter Oldenbourg, 2023: 263–289.

Radonjić, Nemanja. "Drums of Revolution: Veda Zagorac and Zdravko Pečar." In *Nyimpa Kor Ndzidzi*, edited by Ana Sladojević and Emilija Epštajn. Belgrade: Museum of African Art, 2017.

Radonjić, Nemanja. *Slika Afrike u Jugoslaviji.* Beograd: Institut za noviju istoriju Srbije, 2023.

Radonjić, Nemanja. "*Studenti iz Afrike u socijalističkoj i nesvrstanoj Jugoslaviji: Prilog istraživanju slike Drugog.*" *Godišnjak za društvenu istoriju* 3 (2020): 23–53.

Raymond, Janice G. *A Passion for Friends: Toward a Philosophy of Female Affection.* Spinifex Press, 2001.

"Report on Senegal Compiled by the State Secretariat for Foreign Affairs," 15 July 1961. AJ, KPR, I-3-a/103-10.

Ripert Yohann C. "Decolonizing Diplomacy: Senghor, Kennedy, and the Practice of Ideological Resistance." *African Studies Review* 64, no.2 (2021): 292–314

Ripert Yohann C. "Rethinking Négritude: Aimé Césaire & Léopold Sédar Senghor and the Imagination of a Global Postcoloniality." PhD diss., Columbia University, 2017.

Robertson, James. "Small Socialism: The Scales of Self-Management Culture in Postwar Yugoslavia." *The Slavic Review* 79, no. 3 (2020): 601–603.

Rodden, John. *Performing the Literary Interview: How Writers Craft Their Public Selves*. University of Nebraska Press, 2001.

Rosello, Mireille, and Robert Postawsko. "'One More Sea to Cross:' Exile and Intertextuality in Aimé Césaire's Cahier d'un retour au pays natal." *Yale French Studies*, no. 83 (1993): 176–195.

Roshchin, Evgeny. *Friendship Among Nations: History of a Concept*. Manchester University Press, 2020.

Rubinstein, Alvin Z. *Yugoslavia and the Nonaligned World*. Princeton University Press, 1970.

Said, Edward. "Third World Intellectuals and Metropolitan Culture." *Raritan* 9, no. 3 (1990): 27–50.

Salazkina, Masha. *World Socialist Cinema: Alliances, Affinities, and Solidarities in the Global Cold War*. University of California Press, 2023.

Salien, Jean-Marie. "Croyances populaires haïtiennes dans *Hadriana dans tous mes rêves* de René Depestre." *The French Review* 74, no. 1 (2000): 82–93.

Samatar, Sofia. "Martinska-Martinique." *Caribbean Quarterly* 68, no. 2 (2022): 268–279.

Sartre, Jean-Paul. "Black Orpheus." Translated by John MacCombie. *The Massachusetts Review* 6, no. 1 (1964): 13–52.

Saunders, Patricia J. "Fugitive Dreams of Diaspora: Conversations with Saidiya Hartman." *Anthurium* 6, no. 1 (2008).

Schwartz, Joan M., and Terry Cook. "Archives, Records, and Power: The Making of Modern History." *Archival Science* 2 (2002): 1–19.

Senghor, Léopold Sédar. *Anthologie de la nouvelle poésie nègre et malgache de langue française*. Paris: Presses Universitaires de France, 1948.

Senghor, Léopold Sédar. "Balkanisation ou Fédération." *Afrique Nouvelle* (December 1956).

Senghor, Léopold Sédar. "De la Négritude." In *Liberté V: Le dialogue des cultures*. Paris: Seuil, 1993.

Senghor, Léopold Sédar. "Hommage à Pierre Teilhard De Chardin." In *Liberté V: Le dialogue des cultures*. Paris: Seuil, 1993.

Senghor, Léopold Sédar. *Hosties Noires*. Paris: Seuil, 1948.

Senghor, Léopold Sédar. "Je vous dis que la France est un arbre vivant." Address to the French National Assembly, 29 January 1957.

Senghor, Léopold Sédar. "Još se nisam odužio ženi." Interview by Dušan Ed. Grbić. *Ilustrovana Politika*, no. 879, 9 September 1975.

Senghor, Léopold Sédar. "La voie africaine du socialisme: nouvel essai de définition." In *Liberté II: Nation et Voie Africaine du Socialisme*. Paris: Seuil, 1971.

Senghor, Léopold Sédar. *Liberté 1*. Paris: Seuil, 1964.

Senghor, Léopold Sédar. *On African Socialism*. New York: Praeger, 1964.

Senghor, Léopold Sédar. *Pierre Teilhard De Chardin Et La Politique Africaine*. Paris: Seuil, 1962.

Senghor, Léopold Sédar. "Pour une République Fédérale." *Politique étrangère* 21, no. 2 (1956): 165–174.

Senghor, Léopold Sédar. "Preface." In *The New International Economic Order: Philosophical and Socio-Cultural Implications*, edited by Hans Köchler. International Progress Organization, 1980.

Senghor, Léopold Sédar. *Response to the Toast Made by President Josip Broz Tito,* 2 September 1975. AJ, KPR, I-3-a/103-10.

Senghor, Léopold Sédar. Press conference, Struga Poetry Evenings, broadcast on Radio Belgrade, 1975. Radio Belgrade Archive.

Senghor, Léopold Sédar. "Rapport sur la doctrine el le programme du parti," *Nation et voie africaine du socialisme*. Paris: Présence Africaine, 1961.

Sengor, Léopold Sédar. *Poezija: Izbor*. Translated by Aco Šopov. Skopje: Nova Makedonija, 1975.

Sharma, Arvind. *Religious Studies and Comparative Methodology: The Case for Reciprocal Illumination*. Albany: State University of New York Press, 2005.

Sheller, Mimi. *Citizenship from Below: Erotic Agency and Caribbean Freedom*. Duke University Press, 2012.

Sladojević, Ana. "An Anticolonial Museum." *Europe Now*, no. 50, Council for European Studies (2023). https://www.europenowjournal.org/2023/02/21/an-anticolonial-museum/.

Smirnova Tatiana and Ophélie Rillon. "When Malian Women Looked to the USSR (1961–1991): The Challenges of Female Educational Cooperation." *International Journal of African Historical Studies* 54, no. 3 (2021): 457–478.

Smith, Graham M. "Friendship, State, and Nation." In *Friendship and International Relations*, edited by Simon Koschut and Andrea Oelsner. London: Palgrave Macmillan, 2014.

Smole, Jože, and Rudi Štajduhar, eds. *Predsednik Tito u zemljama Azije i Afrike*. Beograd: Kultura, 1959.

Sontag, Susan. *On Photography*. Rosetta Books, 2005.

Southern Constellations: The Poetics of the Non-Aligned. Curated by Bojana Piškur. Translated by Tamara Soban. Ljubljana: Modern galerija, 2019. Exhibition catalog.

Spaskovska, Ljubica. "Comrades, Poets, Politicians: Aco Šopov, Léopold Sédar Senghor and the Cultural Politics of Non-Alignment." Presented at the Toward a Conjuctural Political Economy of Non-Alignment and Cultural Politics Research Workshop, Rijeka, 27–29 September 2021.

Spivak, Gayatri Chakravorty. *Death of a Discipline*. Columbia University Press, 2003.

Stephens, Michelle Ann, and Yolanda Martínez-San Miguel, eds. *Contemporary Archipelagic Thinking: Towards New Comparative Methodologies and Disciplinary Formations*. Rowman & Littlefield, 2020.

Stojaković, Gordana. "Poruke o zaru i feredži u AFŽ štampi na srpskom jeziku (1947–1951): slučaj Kosmet," *Ženski Muzej*, 27 December 2021. https://zenskimuzejns.org.rs/2021/12/27/poruke-o-zaru-i-feredzi-u-afz-stampi-na-srpskom-jeziku-1947-1951-slucaj-kosmet/.

Stojanović, Dubravka. *Prošlost dolazi: Promene u tumačenju prošlosti u srpskim udžbenicima istorije 1913–2021.* Biblioteka XX vek, 2023.

Stubbs, Paul. "Exploring Contradictory Racializations: Socialist Yugoslavia, the Non-Aligned Movement and Decolonial Worldmaking," paper presented at the international conference *Postcolonial, Decolonial, Postimperial, Deimperial*, Rijeka, May 2024.

Stubbs, Paul. "Socialist Yugoslavia and the Antinomies of the Non-Aligned Movement," LeftEast, 17 June 2019. https://lefteast.org/yugoslavia-antinomies-non-aligned-movement/.

Stubbs, Paul. "The Emancipatory Afterlives of Non-Aligned Internationalism," Rosa Luxemburg Stiftung, January 2020. https://www.rosalux.de/en/publication/id/41556/.

Stubbs, Paul, ed. *Socialist Yugoslavia and the Non-Aligned Movement: Social, Cultural, Political, and Economic Imaginaries.* McGill-Queen's University Press, 2023.

Subotic, Jelena, and Srdjan Vucetic, "Performing Solidarity: Whiteness and Status-seeking in the Non-Aligned World." *Journal of International Relations and Development* 22, no. 3 (2019): 722–743.

Šopov, Aco. *Pesna na crnata žena*. Skopje: Misla, 1976.

Šopov, Aco. "Poezija Otkriva Svet." *Politika*, 15 February 1976.

Šopova, Jasmina. *Sengor – Šopov: Paraleli*. Skopje: Sigmapres, 2006.

Táíwò, Olúfémi O. *Elite Capture: How the Powerful Took Over Identity Politics (And Everything Else)*. Haymarket Books, 2022.

Taylor, Astra, and Leah Hunt-Hendrix. "One for All," *The New Republic*, 26 August 2019. https://newrepublic.com/article/154623/green-new-deal-solidarity-solution-climate-change-global-warming.

Telegram from Assistant Secretary of State for Foreign Affairs to the Cabinet of the President of the Republic, 9 June 1961. AJ, KPR, I-3-a/103-10.

Telegram from the Yugoslav Embassy in Dakar to the Ministry of Foreign Affairs, 25 April 1975. AJ, KPR, I-3-a/103-10.

Thébia-Melsan, Annick, and Gérard Lamoureux, eds. *Aimé Césaire: pour regarder le siècle en face*. Maisonneuve & Larose, 2000.

Thompson, Edward P., ed. *The Railway: An Adventure in Construction*. Helsinki: Rab-Rab Press, 2020.

Tlostanova, Madina, Suruchi Thapar-Björkert, and Redi Koobak. "The Postsocialist 'Missing Other' of Transnational Feminism?" *Feminist Review* 121, no. 1 (2019): 81–87.

Todorova, Maria. *Imagining the Balkans*. New York: Oxford University Press, 2009.

Tomšič, Vida. *Izveštaj O Poseti Ženskim Organizacijama U Maliju, Gvineji I Senegalu, 7–19. Februara 1967. godine (Report on the Visit to Women's Organizations in Mali, Guinea, and Senegal, 7–19 February 1967)*. AJ 142 (SSRNJ), A-631.

Tomšič, Vida. Letter to Aoua Kéita, 1967. AJ 142 (SSRNJ), A-631.

Tomšič, Vida. Letter to Aoua Kéita, 7 October 1971. AJ 142 (SSRNJ), A-631.

Tomšič, Vida. *Žena U Razvoju Socijalističke Samoupravne Jugoslavije*. Jugoslovenska stvarnost, 1980. Print.

Turajlić, Mila. "Filmske Novosti: Filmed Diplomacy." *Nationalities Papers* 49, no. 3 (2021): 483–503.

Turajlić, Mila, dir. *Non-Aligned & Ciné-Guerrillas: Scenes from the Labudovic Reels*. 2022.

Turrittin, Jane. "Aoua Kéita and the Nascent Women's Movement in the French Soudan." *African Studies Review* 36, no. 1 (1993): 59–89.

Tyerman, Edward. *Internationalist Aesthetics: China and Early Soviet Culture*. Columbia University Press, 2022.

"Un débat autour des conditions d'une poésie nationale chez les peuples noirs." *Présence Africaine* 4 (1955): 36–38.

Unkovski-Korica, Vladimir. *The Economic Struggle for Power in Tito's Yugoslavia. From World War II to Non-Alignment*. I.B. Tauris, London, 2016.

Unkovski-Korica, Vladimir. "Yugoslavia's Third Way: The Rise and Fall of Self-Management." In *The Routledge Handbook of Balkan and Southeast European History*, edited by John R. Lampe and Ulf Brunnbauer. London: Routledge, 2020.

Vaillant, Janet G. *Black, French, and African: A Life of Léopold Sédar Senghor*. Harvard University Press, 2013.

Vergès, Françoise. "Martinska/Martinique." In *Travelling Communiqué*, edited by Armin Linke, Travelling Communiqué Project Group, Kodwo Eshun, Doreen Mende & Milica Tomić, Spector Books, 2016.

Videkanić, Bojana. *Nonaligned Modernism: Socialist Postcolonial Aesthetics in Yugoslavia, 1945–1985*. McGill-Queen's University Press, 2019.

Weeks, Kathi. *The Problem with Work: Feminism, Marxism, Antiwork Politics, and Postwork Imaginaries*. Duke University Press, 2011.

Wendt, Alexander. *Social Theory of International Politics*. Cambridge University Press, 1999.

Wilder, Gary. *Freedom Time: Negritude, Decolonization, and the Future of the World*. Duke University Press, 2015.

Wilder, Gary. *Concrete Utopianism: The Politics of Temporality and Solidarity*. Fordham University Press, 2022.

Woodward, Susan. *Socialist Unemployment: The Political Economy of Yugoslavia, 1945–1990*. Princeton University Press, 1995.

Wright, Peter. "Challenging Yugoslavia's Internationalist Exceptionalism." In *Re-imagining the Balkans: How to Think and Teach a Region: Festschrift in*

Honor of Professor Maria N. Todorova, edited by Theodora Dragostinova and Veneta Ivanova. Amsterdam: De Gruyter, 2023: 269–278.

Wright, Peter. "'Are there Racists in Yugoslavia?' Debating Racism and Anti-blackness in Socialist Yugoslavia." *Slavic Review* 81, no.2 (2022): 418–441.

Wylie, Hal. Review of *Eros dans un train chinois: Neuf histoires d'amour et un conte de sorcier* by René Depestre. *World Literature Today* 66, no. 1 (1992): 189.

Yacine, Kateb. *Minuit passé de douze heures: écrits journalistiques, 1947–1989.* Paris: Editions du Seuil, 1999.

Yugoslav Ministry of Foreign Affairs. "Information About the Struga Poetry Evening of 1975," 28 August 1975. AJ, KPR, I-3-a/103-10.

Zagorac, Veda. Letter to Kdaž after the Congress of Guinean Women. AJ 142 (SSRNJ), A-631.

Zeilig, Leo. *Frantz Fanon: The Militant Philosopher of Third World Revolution.* London: I.B. Tauris, 2016.